INTRODUCTION TO NETWORK TRAFFIC FLOW THEORY

INTRODUCTION TO NETWORK TRAFFIC FLOW THEORY

Principles, Concepts, Models, and Methods

Wen-Long Jin

Elsevier
Radarweg 29, PO Box 211, 1000 AE Amsterdam, Netherlands
The Boulevard, Langford Lane, Kidlington, Oxford OX5 1GB, United Kingdom
50 Hampshire Street, 5th Floor, Cambridge, MA 02139, United States

Copyright © 2021 Elsevier Inc. All rights reserved.

No part of this publication may be reproduced or transmitted in any form or by any means, electronic or mechanical, including photocopying, recording, or any information storage and retrieval system, without permission in writing from the publisher. Details on how to seek permission, further information about the Publisher's permissions policies and our arrangements with organizations such as the Copyright Clearance Center and the Copyright Licensing Agency, can be found at our website: www.elsevier.com/permissions.

This book and the individual contributions contained in it are protected under copyright by the Publisher (other than as may be noted herein).

Notices

Knowledge and best practice in this field are constantly changing. As new research and experience broaden our understanding, changes in research methods, professional practices, or medical treatment may become necessary.

Practitioners and researchers must always rely on their own experience and knowledge in evaluating and using any information, methods, compounds, or experiments described herein. In using such information or methods they should be mindful of their own safety and the safety of others, including parties for whom they have a professional responsibility.

To the fullest extent of the law, neither the Publisher nor the authors, contributors, or editors, assume any liability for any injury and/or damage to persons or property as a matter of products liability, negligence or otherwise, or from any use or operation of any methods, products, instructions, or ideas contained in the material herein.

Library of Congress Cataloging-in-Publication Data
A catalog record for this book is available from the Library of Congress

British Library Cataloguing-in-Publication Data
A catalogue record for this book is available from the British Library

ISBN: 978-0-12-815840-1

For information on all Elsevier publications
visit our website at https://www.elsevier.com/books-and-journals

Publisher: Joe Hayton
Acquisitions Editor: Brian Romer
Editorial Project Manager: Barbara Makinster
Production Project Manager: Punithavathy Govindaradjane
Designer: Matthew Limbert

Typeset by VTeX

To my parents for nurturing my curiosity in nature and society

Contents

Preface	xiii
Acknowledgments	xvii
Acronyms	xix
Notations	xxi

I
BASICS

1. Introduction

1.1 Transportation system analysis	3
1.2 Traffic flow theory	5
1.3 Principles, concepts, models, and methods in traffic flow theory	8
1.4 A brief overview of the book	9
Notes	11
Problems	12

2. Definitions of variables

2.1 Three traffic scenarios and space-time diagrams	13
2.2 The three-dimensional representation of traffic flow and primary variables	15
2.3 More derived variables in three coordinates	18
2.3.1. In the flow coordinates	18
2.3.2. In the trajectory coordinates	19
2.3.3. In the schedule coordinates	20
2.3.4. Higher-order derivatives of the primary variables	21
2.3.5. Relationships among the secondary variables	21
2.4 Detection	22
2.4.1. Edie's formulas	22
2.4.2. Detectors	24
2.5 Multi-commodity traffic on a multilane road	27
2.5.1. Multi-commodity traffic	27
2.5.2. Lane-changing traffic	28
Notes	29
Problems	31

3. Basic principles

3.1 Conservation laws	33

3.1.1. In the flow coordinates	34
3.1.2. In other coordinates	35
3.1.3. Conservation laws in other traffic systems	35
3.2 Collision-free condition and other first-order constraints	37
3.2.1. Constraints on density and spacing	37
3.2.2. Constraints on speed and pace	37
3.2.3. Constraints on flow-rate and headway	38
3.2.4. Clearance and time gap	38
3.3 Fundamental diagram	39
3.3.1. Derivation and observation	39
3.3.2. General fundamental diagrams	40
3.3.3. The Greenshields fundamental diagram	43
3.3.4. The triangular fundamental diagram	43
3.3.5. Fundamental diagrams in other secondary variables	46
3.3.6. Non-concave flow-density relations and non-decreasing speed-density relations	48
3.3.7. Fundamental diagrams of inhomogeneous roads and lane-changing traffic	49
3.3.8. Multi-commodity fundamental diagrams	50
3.3.9. Network fundamental diagram	51
3.4 Bounded acceleration and higher-order constraints	52
Notes	53
Problems	55

4. Basic concepts

4.1 Steady states	57
4.2 The simple lead-vehicle problem	58
4.3 Stationary states	60
4.3.1. Definition	60
4.3.2. Equilibrium stationary state in a lane-drop/sag/tunnel zone	61
4.3.3. Considering bounded acceleration	62
4.4 Bottlenecks on a road	63
4.4.1. Capacity reduction	64
4.4.2. More on lane-drop bottlenecks	64
4.4.3. Capacity drop	65
4.5 First-in-first-out (FIFO)	66
4.5.1. FIFO multilane traffic	67
4.5.2. Non-FIFO traffic	68
4.6 First-in-first-out and unifiable equilibrium states	69
Notes	70
Problems	71

II
FIRST-ORDER MODELS

5. The Lighthill-Whitham-Richards (LWR) model

- 5.1 Model derivation ... 76
  - 5.1.1. With the Greenshields fundamental diagram ... 76
  - 5.1.2. Equivalent formulations in other coordinates ... 77
  - 5.1.3. Initial and boundary conditions ... 77
- 5.2 Extensions ... 79
- 5.3 The initial value problem with the triangular fundamental diagram and linear transport equation ... 82
  - 5.3.1. Under-critical initial conditions ... 82
  - 5.3.2. Over-critical initial conditions ... 83
  - 5.3.3. Mixed under- and over-critical initial conditions ... 84
- 5.4 General fundamental diagram and characteristic wave ... 85
  - 5.4.1. Steady solutions ... 85
  - 5.4.2. Nearly steady solutions and characteristic wave ... 85
- 5.5 Solutions to the Riemann problem, shock and rarefaction waves, and entropy condition ... 87
  - 5.5.1. Shock wave ... 88
  - 5.5.2. Rarefaction wave ... 89
  - 5.5.3. Entropy condition ... 90
  - 5.5.4. Riemann solutions with the triangular fundamental diagram ... 91
- 5.6 Stationary states and boundary fluxes in Riemann solutions ... 92
- 5.7 Inhomogeneous LWR model ... 94
  - 5.7.1. Location-dependent speed limits ... 94
  - 5.7.2. Location-dependent number of lanes ... 97
- 5.8 An example with a moving bottleneck ... 99
- Notes ... 101
- Problems ... 102

6. The Cell Transmission Model (CTM)

- 6.1 Numerical methods for solving the LWR model ... 105
  - 6.1.1. Finite difference methods ... 107
  - 6.1.2. The Godunov method ... 108
- 6.2 The Cell Transmission Model ... 109
  - 6.2.1. Demand and supply ... 109
  - 6.2.2. Boundary flux function ... 112
  - 6.2.3. Boundary conditions ... 113
  - 6.2.4. The CTM ... 113
  - 6.2.5. Numerical accuracy and computational cost ... 116
- 6.3 Stationary states on a link ... 116
- 6.4 Numerical solutions to the Riemann problem ... 117
  - 6.4.1. Shock wave ... 118
  - 6.4.2. Rarefaction wave ... 118
- 6.5 Generalized CTM for link traffic ... 120
  - 6.5.1. Inhomogeneous roads ... 120

	6.5.2. Multi-commodity models	121
6.6	Junction models	123
	6.6.1. Diverge models	125
	6.6.2. Merge models	126
	6.6.3. General junction models	127
	Notes	127
	Problems	130

7. Newell's simplified kinematic wave model

7.1	The Hamilton-Jacobi equations and the Hopf-Lax formula for the LWR model	133
	7.1.1. The four Hamilton-Jacobi equations equivalent to the LWR model	134
	7.1.2. The variational principle	134
	7.1.3. The Hopf-Lax formula	136
	7.1.4. The Riemann problem	139
7.2	Newell's simplified kinematic wave model	141
	7.2.1. Derivation	143
	7.2.2. Properties	144
	7.2.3. Newell's model in the trajectory coordinates	146
7.3	Queueing dynamics on a road segment	147
	Notes	148
	Problems	149

8. The Link Transmission Model (LTM)

8.1	Basic variables	151
8.2	New link variables: link demand, supply, queue, and vacancy	152
8.3	Continuous Link Transmission Model	156
8.4	Discrete Link Transmission Model	157
8.5	Homogeneous signalized road networks	159
8.6	Stationary states on a link	161
	8.6.1. Definition	161
	8.6.2. Simple boundary value problem for a road segment	161
	Notes	163
	Problems	163

9. Newell's simplified car-following model

9.1	Derivation	165
9.2	Properties	168
	9.2.1. First-order principles	168
	9.2.2. Equivalent formulations	169
9.3	Applications	171
	9.3.1. Simple accelerating problem (queue discharge problem)	171
	9.3.2. Simple braking problem	172

Notes	173
Problems	173

III
QUEUEING MODELS

10. The link queue model

10.1 Link density, demand, and supply	178
10.1.1. Basic relations	178
10.1.2. Definitions of link demand and supply	179
10.2 Link queue model	179
10.2.1. Continuous version	180
10.2.2. Discrete version	180
10.3 Well-defined and collision-free conditions	181
10.4 Simple boundary value problem	182
10.4.1. Stationary states	182
10.4.2. Dynamic solution of a simple boundary value problem	184
10.5 Applications and extensions	185
10.5.1. Network fundamental diagram on a signalized ring road	185
10.5.2. Modified demand function and the queue discharge problem	185
Notes	187
Problems	188

11. Point queue model

11.1 Derivation	191
11.1.1. Point queue as a limit of a road segment	191
11.1.2. Definitions of queue and vacancy sizes and internal demand and supply	193
11.2 Equivalent formulations	194
11.2.1. Continuous versions	194
11.2.2. Discrete versions	195
11.3 Properties	196
11.3.1. Queueing times	196
11.3.2. Integral version	197
11.3.3. With a constant external supply	199
11.4 Departure time choice at a single bottleneck	200
11.4.1. Costs	200
11.4.2. User equilibrium	202
Notes	204
Problems	205

12. The bathtub model

12.1	A unified space dimension	209
	12.1.1. Traditional transportation system analysis	209
	12.1.2. A new paradigm	210
12.2	Definitions of network-wide trip variables	211
	12.2.1. Travel demand	211
	12.2.2. Active trips	215
	12.2.3. Averages speed and completion rates	218
	12.2.4. A network queue	222
12.3	Three conservation equations	223
	12.3.1. Conservation in total number of trips	223
	12.3.2. Conservation in the trip-miles-traveled	223
	12.3.3. Conservation in the relative number of trips	224
	12.3.4. Relationship among the three conservation laws	226
12.4	Three simplification assumptions	227
	12.4.1. The bathtub assumption	227
	12.4.2. Network fundamental diagram	232
	12.4.3. Time-independent negative exponential distribution of trip distances	234
12.5	Bathtub models	236
	12.5.1. Derivation	236
	12.5.2. Vickrey's bathtub model	237
12.6	Numerical methods	238
	12.6.1. A numerical method for solving the integral form	238
	12.6.2. A numerical method for solving the differential form	238
	12.6.3. A numerical example	239
	Notes	239
	Problems	242

Bibliography   **243**
Index   **253**

Preface

Transportation systems serve the trips of passengers and goods and are indispensable for many economic and social activities. Such systems are complex in nature, since there exist interactions among passengers, vehicles, facilities, operators, and other stakeholders. Thus, the transportation sector faces numerous challenges in safety, efficiency, and equity. To better understand, plan, design, manage, and operate such complex systems has been a core task for transportation researchers and engineers.

Most of transportation problems are practice-oriented and are generally solved with heuristic methods (e.g., the gap-out and max-out method for actuated signals). At the same time, numerous mathematical, behavioral, economic, and ethical topics have their roots in transportation problems (e.g., topology and graph theory, congestion and queueing theory, selfish routing, marginal cost pricing, discrete choice models, and the trolley problem). As the focus of this book, traffic flow models and theories describe the formation, propagation, and dissipation of congestion and queues in road networks. Such traffic dynamics are driven by the travel demands of passengers and goods and the supply of limited capacities by individual and multiple bottlenecks in networks; vehicles' driving behaviors and transportation agencies' control policies determine the allocation of resources among vehicles. Traffic flow models have been widely used in planning transportation facilities, designing traffic signals, estimating and forecasting congestion patterns, controlling and managing traffic at bottlenecks, and providing guidance to improve drivers' choices in routes, departure times, modes, and so on.

Since the 1990s, substantial progresses have been made in the area of traffic flow theory. Notable examples include the simplified and equivalent versions of the Lighthill-Whitham-Richards model in different coordinates, as well as the extensions of the Lighthill-Whitham-Richards model for networks and multi-commodity traffic flow. Another significant direction is related to various deterministic queueing models motivated by congestion pricing, signal control, and other applications. The rapid development was also boosted by the availability of many high quality data sets and the observation of interesting phenomena (e.g., the California PeMS and the FHWA NGSIM data sets, capacity drop, and network fundamental diagram). Even though several books and monographs have been published on traffic flow theory, a systematic introduction to such modern traffic flow theories is warranted and long overdue.

In recent years, however, there have been debates over the role of traffic flow theories in the era of connected and autonomous vehicles (CAVs), big data, artificial intelligence, and emerging mobility systems. Many people believe that, with sufficient data, communication capacities, and data processing capabilities, traditional traffic flow models become dispensable. However, it is likely that new technologies will induce more travel demand and lead to more complex transportation systems. To balance safety, efficiency, and equity in such large-scale multi-modal transportation networks, traffic flow theories will be even more important for guiding connected and autonomous vehicles, understanding the intricate interactions among demands and supplies at various bottlenecks, and efficiently managing the transportation facility. For example, to ensure the safety and efficiency in a mixed traffic system with both human-driven and autonomous vehicles, we need to much better understand how human drivers take care of both safety and speed at the same time; for this, we need to develop car-following and lane-changing models that satisfy such constraints as collision-free, bounded acceleration, bounded deceleration, and so on.

Personally, I started to study traffic control problems in 1999, but quickly realized that the lack of an understanding of the capacity drop mechanism prevented me from rigorously assessing various control strategies' effectiveness and developing new strategies. That has led to my journey in traffic flow theory in the past two decades, during which I have systematically studied the network kinematic wave theory, lane-changing traffic, bounded acceleration and capacity drop, non-first-in-first-out traffic, and bathtub models. Initially, I was more interested in mathematical analyses and numerical solutions of various models; along the years I have shifted my focus toward empirical calibration and validation and relationship among different models; more recently, I have emphasized more on the underlying principles and concepts, which have enabled deeper understanding of traffic phenomena and the development of models that are both physically meaningful and mathematically rigorous.

I have always wanted to summarize my findings and understanding of traffic flow theory in a textbook, as it is fundamental to many studies by myself and others. However, the endeavor turns out to be much more challenging than I expected. As this is my first time to write a book, and traffic flow theory is such a challenging topic, it took me a while to just unify the notations. In addition, as I am still actively involved in research on traffic flow theory, my understanding and perspective have been constantly evolving, and I have to constantly revise the finished chapters. Until very recently, I realized that I have to settle down with my best efforts and stop worrying about missing new and better theories, as this is inevitable for a rapidly evolving area.

Nevertheless, I have several rather lofty goals for this book. The first goal is to establish traffic flow theory as a research domain of its own. Historically, the area of transportation studies has borrowed many theories and methods from mathematics, physics, economics, statistics, and other fields. However, transportation systems have many unique features, and I will try to derive and solve traffic flow models based on the first principles and concepts related to individual driving behaviors and observed system characteristics. For example, the collision-free and forward-driving principles are used to replace the Courant-Friedrichs-Lewy condition for the Cell Transmission Model. The second goal is to present traffic flow theories in a systematic and coherent manner. Different theories may be equivalent but differ in formulations, or they are for the same traffic phenomenon but with different levels of details. In the end, the readers can pick a model that is suitable for their applications; in general, a good model should strike a balance among physical realism, mathematical tractability, computational efficiency, and empirical verifiability. The third goal is to write a textbook on traffic flow theory, instead of a research monograph or comprehensive literature review. The choice of the topics and the details largely reflects my personal (and maybe idiosyncratic) views. I have tried to cover the most fundamental principles, concepts, models, and methods, which will likely be used by the broadest range of researchers, including the future self. There is no doubt that there is still a lot of room for improvement in many aspects. I would like to sincerely apologize for any deficiencies and appreciate constructive criticisms and suggestions for future revisions.

Wen-Long Jin
January 24, 2021 at Irvine, CA

Acknowledgments

Foremost, I'd like to thank my former PhD advisor at UC Davis, Professor H. Michael Zhang, for he introduced me to the fantastic area of transportation in general and traffic flow theory in particular. After the first conversation with him, I was immediately attracted by the practical implications of control theory in transportation engineering. Thanks to the flexibility in the Department of Mathematics at UC Davis, I was able to choose Michael, a professor in Civil Engineering, as my major advisor, even though most of my financial support came from the Mathematics department throughout my PhD study. Michael provided a great deal of freedom to me, such that I could choose the research topics that are most interesting to me during my graduate study. For my masters' thesis, I followed him to study second-order traffic flow models, for which he is a world-renown expert; but for my PhD thesis I switched to network kinematic wave models, which were relatively new at the time. I'd also like to thank Professors Carlos Daganzo and Jean-Patrick Lebacque, who are two of my heroes in traffic flow theory; my research on network kinematic wave theory greatly benefited from their pioneering work and private conversations.

I have greatly enjoyed the free atmosphere of the Institute of Transportation Studies at UC Irvine. In particular, I'd like to thank my post-doc advisor, mentor, and colleague, Professor Will Recker. Will has been supportive of me focusing on transportation and traffic theories, which are important but not of the mainstream in transportation engineering. More and more I feel privileged to work at UC Irvine, as I have been able to focus on topics that most interest me; this would be impossible without the selfless support of Will and other colleagues at UC Irvine.

I'd like to thank my students, especially Hao Yang, Qijian Gan, Zhe Sun, Anupam Srivastava, Felipe de Souza, Qinglong Yan, Xuting Wang, Irene Martinez, Ximeng Fan, and others. I consider them as my collaborators and enjoy discussing different kinds of transportation questions with them. The discussions have greatly helped me to refine my theories and explanations. I'd also like to thank Suman Mistra and many other collaborators, with whom my conversations helped to position the network traffic flow theory in the more general context of transportation studies.

I would also like to thank many colleagues at Elsevier, especially Ms. Barbara L. Makinster and Ms. Punithavathy Govindaradjane, for their patience and help. Hopefully, with the uncovering of Vickrey's bathtub model in 2019, the patience from the publisher has paid off, as it represents a new paradigm for network traffic flow modeling and leads to the last chapter of this book.

I'd like to thank my family, especially my wife, Ling, for being sympathetic and encouraging with my endeavors to write the book. My children, Laurel and Christopher, are also acknowledged for being inspirational to writing the book and many other endeavors. I'd like to thank my sister and brothers, Xiu-Lian, Wen-Hu, and Wen-bin, for their continuous support and discussions related to and interest in my research.

Finally, I'd like to dedicate this book to my parents, Jia-Sheng and Jie-Fang, who did not have the privilege of pursuing higher education but have been unconditionally supportive of my education. I inherited from them much of my curiosity in both nature and society, which has been instrumental for my in-depth research in transportation systems.

Acronyms

ACC	Adaptive Cruise Control
CAV	Connected and autonomous vehicle
CFL	Courant-Friedrichs-Lewy condition
CTM	Cell Transmission Model
FHWA	Federal HighWay Administration
FIFO	First-In-First-Out
GPS	Global Positioning System
HCM	Highway Capacity Manual
ITS	Intelligent Transportation System
LQM	Link Queue Model
LTM	Link Transmission Model
LVP	Lead-vehicle problem
LWR	Lighthill-Whitham-Richards
NFD	Network Fundamental Diagram
NGSIM	Next Generation Simulation
OC	Over-critical
ODE	Ordinary differential equation
PDE	Partial differential equation
PeMS	The Caltrans Performance Measurement System
PQM	Point queue model
SLVP	Simple lead-vehicle problem
SOC	Strictly over-critical
SUC	Strictly under-critical
TMT	Trip-miles traveled
UC	Under-critical
VHT	Vehicle-hours traveled
VLHT	Vehicle-lane-hours traveled
VMT	Vehicle-miles traveled
VSL	Variable Speed Limit

Notations

Parameters

a_0	maximum acceleration rate	Δx	cell size
u	free-flow speed	q_0	$= w\kappa$
C	capacity	w	shock wave speed
L	length	E	duration
κ	jam density	κ_c	critical density
τ	time gap	ϵ	infinitesimal number
ζ	jam spacing	ζ_c	critical spacing
ξ	capacity drop ratio	Δt	time-step size
Λ	platoon size	Δn	unit vehicle

Variables

a	acceleration rate	c	lane-changing intensity
d	demand (rate)	f	in-flux
g	out-flux	h	headway
k	density	l	number of lanes
n	vehicle number	p	commodity density proportion
q	flow-rate	s	supply (rate)
t	time	v	speed
v_s	shock wave speed	x	location
z	spacing	G	cumulative out-flow
F	cumulative in-flow	$T(x,n)$	passing time of vehicle n at x
$N(t,x)$	cumulative flow at t and x	Z	cumulative lane miles
$X(t,n)$	location of vehicle n at t	δ	queue size
γ	commodity flow-rate proportion	λ	characteristic wave speed
η	commodity speed ratio	σ	vacancy size
π	effective green ratio	ω	pace
χ	congestion level		

Relations

$A(v)$	acceleration-speed relation	$D(k)$	demand-density relation
$H(\cdot)$	Heaviside function	$H(\cdot)$	Hamiltonian
$K(\chi)$	density-congestion relation	$L(\cdot)$	Lagrangian
$P(k)$	image density	$Q(k)$	flow-density relation
$V(k)$	speed-density relation	$W(z)$	speed-spacing relation
$\Xi(\omega)$	headway-pace relation		

Basics

The grand aim of all science is to cover the greatest number of empirical facts by logical deduction from the smallest number of hypotheses or axioms. - Albert Einstein

CHAPTER 1

Introduction

Toad transportation systems are designed to move people and goods in space and time. They are intrinsically complex systems with many stakeholders and conflicting objectives. Essential to transportation system analysis is to understand the interplay between travel demand and supply in a road network. Traffic flow theory aims to study the formation, propagation, and dissipation of traffic congestion subject to different travel demand levels, driving behaviors, and traffic control measures. This book differs from many existing ones on traffic flow theory, as it systematically covers the fundamental principles, concepts, models, and methods for network traffic flow theory. This chapter presents some introductory discussions on transportation system analysis, traffic flow theory, and an overview of the whole book.

1.1 Transportation system analysis

Road transportation systems are critical for the movement of people and goods in space and time. They can be viewed as control systems, as illustrated in Fig. 1.1. Their performance can be measured with respect to safety, comfort, mobility, costs, environmental impacts, land use, equity, livability, and so on. Various control, management, planning, and design strategies have been devised to drive the systems to the desired states, and their performances are constantly monitored with detection, estimation, and communication technologies. In order to design and compare various control measures, transportation engineers need to have a good understanding of how the entire transportation system performs when certain control measures are implemented. Qualitative and quantitative models built on the first principles of various system components and real-world observations can be helpful for these tasks.

As illustrated in Fig. 1.2, a transportation system has many stakeholders: general public, including pedestrians and bicyclists, drivers, passengers, goods; fleet operators, including transit agencies and Transporta-

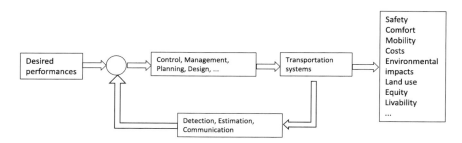

FIGURE 1.1 Transportation systems as control systems.

tion Network Companies (TNCs), delivery companies; vehicles, including buses, cars, and bikes; car manufacturers; and transportation agencies at the city, state, and federal levels. The performance of a multi-modal transportation system results from the complex interactions among different stakeholders, who usually have different objectives, constraints, characteristics, and choice behaviors. In a transportation system, choice behaviors are hierarchical with social, economic, or engineering categories. In the traditional mobility system served by privately operated vehicles, a driver and a vehicle form a driver-vehicle unit, and the driver makes all the choices related to house locations, jobs, trips, destinations, departure times, modes, routes, lanes, parking, speeds, and so on. In the emerging mobility system with connected, autonomous, electric, and shared vehicles, TNCs and autonomous car manufacturers are the additional stakeholders, and many of the choices are handled by the fleet operators and vehicles themselves.

Many road transportation systems, including freeway and city networks, have been plagued with recurrent and non-recurrent traffic congestion. As illustrated in Fig. 1.3, many locations in the Los Angeles freeway network can be congested from 7:30 to 9:00 in the morning of a typical weekday. Indications of congestion include long queues, slow moving speeds, and high concentration of cars. At the system level, congestion is caused by the imbalance between the supply of capacity provided by the infrastructure and the travel demand of passengers and goods, which are determined by the social and economic choice behaviors in house locations, jobs, trips, destinations, departure times, modes, and routes. A road network can have many bottlenecks, where congestion generally initiates. Since congestion patterns and, therefore, travel delays, are usually location- and time-dependent and stochastic, many transportation control, management, planning, and design problems are quite challenging. Without congestion, many transportation problems would not exist; but congestion is inevitable, since trips tend to be spatially and temporally clustered due to the nature of departure time and other choice behaviors.

1.2 Traffic flow theory

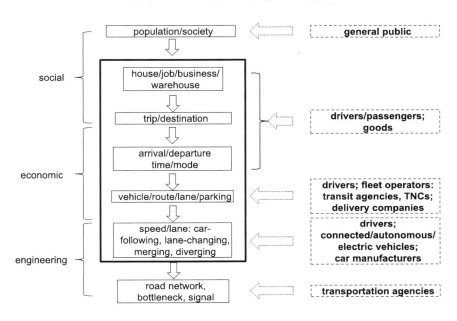

FIGURE 1.2 Stakeholders and their choice behaviors in a transportation system.

It has been observed that congestion still occurs after a road expansion, but the length of the peak period could be shorter. In addition, a road expansion or other measures aiming to improve the supply of capacity could induce more cars to the corresponding road. Traffic congestion is a bane of commuters' lives in many metropolitan areas and deteriorates the performance of a transportation system in terms of safety, comfort, mobility, environmental impacts, and social impacts. Therefore, traffic congestion has been a major motivation of the development of transportation planning and engineering strategies with respect to connected and autonomous vehicle technologies, infrastructure management and control, congestion pricing, and public transit and shared mobility.

1.2 Traffic flow theory

Traffic flow theory is to study how vehicles' driving behaviors, including car-following, lane-changing, merging, and diverging behaviors, would impact the formation, propagation, and dissipation of traffic congestion as well as the travel speeds and delays of individual vehicles in various types of transportation facilities and subject to such control measures as speed limits, signal control, fleet size management, and so on. In essence, traffic flow theory studies the interaction between travel demand

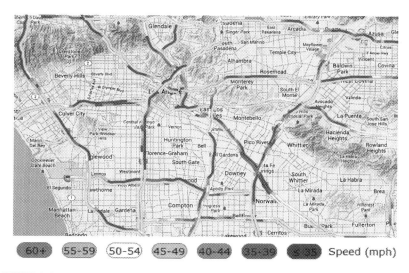

FIGURE 1.3 Traffic congestion patterns in the Los Angeles freeway network at 8:00 AM on June 18, 2013 (Data source: http://pems.dot.ca.gov/).

and supply and their impacts on traffic congestion and trip completion times.

The area of traffic flow theory covers a broad range of topics related to the identification and formulation of traffic flow problems at different bottlenecks and road networks (e.g., signalized intersection, lane-drop, sag/tunnel, merge, diverge, network, etc); definitions of variables for describing road and vehicle characteristics (e.g., capacity, queue length, delay, travel time, etc) as well as traffic phenomena; derivation, inference, calibration, and validation of traffic flow models for the relations among different variables; solutions and analyses of static and dynamic congestion patterns in traffic flow models. Note that economic theories for travelers' choice behaviors in routes, modes, departure times, and origins and destinations are highly related to traffic flow theory as they usually determine the travel demand on a road link or network, but they are not traffic flow theories in our view.

Traffic flow models and theories have been foundational for transportation studies, as well as studies in public health, urban planning, transportation economics, laws, and social systems. For examples, the link performance function, which determines the link travel time from the link's demand, underpins the traffic assignment problem and transportation planning, and Webster's delay formula, which determines the travel delay from the demand at a signalized intersection, is essential for determining and analyzing signal settings. Dynamic traffic flow models have been used to estimate and forecast congestion patterns, control and management of traffic at bottlenecks, and provide guidance to improve drivers' choices in routes, departure times, modes, and so on. In all of these applications, traffic flow models and theories have played a critical role in improving the safety, mobility, and environmental impacts of a transportation system.

There is a saying that every driver is a traffic flow theorist. That is, all drivers have their understandings and hypotheses regarding traffic congestion. For examples, some people believe that left lanes are faster in congested traffic, but others believe otherwise; some people believe that arterial roads can be faster than freeways during the rush hours. People use their traffic flow theories to guide their choices in modes, departure times, routes, lanes, and speeds. Thus, good traffic flow theories can be useful for improving individuals' driving experience.

A systematic development of traffic flow theory is relatively recent. It starts with Greenshields' hypothesis and observation of a speed-density relation, now known as the fundamental diagram of traffic flow, in the 1930s. Then in the 1950s, mathematical models describing the evolution of traffic flow and vehicles' car-following behaviors were proposed by applied mathematicians, and traffic engineers; the most influential is the Lighthill-Whitham-Richards (LWR) model, which combines the fundamental diagram and conservation law in the number of vehicles. Since 1990s, various equivalent formulations of the LWR model with different state variables in different coordinates were presented by transportation researchers; another important direction is the introduction of the network kinematic wave theory, which integrates the LWR model and junction models. These developments are mostly motivated by theoretical investigations and the need to formulate and solve the dynamic traffic assignment problem in a road network. In parallel, since 1960s, deterministic and stochastic queueing models have been introduced to model the queueing process at different types of bottlenecks. In particular, motivated by the applications in congestion pricing, Vickrey introduced the point queue model for a single bottleneck in the 1960s and the bathtub model for a network of bottlenecks in the 1990s; for the latter, the network fundamental diagram is an important component and has been studied since the 1960s.

From the above brief survey of the literature, we can see that the development of traffic flow theory has been propelled by empirical discoveries, theoretical investigations, and applications. With emerging shared mobility systems, connected and autonomous vehicles, and other new technologies, multi-modal transportation systems are becoming ever more complex. For such emerging mobility systems, the availability of more high-quality data will enable more discoveries of interesting and critical traffic phenomena, for which new theories and models are needed to explain the underlying mechanism. To control, manage, and plan such systems more effectively and efficiently, engineers and planners also need new theories and models to analyze and predict the congestion dynamics on different scales. Thus, the field of traffic flow theory will continue to be motivated by empirical discoveries, theoretical investigations, and applications.

1.3 Principles, concepts, models, and methods in traffic flow theory

In the history of mathematics and science, many groundbreaking new theories are started with a set of simple yet intuitive principles, which are also called axioms, assumptions, postulates, or hypotheses. Euclidean geometry is derived from five axioms. Riemann derived a new geometry based on the assumption that "the length of lines is independent of their position". Einstein derived the special theory of relativity based on two postulates: the principle of relativity, and "that light is always propagated in empty space with a definite velocity which is independent of the state of motion of the emitting body".

In this book, we aim to identify a set of simple principles for traffic flow that are consistent with our daily driving experience and empirical observations. From the perspective of individual drivers, traffic flow models should be collision-free and observe the speed limit. At the aggregate level, such values as density and flow in traffic flow are generally non-negative, traffic is unidirectional on many roads, the number of vehicles is conserved, and there exists an approximate relation between speed and density in congested traffic. In addition, the acceleration and deceleration rates as well as the jerk should be bounded, and some principles can be identified for lane-changing, merging, and diverging behaviors. Unfortunately, such basic principles have yet to be sufficiently discussed in existing traffic flow theory, and many efforts have been wasted on solving and analyzing physically meaningless models that violate some of the basic principles. For examples, some models fail to produce a reasonable speed-density relation at the aggregate level, and they cannot be used to describe the congestion dynamics. Other car-following models violate the very basic collision-free principle; this is why we cannot apply these car-following models to guide autonomous vehicles. For some models, one or more key assumptions were not explicitly discussed, and this leads to wrong applications of such models for situations where such implicit assumptions are violated. Hence, to carefully examine basic principles for traffic flow can help to put traffic flow theory on the proper foundation and lead to fruitful developments of highly original theory in the future.

In addition to the domain-specific principles, we also need to pay attention to the basic principles with respect to logic and reasoning. For examples, a correlation may not be a causal relation, one or many examples cannot prove a general conclusion, and the units on the two sides of an equation should match each other. Unfortunately, these could also be forgotten by many modelers in practice. In addition, some theories and models come with essential, but implicit assumptions, and failing to recognize them could lead to improper extensions and applications.

Once basic principles are identified, related concepts need to be introduced to formally define such principles. This generally lead to definitions of variables and states. In traffic flow, the primary variables include vehicles' trajectories, schedules, and flows. Derived variables include densities, flow-rates, speeds, queue length, and so on. Demand and supply can also be defined for road segments, links, or different types of trips. Traffic can be in a steady, stationary, or equilibrium state, depending on whether it is independent of time, location, or speed-density relation.

Further, models describe the relations among variables, and the change in variables. The modeling process can include derivations of different formulations, explanation of the relationship among different formulations, and unification of different models. Models can be derived from basic principles or obtained from regression methods with data.

There is a saying that all models are wrong, but some are useful. To understand when and how models are useful, we need to understand them well enough. Methods for analyzing and solving traffic flow models can be analytical, numerical, or empirical. Many traffic flow models are analytically challenging to solve, as they are genuinely nonlinear. However, for flow-based models, it is helpful to solve the Riemann problem under very special initial conditions. Mathematically, many nonlinear models can admit multiple solutions, and basic principles are needed to pick out unique, physically meaningful ones. Basic mathematical analysis can reveal the limitations of some models; for example, some models predict free-flow travel speed at the jam density, and this renders these models useless for congested traffic. Under general conditions, many traffic flow models have to be solved numerically by discretizing the space and time domain. Numerical analyses can reveal the relationship between the basic space size and the time step-size. In addition, well-defined numerical methods should yield converging solutions with finer grids in space and time. Ultimately models and their solutions should be validated by observations. With observations, we need to first calibrate the parameters in a model and then compare the analytical and numerical solutions with the observations. In this book we will cover all of these methods, which help to reveal the strengths and weaknesses of each model.

1.4 A brief overview of the book

This book is divided into three parts.

The first part covers the basics of traffic flow theory in Chapters 2–4, in addition to this chapter of Introduction. Chapter 2 discusses three traffic scenarios and space-time diagrams, a three-dimensional representation of traffic flow, three primary variables and corresponding coordinate systems, and other variables. Chapter 3 introduces the aggregate principles in conservation laws and fundamental diagrams and the disaggregate principles in collision-free and bounded acceleration. Chapter 4 introduces steady and stationary states and solves them for simple bottlenecks.

The second part covers the basics for kinematic wave theory in Chapters 5–9. Chapter 5 systematically discusses the LWR model. The Riemann problem is solved theoretically with traditional entropy conditions. Numerically the Godunov scheme is presented under general initial conditions. Chapter 6 presents the Cell Transmission Model (CTM), including the demand and supply functions, and the boundary flux function for various types of junctions. Chapter 7 presents Newell's simplified kinematic wave model. It starts with the Hamilton-Jacobi equation of the LWR model and the Hopf-Lax formula. Chapter 8 presents the Link Transmission Model (LTM). It defines the link demand and supply functions from boundary cumulative flows. Chapter 9 presents Newell's simplified car-following model, which satisfies several basic disaggregate, driving principles and the aggregate principles.

The third part covers several queueing models in Chapter 10–12. Chapter 10 presents a link queue model (LQM), which approximates the LWR model with an ordinary differential equation. Chapter 11 discusses formulations and properties of point queue models (PQM), which eliminates the spatial dimension for simplicity as in the LQM. Chapter 12 presents the bathtub models for network trip flows; in these models the space dimension is relatively for all trips.

Homework problems are presented at the end of each chapter. They can be related to literature review, opinion essays, mathematical proofs and derivations, numerical solutions, or data analysis. For numerical solutions and data analysis, the following programming languages can be used: Excel, Matlab®, and Jupyter Notebooks.

Throughout the book, we cannot avoid applications of advanced systems theories and mathematics. However, I will carefully explain any required mathematics so that they are accessible by anyone with basic training in calculus. In addition, I have tried my best to explain the physical meanings of equations and theorems. For examples, shock/rarefaction waves are explained by scenarios with red/green lights, Lax's entropy condition for shock and rarefaction waves is explained with the Ansorge's acceleration/deceleration rule, the Riemann problem is equivalent to the lead-vehicle problem, and the Courant-Friedrichs-Lewy (CFL) condition is explained by the collision-free condition.

In this book, many topics are only touched upon or totally omitted due to the limitation of space. Examples include higher-order continuum and car-following models, pedestrian traffic flow models, traffic flow models for signalized road networks, advanced mathematical theories for multi-commodity network traffic flow models, models for shared mobility and transit systems, and stochastic models. However, the basic principles, concepts, models, and methods introduced in the book will be helpful to understand existing theories or develop new theories for these and other traffic systems.

Notes

Note 1.1. *For the traditional transportation network analysis methods, please refer to (Cascetta, 2009).*

Note 1.2. *A number of Nobel prize winners' works have been directly applied or even started in transportation studies. For examples, the 1970 Economics prize's winner, Samuelson, was among the first to study spatial price equilibrium, which has a lot of similarity with user equilibrium. The 1977 Chemistry prize's winner, Prigogine, co-authored a book entitled "Kinetic theory of vehicular traffic" in 1971 and proposed the two-fluid theory of arterial traffic. The 1994 Economics prize's winner, Nash, introduced the concept of Nash equilibrium and presented a proof based on the fixed-point theorem, which have been applied to study user equilibrium. The 1996 Economics prize's winner, Vickrey, wrote a seminal paper, "Congestion Theory and Transport Investment" in 1969, which is among the first to study congestion pricing. Columbia University's Rare Book & Manuscript Library, https://findingaids.library.columbia.edu/ead/nnc-rb/ldpd_5455879/dsc/3#subseries_8, collects 131 manuscripts of Vickrey's on transportation studies. The 2000 Economics prize's winner, McFadden, wrote the seminal book "Conditional logit analysis of qualitative choice behavior" in 1973, which introduces the discrete choice model.*

Note 1.3. *Newell wrote a really nice piece for the early history of traffic flow theory in (G. Newell, 2002). As he correctly commented, many of the fundamental theories, models, and algorithms before 1990's were developed by established researchers in other fields, and there was no theory to explain the effectiveness of ramp metering and other traffic control measures. However, the situation has been substantially improved since seminal works by himself, Daganzo, and other researchers of the Berkeley school of traffic flow theory since late 1990's. This book will try to highlight the unique contributions made by these transportation researchers. In addition, this book will present a theory for capacity drop, which is the mobility motivation of ramp metering (Banks, 1991a; Papageorgiou et al., 2003).*

Note 1.4. *Congestion still occurs after a road expansion, but the length of the peak period could be shorter. This is called the shifting-peak phenomenon in (Small, 1992). A systematic discussion on traffic congestion was made in (Downs, 2004).*

Note 1.5. *Departure time and route choice behaviors underlay the traffic assignment problem, transportation planning, and congestion pricing (Sheffi, 1984;*

Yang and Huang, 2005; Small, 2013), and mode choice behaviors underly the travel demand forecast (Akiva and Lerman, 1985).

Note 1.6. *See https://www.youtube.com/watch?v=u4fuHV5rr7s for a beautiful night view of traffic flow from ORIX Building in Osaka City, Japan.*

Note 1.7. *The Revised Monograph on Traffic Flow Theory by the U.S. Department of Transportation, Federal Highway Administration is available at https://www.fhwa.dot.gov/publications/research/operations/tft/.*

Note 1.8. *The English translations of Riemann's papers have been published in (Baker et al., 2004). Even though I did not understand most of his advanced mathematics, I was amazed by how he was able to arrive at the original and deep results from a few fundamental first principles. For example, in the article entitled "The hypothesis on which geometry is based", he started by examining the assumptions in existing geometry from Euclid to Legendre and then tried to seek "the simplest facts" for geometry. Later he arrived at the assumption that "the length of lines is independent of their position", which has led to Riemannian and modern geometry. This is also the case when Einstein derived his theory of special relativity http://www.fourmilab.ch/etexts/einstein/specrel/www/. In particular, he started with one conjecture of "Principle of Relativity" and a postulate "that light is always propagated in empty space with a definite velocity c which is independent of the state of motion of the emitting body".*

Problems

Problem 1.1. *As a driver or rider, you might have contrived a theory or trick to improve your safety, speed, or fuel efficiency in congestion. This could be a traffic flow theory. Describe the underlying principle and discuss why it works for you and whether it is helpful for the overall transportation system if many drivers follow suit.*

Problem 1.2. *Write a critical review on "Memoirs on highway traffic flow theory in the 1950s" by GF Newell, published in Operations Research, 2002. Discuss any principles, concepts, models, and methods that are interesting to you.*

Problem 1.3. *Critically review (Vickrey, 2019).*

CHAPTER 2

Definitions of variables

The mobility of vehicles, passengers, goods, or other entities in a space-time domain forms traffic flow. The time and space dimensions can vary for different traffic systems. This chapter defines some basic variables for describing traffic flow, which will be used to introduce fundamental principles, concepts, models, and methods in the rest of the book.

2.1 Three traffic scenarios and space-time diagrams

Traffic flow is formed by the movements of vehicles, passengers, goods, and other objects in a space-time domain. The following are three scenarios of traffic flow and the corresponding space-time diagrams.

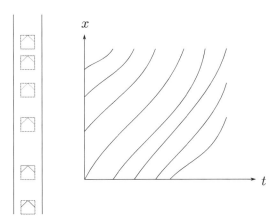

FIGURE 2.1 Traffic flow on a road.

For vehicles moving on a road during a day, as illustrated in the left figure of Fig. 2.1, a natural choice of space is the distance from a point on the road. If the road is unidirectional and no backward traveling is allowed, vehicles travel in the positive direction of the x coordinate. On the right-hand side, the trajectories are illustrated in the absolute space-time diagram. Here t represents the within-day time.

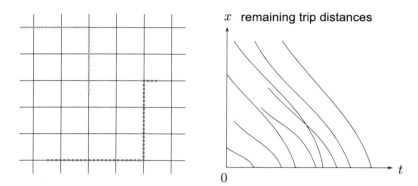

FIGURE 2.2 Traffic flow on a road network.

For trips of vehicles, passengers, or goods in a road network during a day, whose paths are illustrated by the dotted lines on the left figure of Fig. 2.2, their absolute space coordinates would be different as they can have different links, paths, origins, and destinations. However, the remaining trip distance can be used as the unified space coordinate, and the trip trajectories can be illustrated in the relative space-time diagram on the right-hand side. Here t represents the within-day time.

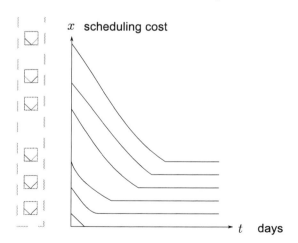

FIGURE 2.3 Traffic flow on an imaginary road.

When passengers choose their departure times from day to day, they would like to choose an arrival time that is uncongested and has a smaller scheduling cost (penalty for early or late arrivals). Then they are traveling on an imaginary road in the direction of reducing scheduling costs, as illustrated by the left figure of Fig. 2.3. Their trajectories in the imaginary space-time diagram are illustrated on the right-hand side. Here t represents days.

In addition to traffic flow in such an economic space, the movements of people in a social system could lead to traffic flow in an imaginary, social space, in an even larger time span.

Traffic flow theory is to describe and predict the movements of vehicles in these space-time diagrams. In the following sections, we introduce some basic variables and concepts for the first, vehicular traffic system in the absolute physical space during a period of time within a day. But they also apply to other traffic systems with the corresponding space and time dimensions.

2.2 The three-dimensional representation of traffic flow and primary variables

During peak periods, traffic congestion patterns in an urban road network are determined by daily commuters' origins, destinations, schedules, and route choices. From the snapshots of speed profiles in the Los Angeles freeway network during the morning peak hours on June 18, 2013, as shown in Fig. 1.3, different links can have different speed profiles, queue lengths, and bottleneck locations. A general road network has the following components:

1. $\mathcal{R}$: the set of origin links; $\mathcal{Y}$: the set of destination links; $\mathcal{B}$: the set of regular links; $\mathcal{B}' = \mathcal{R} \cup \mathcal{Y} \cup \mathcal{B}$: the set of all links.
2. $\mathcal{M}$: the set of commodities, where vehicles using the same path or sharing the same characteristics belong to a commodity; $\mathcal{M}_b$: the set of commodities using link $b \in \mathcal{B}'$.
3. $\mathcal{J}$: the set of junctions; $\mathcal{I}_j$: the set of upstream (incoming) links of junction $j \in \mathcal{J}$; $\mathcal{O}_j$: the set of downstream (outgoing) links of junction j.

When we zoom in the traffic map, traffic congestion patterns on each road link are determined by the relative locations of vehicles, as illustrated in Fig. 2.4, where we use the rear bumper as the reference point of a vehicle and label vehicles in an increasing order from leaders to followers. On the left are the initial locations of six vehicles. We denote the vehicle number by n, the location by x, which increases in the traffic direction, and the time by t. The right figure shows the trajectories in the (t, x)-space of eight vehicles; i.e., their locations at different times, which can be collected from GPS devices or video cameras mounted along the road side. On a road segment from $x = 0$ to $x = L$ during the time interval between $t = 0$ and

$t = E$, as shown in the figure, the traffic condition is determined by all vehicles' trajectories.

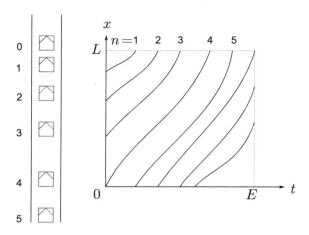

FIGURE 2.4 Vehicle trajectories on a road.

If denoting $N(t, x)$ as the cumulative flow or the cumulative number of vehicles passing location x at t after a reference vehicle, we can plot the cumulative flows at different locations and different time instants as in Fig. 2.5. In the figure, the cumulative flows are piecewise constant staircases, but we can approximate them with continuous (dashed) curves by connecting the cusps. A further simplification is to assume that $N(t, x)$ is smooth and differentiable.

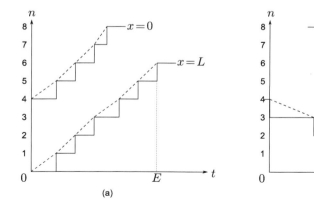

FIGURE 2.5 Cumulative flows.

The cumulative flows form a three-dimensional surface, as shown in Fig. 2.6, where the level curves represent vehicles' trajectories. The surface

2.2 Primary variables

can be represented by

$$n = N(t, x), \qquad (2.1)$$

where t and x are independent variables, and n the dependent variable. Similarly, the surface can also be represented by

$$x = X(t, n), \qquad (2.2)$$

where t and n are independent variables, and $X(t, n)$ is the location (trajectory) of vehicle n at t; or

$$t = T(n, x), \qquad (2.3)$$

where x and n are independent variables, and $T(n, x)$ is the time (schedule) for vehicle n to pass x.

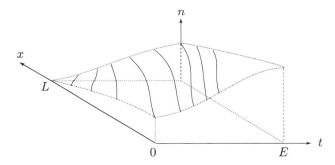

FIGURE 2.6 The t-x-n surface for a traffic stream.

The three representations are equivalent but with different coordinates. $N(t, x)$ describes the flow, and (t, x) form the flow (or Eulerian) coordinates. $X(t, n)$ describes the trajectory, and (t, n) forms the trajectory (or Lagrangian) coordinates. $T(n, x)$ describes the schedule, and (n, x) forms the schedule coordinates. We call t, x, and n the primary variables of traffic flow, from which many other variables can be derived. The $t - x - n$ trinity for traffic flow is illustrated in Fig. 2.7.

At t, the cumulative number at $X(t, n)$ should be n; thus we have the following equality:

$$n = N(t, X(t, n)). \qquad (2.4a)$$

Similarly, we have

$$x = X(t, N(t, x)), \qquad (2.4b)$$
$$x = X(T(n, x), n), \qquad (2.4c)$$

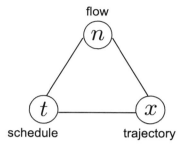

FIGURE 2.7 The *t-x-n* trinity for traffic flow.

$$t = T(n, X(t,n)). \tag{2.4d}$$
$$t = T(N(t,x), x), \tag{2.4e}$$
$$n = N(T(n,x), x), \tag{2.4f}$$

$N(t,x)$, $X(t,n)$, and $T(n,x)$ are symmetrical. That is, all of the three functions are related. In particular, at a given time t, $X(t,n)$ and $N(t,x)$ are inverse functions of each other. There is a similar relation between $X(t,n)$ and $T(n,x)$, and between $N(t,x)$ and $T(n,x)$.

2.3 More derived variables in three coordinates

Even though traffic flow can be described by the 3-D surface, $N(t,x)$, $X(t,n)$, or $T(n,x)$, it could be costly to obtain such complete information of all vehicles' trajectories. Thus, sometimes traffic states are described by the derivatives of the primary variables.

This section defines the first- and second-order variables, which are respectively the first- and second-order derivatives of the primary variables. In contrast, t, x, and n are the zeroth-order variables.

2.3.1 In the flow coordinates

The number of vehicles passing x from $t - \Delta t$ to t equals $\Delta N([t - \Delta t, t], x) = N(t,x) - N(t - \Delta t, x)$, which is non-negative, and the average *flow-rate* is then

$$\frac{\Delta N([t - \Delta t, t], x)}{\Delta t} = \frac{N(t,x) - N(t - \Delta t, x)}{\Delta t}.$$

Letting $\Delta t \to 0$, we obtain the instantaneous flow-rate at x and t:

$$q(t,x) = \lim_{\Delta t \to 0} \frac{N(t,x) - N(t - \Delta t, x)}{\Delta t}$$

2.3 Derived variables

$$\frac{\partial N(t,x)}{\partial t} = N_t(t,x), \quad (2.5)$$

which is the partial derivative of the cumulative flow with respect to time. Correspondingly, if the flow-rates are given, the number of vehicles passing x from $t - \Delta t$ to t can be calculated by integration:

$$\Delta N([t - \Delta t, t], x) = \int_{y=t-\Delta t}^{t} q(y, x) dy.$$

The number of vehicles at t from $x - \Delta x$ to x equals $\Delta N(t, [x - \Delta x, x]) = N(t, x - \Delta x) - N(t, x)$, since a vehicle passes $x - \Delta x$ earlier than x. The average *density* is

$$\frac{\Delta N(t, [x - \Delta x, x])}{\Delta x} = \frac{N(t, x - \Delta x) - N(t, x)}{\Delta x}.$$

Let $\Delta x \to 0$, we obtain the density at x and t:

$$\begin{aligned} k(t, x) &= \lim_{\Delta x \to 0} \frac{N(t, x - \Delta x) - N(t, x)}{\Delta x} \\ &= -\frac{\partial N(t, x)}{\partial x} = -N_x(t, x), \end{aligned} \quad (2.6)$$

which is the negative partial derivative of the cumulative flows with respect to location.

2.3.2 In the trajectory coordinates

The traveling distance of vehicle n from $t - \Delta t$ to t equals $\Delta X([t - \Delta t, t], n) = X(t, n) - X(t - \Delta t, n)$. The average speed is

$$\frac{\Delta X([t - \Delta t, t], n)}{\Delta t} = \frac{X(t, n) - X(t - \Delta t, n)}{\Delta t},$$

and the instantaneous speed is

$$\begin{aligned} v(t, n) &= \lim_{\Delta t \to 0} \frac{X(t, n) - X(t - \Delta t, n)}{\Delta t} \\ &= \frac{\partial X(t, n)}{\partial t} = X_t(t, n), \end{aligned} \quad (2.7)$$

which is the partial derivative with respect to time. The acceleration rate is

$$\begin{aligned} a(t, n) &= \lim_{\Delta t \to 0} \frac{X_t(t + \Delta t, n) - X_t(t, n)}{\Delta t} \\ &= \frac{\partial X_t(t, n)}{\partial t} = X_{tt}(t, n). \end{aligned} \quad (2.8)$$

From a vehicle's speeds and acceleration rates along a trajectory, emission models can be used to calculate the amount of fuel consumption and vehicle emissions. See Note 2.4 for such models.

The distance between vehicles n and $n - \Delta n$ at t equals $\Delta X(t, [n - \Delta n, n]) = X(t, n - \Delta n) - X(t, n)$, since vehicle $n - \Delta n$ is in the front of vehicle n. The average spacing is

$$\frac{\Delta X(t, [n - \Delta n, n])}{\Delta n} = \frac{X(t, n - \Delta n) - X(t, n)}{\Delta n}.$$

If we let $\Delta n \to 0$, the spacing of vehicle n at t is

$$\begin{aligned} z(t, n) &= \lim_{\Delta n \to 0} \frac{X(t, n - \Delta n) - X(t, n)}{\Delta n} \\ &= -\frac{\partial X(t, n)}{\partial n} = -X_n(t, n). \end{aligned} \quad (2.9)$$

2.3.3 In the schedule coordinates

The traveling time of vehicle n from $x - \Delta x$ to x equals $\Delta T(n, [x - \Delta x, x]) = T(n, x) - T(n, x - \Delta x)$. The average *pace* is

$$\frac{\Delta T(n, [x - \Delta x, x])}{\Delta x} = \frac{T(n, x) - T(n, x - \Delta x)}{\Delta x},$$

and the pace at x of vehicle n is

$$\begin{aligned} \omega(n, x) &= \lim_{\Delta x \to 0} = \frac{T(n, x) - T(n, x - \Delta x)}{\Delta x} \\ &= \frac{\partial T(n, x)}{\partial x} = T_x(n, x), \end{aligned} \quad (2.10)$$

which is the partial derivative with respect to location.

The time difference between vehicles $n - \Delta n$ and n passing x equals $\Delta T([n - \Delta n, n], x) = T(n, x) - T(x, n - \Delta n)$. The average *headway* is

$$\frac{\Delta T([n - \Delta n, n], x)}{\Delta n} = \frac{T(n, x) - T(n - \Delta n, x)}{\Delta n}.$$

If we let $\Delta n \to 0$, the headway of vehicle n at x is

$$\begin{aligned} h(n, x) &= \lim_{\Delta n \to 0} \frac{T(n, x) - T(n - \Delta n, x)}{\Delta n} \\ &= \frac{\partial T(n, x)}{\partial n} = T_n(n, x). \end{aligned} \quad (2.11)$$

2.3.4 Higher-order derivatives of the primary variables

We denote a variable in the flow coordinates by $\phi(t,x)$ and its counterpart in the trajectory coordinates by $\Phi(t,n)$, such that they are equal on the traffic surface:

$$\Phi(t,n) = \phi(t, X(t,n)).$$

Then their derivatives can be converted between the two coordinates. For example,

$$\begin{aligned}\frac{\partial \Phi(t,n)}{\partial t} &= \frac{\partial \phi(t, X(t,n))}{\partial t} + \frac{\partial \phi(t, X(t,n))}{\partial x} \frac{\partial X(t,n)}{\partial t} \\ &= \frac{\partial \phi(t,x)}{\partial t} + v(t,x) \frac{\partial \phi(t,x)}{\partial x}.\end{aligned}$$

With $\Phi(t,n) = v(t,n)$, the acceleration rate

$$a(t,n) = v_t(t,x) + v(t,x) v_x(t,x).$$

Higher-order derivatives of the primary variables can be converted among the three coordinates in the similar fashion. See Problem 2.2 for more problems.

2.3.5 Relationships among the secondary variables

Among the many variables, k, q, v, z, h, and ω are the first-order derivatives of the primary variables, and are called secondary variables. All of them can be defined in any of the three coordinates. For example, traffic density $k(t,x)$ in the trajectory and schedule coordinates can be written as $k(t,n)$ and $k(n,x)$, respectively.

Taking the derivative of both sides of (2.4a) with respect to n, we have

$$k(t,x) = \frac{1}{z(t,n)}.$$

That is, at a point on the three-dimensional surface, the density and spacing are inverse to each other. Taking the derivative of both sides of (2.4b) with respect to x, we can also reach (2.12a). Similarly, from (2.4c) or (2.4d) we have

$$v(t,n) = \frac{1}{\omega(n,x)},$$

and from (2.4e) or (2.4f) we have

$$h(n,x) = \frac{1}{q(t,x)}.$$

If we extend the definitions of these variables into all three coordinates, their inverse relationships hold in all coordinates or are independent of coordinates. That is, in all coordinates,

$$kz = 1, \tag{2.12a}$$
$$v\omega = 1, \tag{2.12b}$$
$$qh = 1. \tag{2.12c}$$

Such inverse relationships are also valid for the average values of these variables. See Problem 2.1. These relations suggest that among the six secondary variables, only three are independent. For example, if k, v, and q are known, then z, ω, and z can be calculated.

Differentiating both sides of (2.4a) with respect to t leads to

$$0 = N_t(t, x) + N_x(t, x) X_t(t, n),$$

or equivalently, the following constitutive law,

$$q = kv, \tag{2.13}$$

which is also independent of the coordinates. Thus, if two of k, v, and q are known, the third one can be calculated. This also leads to a similar relation among h, z, and ω.

2.4 Detection

2.4.1 Edie's formulas

For a traffic stream, we can define three domains in the three coordinates: $\Omega(t, x)$, $\Omega(t, n)$, and $\Omega(n, x)$. In Fig. 2.6, the three domains are $\Omega(t, x) = [0, E] \times [0, L]$, $\Omega(t, n) = [0, E] \times [N(t, L), N(t, 0)]$, and $\Omega(n, x) = [0, L] \times [N(0, x), N(E, x)]$. That is, the (t, x)-domain is the rectangular area on the (t, x) plane, the (t, n)-domain is bounded by the two cumulative flows at $x = L$ and $x = 0$, as shown in Fig. 2.5(a), and the (n, x)-domain is bounded by the two cumulative flows at $t = 0$ and $t = E$, as shown in Fig. 2.5(b). These domains are the projections of the (t, x, n)-surface on the three coordinates.

The areas of the three domains are

$$|\Omega(t, x)| = EL,$$
$$|\Omega(t, n)| = \int_{t=0}^{E} N(t, 0) - N(t, L) dt,$$
$$|\Omega(n, x)| = \int_{x=0}^{L} N(E, x) - N(0, x) dx.$$

2.4 Detection

Apparently, $|\Omega(t,n)|$ equals the total travel time of all vehicles inside the (t,x)-domain and is therefore the vehicle-hours traveled (VHT), and $|\Omega(n,x)|$ equals the total travel distance of all vehicles inside the (t,x)-domain and is therefore the vehicle-miles traveled (VMT). Both VHT and VMT can be approximately calculated from individual vehicles' trajectories: Assuming that a plot of Λ vehicles travel inside the road segment from 0 to L during 0 and E and vehicle i's time and distance inside the (t,x)-domain are denoted by ΔT_i and ΔX_i, then

$$VHT = |\Omega(t,n)| \approx \sum_{i=1}^{\Lambda} \Delta T_i, \qquad (2.14)$$

$$VMT = |\Omega(n,x)| \approx \sum_{i=1}^{\Lambda} \Delta X_i. \qquad (2.15)$$

Then we can use Edie's formulas to calculate the average density, flow-rate, and speed in the domain:

$$\bar{k}(\Omega(t,x)) = \frac{VHT}{|\Omega(t,x)|}, \qquad (2.16a)$$

$$\bar{q}(\Omega(t,x)) = \frac{VMT}{|\Omega(t,x)|}, \qquad (2.16b)$$

$$\bar{v}(\Omega(t,x)) = \frac{VMT}{VHT}. \qquad (2.16c)$$

With this definition, the constitutive law, (2.13), is still satisfied by the average values.

Edie's formulas can be extended for a road network. The length of road b is denoted by L_b, and the average density and flow-rate on the link during a time interval E are $\bar{k}_b$ and $\bar{q}_b$, respectively. Thus the area of the (t,x)-domain, VHT, and VMT on the link are EL_b, $\bar{k}_b E L_b$, and $\bar{q}_b E L_b$. For a network whose set of links is denoted by $\mathcal{B}$, we have

$$|\Omega(t,x)| = \sum_{b \in \mathcal{B}} E L_b,$$

$$VHT = \sum_{b \in \mathcal{B}} \bar{k}_b E L_b,$$

$$VMT = \sum_{b \in \mathcal{B}} \bar{q}_b E L_b,$$

from which we have the average density, flow-rate, and speed for the whole network

$$\bar{k} = \frac{\sum_{b \in \mathcal{B}} \bar{k}_b L_b}{\sum_{b \in \mathcal{B}} L_b},$$

$$\bar{q} = \frac{\sum_{b\in\mathcal{B}} \bar{q}_b L_b}{\sum_{b\in\mathcal{B}} \bar{L}_b},$$

$$\bar{v} = \frac{\sum_{b\in\mathcal{B}} \bar{q}_b L_b}{\sum_{b\in\mathcal{B}} \bar{k}_b L_b}.$$

2.4.2 Detectors

There are many types of traffic detectors. At a point, stopwatches, hand tallies or pneumatic tubes, and radar or microwave detectors can be used to collect cumulative counts and passing times, from which flow-rates and headways can be calculated. For a short section, paired pneumatic tubes, inductive loop detectors, and video cameras can collect flow-rates, densities, and speeds. On a road segment, aerial photography through cameras mounted on tall buildings, helicopters, or drones can collect vehicles' trajectories. Moving observers through floating cars and probe vehicles with GPS devices can sample individual vehicles' trajectories. In wide-area Intelligent Transportation Systems (ITS), electronic toll collection (ETC) and automatic vehicle re-identification (AVI) can collect vehicles' entrance and exit times.

Consider a loop detector, whose length is quite short at L (around 6 ft or 2 m). Λ vehicles pass the detector during a time interval of E, and vehicle i's passing speed is denoted by v_i. Vehicles' trajectories passing a loop detector are illustrated in Fig. 2.8.

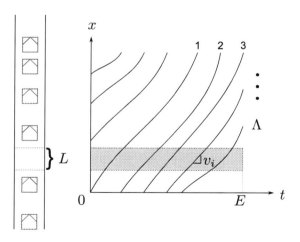

FIGURE 2.8 Vehicles' trajectories passing a loop detector.

There are generally two ways to calculate the average speed of these vehicles:

2.4 Detection

$$\bar{v}_1 = \frac{\sum_{i=1}^{\Lambda} v_i}{\Lambda},$$

$$\bar{v}_2 = \frac{\Lambda}{\sum_{i=1}^{\Lambda} \frac{1}{v_i}},$$

where $\bar{v}_1$ is the arithmetic mean and usually called the time-mean speed, and $\bar{v}_2$ is the harmonic mean and usually called the space-mean speed. There are also other ways to find the average speed. Then which average should we use?

In the following, we demonstrate that the space-mean speed is consistent with Edie's definition. The (t, x)-domain is $\Omega(t, x) = [0, E] \times [0, L]$, illustrated by the shaded region in Fig. 2.8. Since L is small, we assume that all vehicles are able to traverse the whole detector; thus $\Delta X_i = L$, and $\Delta T_i = \frac{L}{v_i}$. From Edie's formulas, $VHT = \sum_{i=1}^{\Lambda} \frac{L}{v_i}$, $VMT = \Lambda L$, $|\Omega(t, x)| = EL$, and

$$\bar{k}(\Omega(t, x)) = \frac{\sum_{i=1}^{\Lambda} \frac{1}{v_i}}{E},$$

$$\bar{q}(\Omega(t, x)) = \frac{\Lambda}{E},$$

$$\bar{v}(\Omega(t, x)) = \frac{\Lambda}{\sum_{i=1}^{\Lambda} \frac{1}{v_i}},$$

where the average speed equals the space-mean speed.

Still for a loop detector over a road segment between 0 and L, the occupancy during a time interval E is defined as the percentage of time when the detector is covered by a vehicle. A loop detector's magnetic field changes whenever the metallic body of a vehicle is over it; thus it is covered when a vehicle's front bumper touches $x = 0$ until the rear bumper leaves $x = L$. Hence the occupancy in the (t, x)-domain is

$$o = \frac{\sum_{i=1}^{\Lambda} \frac{\zeta_i + L}{v_i}}{E}, \quad (2.17)$$

where ζ_i is the length of vehicle i. If all vehicles have the same length, ζ, then

$$o = (\zeta + L) \frac{\sum_{i=1}^{\Lambda} \frac{1}{v_i}}{E} = (\zeta + L)\bar{k},$$

or equivalently,

$$\bar{k} = \frac{1}{\zeta + L} o. \quad (2.18)$$

That is, the density is proportional to the occupancy. Refer to Problem 2.3 for the case when vehicles have different lengths but same speed. A loop detector can count the number of passing vehicles, Λ, during a time interval. Thus it can detect the average flow-rate, $\bar{q} = \frac{\Lambda}{E}$. From the constitutive law, we can calculate the space-mean speed

$$\bar{v} = (\zeta + L)\frac{\Lambda}{Eo}.$$

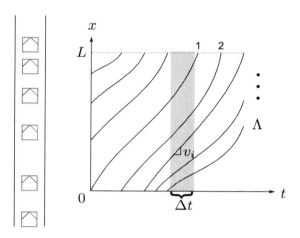

FIGURE 2.9 Vehicles' trajectories passing a camera detector.

Consider a video camera detector, which covers a range of L. At a time instant, it detects Λ vehicles, and vehicle i's speed is v_i. Vehicles' trajectories passing the detector are illustrated in Fig. 2.9. In this case, the (t, x)-domain is $\Omega(t, x) = [0, \Delta t] \times [0, L]$, illustrated by the shaded region in Fig. 2.9, where Δt is very small. Inside the domain, vehicle i's travel time and distance are Δt and $v_i \Delta t$, respectively. From Edie's formulas, the average density is

$$\bar{k} = \frac{\Lambda}{L},$$

the average flow-rate is

$$\bar{q} = \frac{\sum_{i=1}^{\Lambda} v_i}{L},$$

and the average speed is

$$\bar{v} = \frac{\sum_{i=1}^{\Lambda} v_i}{\Lambda},$$

where $\bar{v}$ is the arithmetic mean.

2.5 Multi-commodity traffic on a multilane road

2.5.1 Multi-commodity traffic

Vehicles traveling on a road can be separated into different commodities based on their attributes, including their lanes, classes, aggressiveness, paths, and so on. Many kinematic wave models have been proposed to describe multi-commodity traffic dynamics in the evolution of both total and commodity densities, speeds, and flow-rates. For an M-commodity traffic, we can denote the cumulative flow, density, speed, and flow-rate of commodity m ($m = 1, \cdots, M$) in the flow coordinates by $N_m(t, x)$, $k_m(t, x)$, $v_m(t, x)$, and $q_m(t, x)$, respectively. Correspondingly, the total cumulative flow, traffic density, speed, and flow-rate are denoted by $N(t, x)$, $k(t, x)$, $v(t, x)$, and $q(t, x)$, respectively. Hereafter (t, x) is omitted unless necessary.

Then we have the following relations:

- Additive relations between commodity and total cumulative flows, densities and flow-rates:

$$N = \sum_{m=1}^{M} N_m, \tag{2.19a}$$

$$k = \sum_{m=1}^{M} k_m, \tag{2.19b}$$

$$q = \sum_{m=1}^{M} q_m. \tag{2.19c}$$

- Commodity and total constitutive laws ($m = 1, \cdots, M$):

$$q_m = k_m v_m, \tag{2.20a}$$
$$q = kv. \tag{2.20b}$$

Hence the total speed is the weighted average of commodity speeds

$$v = \frac{\sum_{m=1}^{M} k_m v_m}{\sum_{m=1}^{M} k_m} = \sum_{m=1}^{M} p_m v_m, \tag{2.21}$$

where p_m is the commodity density proportion:

$$p_m = \frac{k_m}{k}.$$

Thus

$$p_m \in [0, 1],$$

$$\sum_{m=1}^{M} p_m = 1.$$

Denote the commodity speed proportion by η_m:

$$\eta_m = \frac{v_m}{v},$$

which is non-negative but can be greater than 1. Then (2.21) can be rewritten as

$$\sum_{m=1}^{M} p_m \eta_m = 1,$$

or equivalently

$$\sum_{m=1}^{M} p_m (\eta_m - 1) = 0.$$

Denote the commodity flow-rate proportion by γ_m:

$$\gamma_m = \frac{q_m}{q} = p_m \eta_m.$$

Thus

$$\gamma_m \in [0, 1],$$

$$\sum_{m=1}^{M} \gamma_m = 1.$$

We denote the location of vehicle n of commodity m at time t by $X_m(t, n)$, and the location of vehicle n of the total traffic stream at t by $X(t, n)$. Note that there is no additive relation among the locations.

2.5.2 Lane-changing traffic

On a multilane road, vehicles can change their lanes. Fig. 2.10 shows some longitudinal trajectories in a (t, x)-domain, in which the red (thick) line segments denote the trajectories when they are changing lanes. During the lane-changing process, a vehicle occupies two lanes and equals two vehicles effectively. Thus on all lanes the total vehicle-lane-hours-traveled equal

$$VLHT = \sum_{i=1}^{\Lambda} \Delta T_i + \Sigma \varphi,$$

where Σ is the number of lane changes, and φ is the average lane-changing duration.

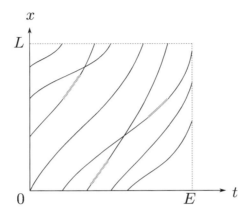

FIGURE 2.10 Longitudinal trajectories of lane-changing vehicles inside a lane-changing area.

We define the *lane-changing intensity* by the ratio of the total lane-changing time to the total travel time; i.e.,

$$c = \frac{\Sigma \varphi}{\sum_{i=1}^{\Lambda} \Delta T_i}. \qquad (2.22)$$

Thus the effective total density inside a lane-changing zone equals

$$\hat{k} = (1+c)k. \qquad (2.23)$$

Inside a lane-changing zone downstream to an on-ramp, the number of lane changes depends on the on-ramp flow-rate and the number of freeway lanes. The lane-changing duration is in the order of 5 seconds.

Thus the lane-changing intensity captures the disruption effect of systematic lane changes.

Notes

Note 2.1. *Traditionally, traffic flow theory deals with the movement of vehicles in an absolute space on a network of roads, as illustrated in Fig. 2.1. The relative space with respect to the remaining trip distances illustrated in Fig. 2.2 was first* introduced in (Vickrey, 2020; Jin, 2020). Day-to-day traffic flow in the imaginary space illustrated in Fig. 2.3 was introduced for day-to-day departure time choice at a single bottleneck in (Jin et al., 2020).

Note 2.2. *The cumulative number of vehicles $N(t, x)$ was first used by the legendary CalTrans traffic engineer, Moskowitz, to describe traffic conditions Moskowitz (1965). The three-dimensional representation of traffic flow in Fig. 2.6 was introduced in Makigami et al. (1971). In the reference, such a representation was applied to multi-lane traffic where vehicles' can overtake each other, and a scheme was proposed to obtain equivalent FIFO trajectories from non-FIFO ones. However, such a scheme is not unique. See the homework problem 4.7.*

Note 2.3. *The symmetry among the three primary variables and corresponding coordinates was systematically discussed in (Laval and Leclercq, 2013). Even though the flow (Eulerian) and trajectory (Lagrangian) coordinates have been used in studying fluid dynamics, the schedule coordinates, (n, x), seem to be unique for traffic flow, and have been used in (Vaughan et al., 1984).*

Note 2.4. *Examples of emission models include the MOVES https://www.epa.gov/moves, CMEM (Barth et al., 2001), and VT-Micro (Rakha et al., 2003). Among them, VT-Micro has the simplest implementation with explicit formulas to calculate emission rates from speeds and acceleration rates.*

Note 2.5. *In the literature, there is no consensus on the term for $T_x(n, x)$. It has been called time, travel time (per unit distance), delay, response rates, pace, latency, travel rate, and tardity (Vaughan et al., 1984). Here we call it pace, which is popular to describe how fast a person runs.*

Note 2.6. *A systematical way to derive the relationships among different variables in the three coordinates was presented in (Jin, 2016).*

Note 2.7. *In this book, flow equals cumulative flow to represent the number of vehicles during a time interval; flow-rate equals the number of vehicles passing a point during a unit time interval; and demand equals the number of vehicles desiring to pass a point during a unit time. In the transportation literature, the distinction is unclear: flow and flow-rate are usually used interchangeably, volume can mean flow, flow-rate, or even the number of vehicles on a road, and demand equals the number of vehicles during a time interval.*

Note 2.8. *The concept of lane-changing intensity in (2.22) was first introduced in (Jin, 2010a). Lane-changing durations were estimated in (Toledo and Zohar, 2007) and (Jin, 2010b).*

Note 2.9. *This chapter does not discuss stochastic features of traffic flow, for which (Haight, 1963) is a good reference.*

Problems

Problem 2.1. *Answer the following three questions.*

1. At a time instant, there is a platoon of Λ vehicles on a road segment of length L. What is the average density and the average spacing?
2. A platoon of Λ vehicles pass a location during a time interval of E. What is the average flow-rate and the average headway?
3. A vehicle travels a distance of L during a time interval of E. What is the average speed and the average tardity?

Problem 2.2. *What are the equivalent forms of the speed difference, $X_{tn}(t,n)$, in the flow and schedule coordinates? What are the equivalent forms of the speed gradient, $v_x(t,x)$, in the trajectory and schedule coordinates? What are the equivalent forms of the pace gradient, $\omega_x(n,x)$, in the flow and trajectory coordinates?*

Problem 2.3. *At a loop detector, if all vehicles have different lengths but the same speed during a time interval, what is the relationship between the occupancy and density?*

Problem 2.4. *This can be a group project. A stretch (900 ft) of I-80 in San Francisco, CA, is shown in the following figure. Four data sets (derived from the NGSIM project) are provided at https://www.dropbox.com/s/8t8iyt80pugw7cx/problem2.4-datasets.zip?dl=0, and each of them has been split into a number of subsets. Each subset has five columns:*

1. Vehicle ID
2. Frame ID: each frame equals 1/15 second in data set 1, and 1/10 second in other data sets.
3. Longitudinal distance from the upstream boundary: The upstream boundary is 0, and the downstream boundary is 900 ft.
4. Vehicle class: 2 for cars, and 3 for trucks. Motorcycles have been removed.
5. Lane ID: 1 for the left-most HOV lane, 2 and 6 from left to right are the regular lanes.

Each subset contains three minutes of data between $[t, t+3]$, and t is different for different subsets. For each subset, use Edie's formulas to calculate the average densities, speeds, and flow-rates (1) of each individual lanes, (2) of regular lanes, and (3) of all lanes. The units should be vpm, mph, and vph, respectively.

CHAPTER 3

Basic principles

This chapter discusses some basic principles for traffic flow at both the aggregate and disaggregate levels. These principles are consistent with our daily driving experiences, traffic rules, vehicle characteristics, and empirical observations. The principles are defined by equations or inequalities in different variables. They could be different from different types of traffic systems. Many of the constraints have been incorporated into the standardized Adaptive Cruise Control (ACC) system (ISO 15622).

For the primary variable of cumulative flow, the number of vehicles is conserved, and this leads to conservation of flows. This is the zeroth-order principle.

The secondary variables are generally non-negative and bounded; i.e., they should satisfy the collision-free and other conditions. In addition, empirical observations demonstrate the existence of a relation between speed and density, and this leads to the so-called fundamental diagram. These are the first-order principles.

In addition, acceleration and deceleration rates are also bounded, due to the limitations in the mechanical properties of vehicles as well as drivers' reaction times. These are the second-order principles.

There can also be the third-order principles with respect to jerk, which is closely related to the comfort level of driving.

Ideally, all of these principles should be satisfied by a well-defined traffic flow model, both analytically and numerically. That is, analytical and numerical solutions of a traffic flow model should be consistent with the principles, based on which the model is defined and derived. As a model could become too complicated to satisfy all of them, models for many applications in traffic planning and management only need to satisfy the zeroth and first-order principles.

3.1 Conservation laws

It is self-evident that the number of vehicles is conserved in a traffic system, if vehicles are not generated or demolished for whatever reason. This is the *conservation law* in the number of vehicles, which is a fundamental principle of traffic flow theory. It can take various forms in different coordinates under different situations.

3.1.1 In the flow coordinates

In the flow coordinates, the in- and out-flows of the road segment from 0 to t are denoted by $F(t)$ and $G(t)$, which can be observed from various traffic counters, including loop detectors. Then $F(0) = G(0) = 0$, and

$$F(t) = N(t,0) - n_0, \qquad (3.1)$$
$$G(t) = N(t,L), \qquad (3.2)$$

where $n_0 = N(0,0)$ is the initial number of vehicles on the road, $F(E)$ is the number of vehicles passing the upstream boundary at $x = 0$ from 0 to E, and $G(E)$ the number of vehicles passing the downstream boundary at $x = L$. If we denote n_E as the number of vehicles on the road segment at $t = E$, then from Fig. 2.6 we have the following relation:

$$n_0 + F(E) = G(E) + n_E; \qquad (3.3)$$

i.e., the initial number of vehicles plus the in-flow equals the out-flow plus the remaining number of vehicles. Equivalently, we update the number of vehicles on a road segment by adding the in-flow and subtracting the out-flow from the initial number of vehicles.

Further, for the domain of $\Omega = [t, t + \Delta t] \times [x, x + \Delta x]$, the conservation law, (3.3), can be written as

$$\Delta N(t, [x, x + \Delta x]) + \Delta N([t, t + \Delta t], x) = \qquad (3.4)$$
$$\Delta N([t, t + \Delta t], x + \Delta x) + \Delta N(t + \Delta t, [x, x + \Delta x]), \qquad (3.5)$$

which leads to, by letting $\Delta t \to 0$,

$$\frac{\partial \Delta N(t, [x, x + \Delta x])}{\partial t} = q(t,x) - q(t, x + \Delta x). \qquad (3.6)$$

Further dividing both sides by Δx and letting $\Delta x \to 0$, we have

$$\frac{\partial k(t,x)}{\partial t} + \frac{\partial q(t,x)}{\partial x} = 0, \qquad (3.7)$$

which can also be derived from

$$\frac{\partial^2 N(t,x)}{\partial t \partial x} = \frac{\partial^2 N(t,x)}{\partial x \partial t}.$$

Both of the above equations are different forms of the conservation law. They are the direct consequences of the definitions of the corresponding variables.

Let's consider the physical meaning of (3.7) during the peak period between 7:30 and 9:00. In the beginning of the peak period, the flow-rate generally decreases in location; i.e., $\frac{\partial q(t,x)}{\partial x} < 0$, and queues build up since $\frac{\partial k(t,x)}{\partial t} > 0$. Near the end of the peak period, the flow-rate generally increases in location; i.e., $\frac{\partial q(t,x)}{\partial x} > 0$, and queues dissipate since $\frac{\partial k(t,x)}{\partial t} < 0$.

3.1.2 In other coordinates

In the trajectory coordinates, we have the following conservation laws:

$$\Delta X(t, [n - \Delta n, n]) + \Delta X([t, t + \Delta t], n - \Delta n) = \Delta X([t, t + \Delta t], n) + \Delta X(t + \Delta t, [n - \Delta n, n]),$$

and

$$\frac{\partial z(t,n)}{\partial t} + \frac{\partial v(t,n)}{\partial n} = 0. \qquad (3.8)$$

In the schedule coordinates, we have

$$\Delta T([n - \Delta n, n], x) + \Delta T(n, [x, x + \Delta x]) = \Delta T(n - \Delta n, [x, x + \Delta x]) + \Delta T([n - \Delta n, n], x + \Delta x),$$

and

$$\frac{\partial \omega(n,x)}{\partial n} - \frac{\partial h(n,x)}{\partial x} = 0. \qquad (3.9)$$

3.1.3 Conservation laws in other traffic systems

The above conservation laws of vehicles are for a traffic stream on a road segment. The conservation law holds for other traffic systems on a road network or facilities, as long as vehicles cannot be generated or demolished on the road.

We denote the number of vehicles in a traffic system by $\Phi(t)$. The in- and out-fluxes are denoted by $f(t)$ and $g(t)$, respectively. Then the conservation equation for the whole system can be written as

$$\frac{d}{dt}\Phi(t) = f(t) - g(t). \qquad (3.10)$$

If denoting $F(t)$ and $G(t)$ as the cumulative in- and out-flows between 0 and t, we then have

$$\frac{d}{dt}F(t) = f(t), \qquad (3.11)$$

$$\frac{d}{dt}G(t) = g(t), \qquad (3.12)$$

where $f(t)$ and $g(t)$ are referred to as in- and out-fluxes, respectively. Thus we have from 0 to t

$$\Phi(t) = \Phi(0) + F(t) - G(t), \qquad (3.13)$$

which is equivalent to

$$\Phi(0) + F(t) = \Phi(t) + G(t). \qquad (3.14)$$

From t to $t + \Delta t$, we have

$$\Phi(t) + f(t)\Delta t = \Phi(t + \Delta t) + g(t)\Delta t, \qquad (3.15)$$

or

$$\Phi(t + \Delta t) = \Phi(t) + (f(t) - g(t))\Delta t. \qquad (3.16)$$

Consider a segment of road between x and $x + \Delta x$. The in- and out-fluxes are denoted by $q(t, x)$ and $q(t, x + \Delta x)$. In addition, there can be on- and off-ramps at x_i ($i = 1, \cdots, I$), and the ramp flux at x_i is denoted by $\phi_i(t)$, which is positive for an on-ramp and negative for an off-ramp. We introduce the indicator function $R(x_i; [x, x + \Delta x])$:

$$R(x_i; [x, x + \Delta x]) = \begin{cases} 1, & x_i \in [x, x + \Delta x]; \\ 0, & \text{otherwise.} \end{cases} \qquad (3.17)$$

Thus the conservation equation can be written as

$$k(t + \Delta t, x)\Delta x = k(t, x)\Delta x + (q(t, x) - q(t, x + \Delta x))\Delta t$$
$$+ \sum_{i=1}^{I} R(x_i; [x, x + \Delta x])\phi_i(t)\Delta t.$$

Dividing both sides by $\Delta x \Delta t$ and let $\Delta x \to 0^+$ and $\Delta x \to 0^+$, we have

$$\frac{\partial k(t, x)}{\partial t} + \frac{\partial q(t, x)}{\partial x} = \sum_{i=1}^{I} \lim_{\Delta x \to 0^+} \frac{R(x_i; [x, x + \Delta x])}{\Delta x} \phi_i(t). \qquad (3.18)$$

If vehicles keep their commodities, the conservation law of commodity m ($m = 1, \cdots, M$) in the space-time domain (t, x) can be written as:

$$\frac{\partial k_m(t, x)}{\partial t} + \frac{\partial q_m(t, x)}{\partial x} = 0. \qquad (3.19)$$

An obvious effect is that lane changes enable the exchange of flows among different lanes. We denote the density and flow-rate on lane m at time t and location x by $k_m(t, x)$ and $q_m(t, x)$, respectively, and the flow exchange rate from lane $m-1$ to m by $\phi_{m-1\to m}(t,x)$, whose unit is vehicles per unit time and unit length. Then the conservation equation (3.19) can be extended as

$$\frac{\partial k_m(t,x)}{\partial t} + \frac{\partial q_m(t,x)}{\partial x} = \phi_{m-1\to m}(t,x) - \phi_{m\to m+1}(t,x). \quad (3.20)$$

Thus, $\int_{t=t}^{t+\Delta t}\int_{x=x}^{x+\Delta x}\phi_{m-1\to m}(t,x)dxdt$ equals the number of lane changes from lane $m-1$ to lane m in the spatial-temporal domain: $[t, t+\Delta t] \times [x, x+\Delta x]$. If the number of lane changes are induced by on-ramp traffic, then the number of lane changes would be proportional to the number of entering vehicles. In addition, the number of lane changes linearly decreases from the right to the left lanes.

3.2 Collision-free condition and other first-order constraints

This section introduces a set of constraints on the secondary variables. Note that the secondary variables can be defined in any coordinates. Thus the coordinates are omitted unless necessary. Note that many of these constraints should be interpreted statistically: on one hand, the bounds are inferred from observations and subject to statistical errors in the order of 10%; on the other hand, individual drivers and vehicles can have substantially different bounds.

3.2.1 Constraints on density and spacing

In the real world, traffic has to be collision-free; i.e., the spacing cannot be smaller than the jam spacing, when vehicles are bumper to bumper:

$$z \geq \zeta. \quad (3.21)$$

Correspondingly, traffic density cannot be greater than the jam density, κ. That is,

$$0 \leq k \leq \kappa. \quad (3.22)$$

Here $\zeta = \frac{1}{\kappa}$. The jam density depends on vehicles' lengths and drivers' safety margins; it is around 150 veh/km or 1/7 vehicle/meter. Thus, the jam spacing is about 7 meters. The average length of a car is about 4 meters, and drivers leave a safety cushion of 3 meters.

3.2.2 Constraints on speed and pace

Under normal traffic conditions, vehicles travel forward; i.e.,

$$v \geq 0. \quad (3.23)$$

In addition, there is usually a speed limit, u, such that

$$v \leq u. \tag{3.24}$$

Corresponding, the pace cannot be smaller than $\frac{1}{u}$, which is the minimum pace:

$$\omega \geq \frac{1}{u}. \tag{3.25}$$

The speed limit can be impacted by traffic laws, road geometry, vehicles' features, and/or drivers' aggressiveness. It needs to be calibrated for a particular location.

In addition, the speed limit can be dynamically changed for a road segment or individual vehicles so as to improve traffic conditions. This is the Variable Speed Limit (VSL) method. Traditionally, VSL has been implemented for a segment of freeway. With the connected vehicle technology, it is possible to implement VSL for individual vehicles. VSL can help to smooth the stop-and-go traffic conditions on both freeways and arterial roads.

3.2.3 Constraints on flow-rate and headway

The flow-rate should be non-negative. Observations suggest that the flow-rate is limited by C. The maximum flow-rate is called capacity, or the saturation flow-rate. That is,

$$0 \leq q \leq C.$$

Correspondingly, the headway cannot be smaller than $\frac{1}{C}$, which is called the saturation headway:

$$h \geq \frac{1}{C}. \tag{3.26}$$

Related to the speed limit, the capacity is impacted by traffic laws, road geometry, vehicles' features, and/or drivers' aggressiveness. It could also be impacted by lane changes, the number of lanes, slopes, and other factors. The Highway Capacity Manual (HCM) is dedicated to statistically determine the capacities at different locations. The capacity of a road represents its supply and is an important decision variable for transportation infrastructure planning.

3.2.4 Clearance and time gap

The clearance of vehicle n at t is denoted by $z(t, n) - \zeta$; i.e., the distance between the follower's front bumper and the leader's rear bumper. The time gap of vehicle n at t is defined by

$$\tau(t,n) = \frac{z(t,n) - \zeta}{v(t,n)}. \tag{3.27}$$

The time gap approximately equals the duration of time for vehicle n to collide into the leading vehicle $n-1$, if the leading vehicle suddenly stops. Thus, the time gap should be sufficiently long for the following driver and vehicle to react under emergency situation.

Observations suggest that the time gap is relatively constant at about 1.5 seconds in congested traffic. For a constant time gap τ, (3.27) leads to

$$v(t,n) = \frac{z(t,n) - \zeta}{\tau}. \tag{3.28}$$

For autonomous vehicles or vehicles equipped with Adaptive Cruise Control, the time gap can be substantially smaller, e.g., 0.5 second.

3.3 Fundamental diagram

Fundamental diagrams are also statistically meaningful. They are accurate only for the average or ideal situations. In a sense, the existence of fundamental diagrams is a simplification assumption, which is absolutely violated but useful for certain applications.

3.3.1 Derivation and observation

It is reasonable to assume that a vehicle travels as fast as possible, subject to the constraints in the speed limit, (3.24), and a constant time gap, (3.28). That is, the speed of $v(t,n)$ is determined by the following optimization problem:

$$\max v(t,n) \tag{3.29}$$

s.t. $v(t,n) \leq u$ and $v(t,n) = \frac{z(t,n) - \zeta}{\tau}$. The solution is simple:

$$v = \min\{u, \frac{z - \zeta}{\tau}\}, \tag{3.30}$$

which is a speed-spacing relation. As $z = \frac{1}{k}$ and $\zeta = \frac{1}{\kappa}$, there also exists a speed-density relation:

$$v = \min\{u, \frac{\frac{1}{k} - \frac{1}{\kappa}}{\tau}\}, \tag{3.31}$$

which leads to the following flow-density relation, a.k.a., the triangular fundamental diagram:

$$q = \min\{uk, \frac{1}{\tau}(1 - \frac{k}{\kappa})\}. \tag{3.32}$$

Hence the speed limit, the constant time gap, and the maximum speed lead to the fundamental diagram. Clearly, a fundamental diagram also exists when the time gap τ is a function of the density or spacing.

Fig. 3.1 shows the relation between the average occupancy and flow-rate for four lanes observed by loop detectors on the Eastbound SR-91 between Valley View St and Knott Ave in Buena Park, California. The relation is quite scattered for 30-second raw data. However, for 10-minute average data, a functional relation emerges between the flow-rate and occupancy. Further, if only near-stationary states are picked, the functional relation is much clearer with a triangular shape, as shown in Fig. 3.1(c). Detailed discussions on stationary states are provided in Chapter 4. As the traffic density is linear to the occupancy, as in (2.18), the observations suggest a flow-density relation in the average or near-stationary traffic states:

$$q = Q(k). \tag{3.33}$$

Further with the constitutive law, $q = kv$, there exists a corresponding speed-density relation:

$$v = V(k) \equiv \frac{Q(k)}{k}. \tag{3.34}$$

3.3.2 General fundamental diagrams

In general, the speed-density relation has the following properties:

1. The speed is non-negative; i.e., $V(k) \geq 0$, for $k \in [0, \kappa]$.
2. The jam speed is zero; i.e., $V(\kappa) = 0$.
3. The speed is bounded by the free-flow speed: $V(k) \leq u$.
4. The speed-density relation is usually non-increasing:

$$V'(k) \leq 0. \tag{3.35}$$

This is consistent with our driving experiences under normal conditions: at higher densities, the distances among vehicles are smaller, and it is safer to drive at lower speeds. But, it may not be so for night traffic, where people feel more comfortable and drive faster with relatively higher density, and other special traffic systems.

The flow-density relation has the following properties:

3.3 Fundamental diagram

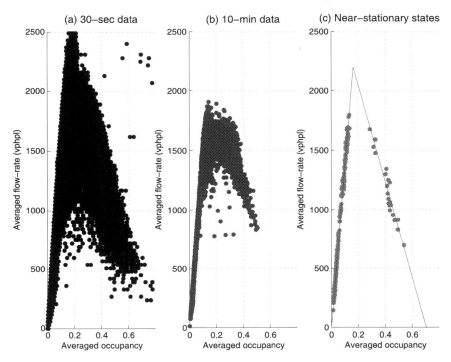

FIGURE 3.1 Observed flow-occupancy relations in: (a) 30-second raw data; (b) 10-minute average data; (c) near-stationary states.

1. The flow-rate is non-negative: $Q(k) \geq 0$ when $k \in [0, \kappa]$.
2. The flow-rate equals zero when $k = 0$ or $k = \kappa$; i.e., $Q(0) = Q(\kappa) = 0$. This can be derived from the constitutive law, $q = kv$, and the second and third properties of the speed-density relation.
3. The flow-density relation is unimodal with the maximum value, C, at the critical density κ_c: $Q'(k) > 0$ for $k < \kappa_c$, and $Q'(k) < 0$ for $k > \kappa_c$. That is, it increases with the density below the critical density, but decreases otherwise. Here $C = Q(\kappa_c)$ is the capacity, and $u_c = V(\kappa_c)$ the critical speed.
4. Generally, the flow-density relation is concave; i.e.,

$$Q''(k) \leq 0. \qquad (3.36)$$

But for some traffic systems this may not be true.

A traffic state is said to be in *equilibrium* if $q = Q(k)$ or $v = V(k)$. An equilibrium traffic state can be categorized into three mutually exclusive and collectively exhaustive types: (i) critical (C) when $k = \kappa_c$; (ii) strictly under-critical (SUC) when $k < \kappa_c$; and (iii) strictly over-critical (SOC) when

$k > \kappa_c$. Further a UC state can be either SUC or C, and an OC state can be either SOC or C. The critical density is also called a sonic point; thus, an SUC state is subsonic, and an SOC state supersonic.

Traffic in equilibrium has two modes or phases: UC (uncongested, free-flow, under-saturated) or OC (congested, over-saturated). For a density k, its image density, $P(k)$, has the same flow-rate but in a different mode; i.e.,

$$Q(P(k)) = Q(k), \quad (P(k) - \kappa_c)(k - \kappa_c) \leq 0. \tag{3.37}$$

Since $Q(k)$ is unimodal, $P(k)$ exists and is unique. In addition,

$$P(P(k)) = k.$$

The characteristic wave speed is defined as

$$\lambda(k) = Q'(k) = V(k) + kV'(k). \tag{3.38}$$

Since the flow-density relation is unimodal, $\lambda(k) > 0$ for $k < \kappa_c$, and $\lambda(k) < 0$ for $k > \kappa_c$. If the flow-density relation is concave, the characteristic wave speed is non-increasing in density: $\lambda(0) \geq \lambda(k) \geq \lambda(\kappa)$. For a concave flow-density relation, the Legendre transformation is defined as ($b \in [\lambda(\kappa), \lambda(0)]$)

$$L(b) = \max_{k \in [0,\kappa]} Q(k) - bk. \tag{3.39}$$

Since $Q(k) - bk$ is the flow-rate passing an observer traveling at a speed of b, $L(b)$ is the maximum flow-rate, which is non-negative. The observer can be in a floating car or a flying drone. For a stationary observer, $b = 0$, and $L(b)$ equals the capacity.

We have the following properties regarding general fundamental diagrams.

Theorem 3.3.1. 1. *The speed-density relation in SOC states is always decreasing, since the flow-density relation is unimodal.*
2. *The characteristic wave speed is not greater than vehicles' speed for non-increasing speed-density relations.*
3. *The concavity condition, (3.36), is equivalent to*

$$kV''(k) + 2V'(k) \leq 0. \tag{3.40}$$

4. *For a non-increasing speed-density relation and a concave flow-density relation,*
   (a) $(\kappa - k)kV'(k) + \kappa V(k)$ *is non-increasing in k.*
   (b) $0 \leq \frac{Q(k)}{\kappa - k} \leq -Q'(\kappa) = -\kappa V'(\kappa).$

3.3.3 The Greenshields fundamental diagram

Such relations were first discovered by Greenshields in 1935. Using video cameras, he observed 1180 groups of 100 vehicles, with fewer than 10% of trucks. He then fit the speed-density relation with a linear relation:

$$V(k) = u(1 - \frac{k}{\kappa}), \qquad (3.41a)$$

where u is the free-flow speed (43 mph), and κ the jam density. Then the flow-density relation is quadratic:

$$Q(k) = uk(1 - \frac{k}{\kappa}). \qquad (3.41b)$$

In the Greenshields fundamental diagram, (3.41), the speed-density relation is strictly decreasing, and the flow-density relation is concave. Thus Theorem 3.3.1 holds.

Both the density and flow-rate can be written as functions of the speed:

$$k = \kappa(1 - \frac{v}{u}),$$
$$q = \kappa u(1 - \frac{v}{u}).$$

The critical density $\kappa_c = \frac{1}{2}\kappa$, the critical speed $u_c = \frac{1}{2}u$, and the capacity $C = \frac{1}{4}\kappa u$. On a freeway, $u = 65$ mph, $\kappa = 240$ vpmpl (vehicles per mile per lane), and $C = 3900$ vphpl (vehicles per hour per lane), which is too high. This is another indication that the Greenshields fundamental diagram is not realistic, even though it is quite simple.

The image density $P(k) = \kappa - k$. The characteristic wave speed is

$$\lambda(k) = u(1 - 2\frac{k}{\kappa}),$$

and the Legendre transformation is ($b \in [-u, u]$)

$$L(b) = \max_{k \in [0,\kappa]} uk(1 - \frac{k}{\kappa}) - bk = \frac{\kappa(u-b)^2}{4u}.$$

The Greenshields fundamental diagram is shown in Fig. 3.2.

3.3.4 The triangular fundamental diagram

Recent observations suggest that the triangular flow-density relation is more reasonable:

$$Q(k) = \min\{uk, w(\kappa - k)\}, \qquad (3.42a)$$

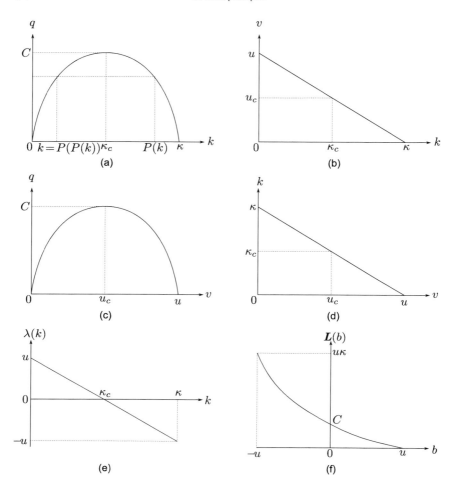

FIGURE 3.2 The Greenshields fundamental diagram.

$$V(k) = \min\{u, w(\frac{\kappa}{k} - 1)\}. \tag{3.42b}$$

In the triangular fundamental diagram, (3.42), the speed-density relation is non-increasing, and the flow-density relation is concave. Thus Theorem 3.3.1 holds.

The flow-density relation is piecewise linear, and the critical density and capacity are at the intersection points:

$$\kappa_c = \frac{w}{u+w}\kappa,$$

$$C = u\kappa_c = \frac{uw}{u+w}\kappa = \frac{\kappa}{\frac{1}{u}+\frac{1}{w}}.$$

Thus the speed- and flow-density relation can also be written as

$$V(k) = \begin{cases} u, & 0 \leq k \leq \kappa_c; \\ w(\frac{\kappa}{k} - 1), & \kappa_c < k \leq \kappa; \end{cases}$$

$$Q(k) = \begin{cases} uk, & 0 \leq k \leq \kappa_c; \\ w(\kappa - k), & \kappa_c < k \leq \kappa. \end{cases}$$

We denote the q-intercept of $q = w(\kappa - k)$ by $q_0 = w\kappa$, and the time gap $\tau = \frac{1}{q_0} = \frac{1}{w\kappa}$.

The flow-density relation can be written as

$$Q(k) = C - \frac{u-w}{2}(\kappa_c - k) - \frac{u+w}{2}|\kappa_c - k|. \qquad (3.43)$$

The image density $P(k)$ can be written as

$$P(k) = \begin{cases} \frac{q_0 - uk}{w}, & 0 \leq k \leq \kappa_c; \\ \frac{q_0 - wk}{u}, & \kappa_c \leq k \leq \kappa. \end{cases}$$

In OC states when $k \geq \kappa_c$, $q = w(\kappa - k)$, and $v = w(\frac{\kappa}{k} - 1)$. Then k and q can also be written as functions in v:

$$k = \frac{w}{v+w}\kappa,$$

$$q = \frac{vw}{v+w}\kappa,$$

and k and v can be written as functions in q:

$$k = \kappa - \frac{q}{w} = \frac{q_0 - q}{w},$$

$$v = \frac{q}{q_0 - q}w.$$

The characteristic wave speed

$$\lambda(k) = \begin{cases} u, & 0 \leq k < \kappa_c; \\ -w, & \kappa_c < k \leq \kappa; \end{cases}$$

and the Legendre transformation is ($b \in [-w, u]$)

$$L(b) = \max_{k \in [0,\kappa]} \min\{uk, w(\kappa - k)\} - bk$$

$$= (u - b)\kappa_c = C - \kappa_c b. \qquad (3.44)$$

Thus $L(0) = C$, $L(u) = 0$, and $L(-w) = w\kappa = q_0$. Thus q_0 is the maximum flow-rate passing a reasonable observer, whose speed is between $-w$ and u.

The triangular fundamental diagram is shown in Fig. 3.3.

In the NGSim data, the values of the parameters are $\tau = 1.6$ s, $\kappa = \frac{1}{7}$ veh/m=229 vpm=143 veh/km, and $u = 65$ mph=105 km/h=29 m/s. Thus $w \approx 10$ mph, $\kappa_c \approx 30$ vpm, and $C \approx 1950$ vph. In Fig. 3.1, the critical occupancy is 0.164, the jam occupancy is 0.705, and the capacity equals 2198 vphpl.

Any concave fundamental diagram is bounded by a triangular fundamental diagram.

Theorem 3.3.2. *For a concave fundamental diagram, $q = Q(k)$, it is bounded from above by a triangular fundamental diagram: $q = \min\{Q_k(0)k, -(\kappa - k)Q_k(\kappa)\}$. That is*

$$Q(k) \leq \min\{Q_k(0)k, -(\kappa - k)Q_k(\kappa)\}. \tag{3.45}$$

3.3.5 Fundamental diagrams in other secondary variables

The fundamental diagram can be represented by the speed-spacing relation:

$$v = W(z) = V\left(\frac{1}{z}\right). \tag{3.46}$$

For the triangular fundamental diagram ($z \geq \zeta$),

$$W(z) = \min\{u, w(\frac{z}{\zeta} - 1)\} = \min\{u, \frac{z-\zeta}{\tau}\}$$
$$= \min\{u, q_0 z - w\}.$$

The fundamental diagram can also be represented by the headway-pace relation:

$$h = \Xi(\omega) = \frac{1}{Q(\frac{1}{W^{-1}(\frac{1}{\omega})})} \tag{3.47}$$

The relation is well-defined when the speed-spacing relation is strictly increasing; or equivalently when the speed-density relation is strictly decreasing. However, for the triangular fundamental diagram, we can still have the following pace-headway relation:

$$h \begin{cases} \geq \frac{1}{C}, & \omega = \frac{1}{u}; \\ = \tau + \zeta\omega, & \omega > \frac{1}{u}, \end{cases}$$

3.3 Fundamental diagram

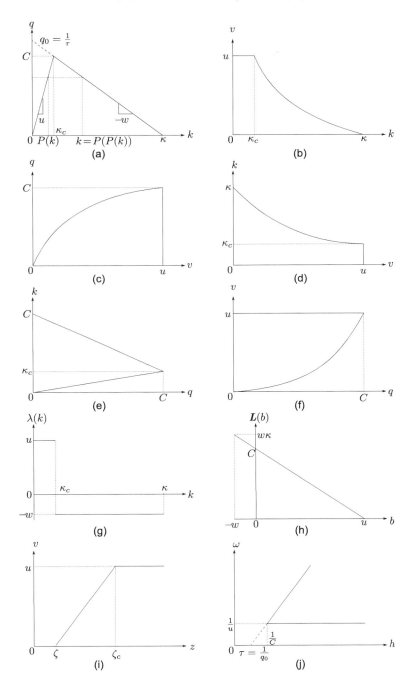

FIGURE 3.3 The triangular fundamental diagram.

which is not a functional relation but can be considered the limit of a functional headway-pace relation. See Note 3.12.

These relations are shown in Fig. 3.3(i)-(j).

3.3.6 Non-concave flow-density relations and non-decreasing speed-density relations

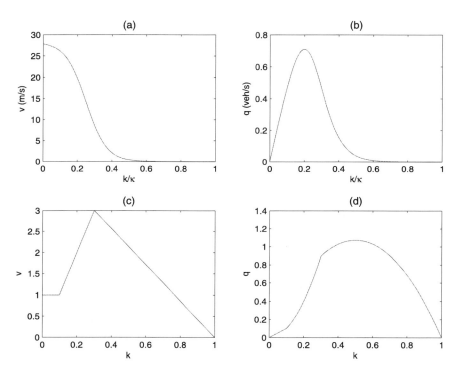

FIGURE 3.4 Two non-concave fundamental diagrams: (a) and (b) for the Kerner-Konhäuser fundamental diagram; (c) and (d) for the LeVeque fundamental diagram.

For some traffic systems, the flow-density relations may not be concave. For example, in the Kerner-Konhäuser fundamental diagram,

$$V(k) = 5.0461[(1 + \exp\{[k/\kappa - 0.25]/0.06\})^{-1} - 3.73 \times 10^{-6}]L/\Upsilon, \quad (3.48)$$

where the unit length $L = 28$ m, the relaxation time $\Upsilon = 5$ s, and the jam density $\kappa = 0.18$ veh/m. The speed-density relation is decreasing, but the flow-density relation is concave for uncongested traffic but non-concave for congested traffic.

In the LeVeque fundamental diagram for night traffic,

$$V(k) = \begin{cases} 1, & 0 \le k \le 0.1; \\ 10k, & 0.1 < k < 0.3; \\ \frac{30}{7}(1-k), & 0.3 \le k \le 1; \end{cases}$$

where both the density and speed are normalized. The speed-density relation is non-decreasing, and the flow-density relation is non-concave in uncongested traffic. The characteristic wave speed is

$$\lambda(k) = \begin{cases} 1, & 0 \le k \le 0.1; \\ 20k, & 0.1 < k < 0.3; \\ \frac{30}{7}(1-2k), & 0.3 \le k \le 1. \end{cases} \qquad (3.49)$$

Thus the characteristic wave speed is faster than vehicles' speed when $0.1 < k < 0.3$, since more vehicles encourage drivers to drive faster in this case.

These fundamental diagrams are shown in Fig. 3.4.

3.3.7 Fundamental diagrams of inhomogeneous roads and lane-changing traffic

On an inhomogeneous road, its number of lanes, curvature, slope, speed limit, and lane-changing activities can vary from location to location. Such inhomogeneity can be captured by the fundamental diagram, which can be written as

$$q = Q(x, k). \qquad (3.50)$$

More general are fundamental diagram which also depend on time-related events, such as weather and incidents/accidents: $q = Q(t, x, k)$.

For a road with l lanes, where l may not be integer as in the lane-drop zone, we assume that all lanes have the same characteristics. Denote k, v, and q as the total density, speed, and flow-rate. Thus for each lane, the density, speed, and flow-rate are $\frac{k}{l}$, v, and $\frac{q}{l}$, respectively. If the speed-density relation for each lane is $v = V\left(\frac{k}{l}\right)$, the flow-density relation for all lanes is

$$q = kv = kV\left(\frac{k}{l}\right).$$

For the triangular fundamental diagram, if κ is the per-lane jam density, the multilane fundamental diagram can be written as

$$q = \min\{uk, w(l\kappa - k)\} = \min\{uk, lq_0 - wk\}, \qquad (3.51)$$

where $q_0 = \frac{1}{\tau}$. The critical density is $l\kappa_c$, where $\kappa_c = \frac{w}{v+w}\kappa$ is the critical density per lane, and the capacity is lC, where $C = u\kappa_c$ is the capacity per lane. Thus in OC states when $k \geq l\kappa_c$, we have

$$k = \frac{lq_0 - q}{w},$$

$$v = \frac{q}{lq_0 - q}w.$$

If there are systematic lane changes on a road with l lanes, the effective total density equals $(1+c)k$, where c is the lane-changing intensity defined in Section 2.5.2. Thus the effective density on each lane is $\frac{(1+c)k}{l}$, and the speed is $v = V\left(\frac{(1+c)k}{l}\right)$. The fundamental diagram with lane-changing effects is

$$q = kV\left(\frac{(1+c)k}{l}\right) = kV\left(\frac{k}{\tilde{l}}\right),$$

where the effective number of lanes is

$$\tilde{l} = \frac{l}{1+c}. \tag{3.52}$$

Therefore, systematic lane changes effectively reduce the number of lanes and make the road more congested. This is consistent with our daily experience.

3.3.8 Multi-commodity fundamental diagrams

For M commodities, the vector of commodity density proportions is denoted by $\vec{p} = \sum_{m=1}^{M} p_m \vec{e}_m$. Here $\vec{e}_m$ is the unit vector whose mth element is 1, and the other elements are zeros. Correspondingly, the total traffic density, speed, and flow-rate are denoted by k, v, and q, respectively.

Commodity speed-density relations ($m = 1, \cdots, M$) are defined by

$$v_m = V_m(k, \vec{p}), \tag{3.53}$$

where commodity m's speed is determined by all commodity densities. Thus, from (2.19) and (2.20), the total traffic speed is also a function of all commodity densities:

$$v = V(k, \vec{p}) \equiv \sum_{m=1}^{M} p_m V_m(k, \vec{p}). \tag{3.54}$$

Correspondingly the commodity and total flow-rates are

$$q_m = Q_m(k, \vec{p}) \equiv k_m V_m(k, \vec{p}), \tag{3.55}$$

$$q = Q(k, \vec{p}) \equiv kV(k, \vec{p}). \tag{3.56}$$

3.3.9 Network fundamental diagram

In our daily experience, all streets become similarly congested in a central business area during the rush hours. This is because drivers would switch their routes, job locations, and house locations, to take advantage of less congested roads and sub-areas. On average, therefore, congested streets can be undifferentiated, and there exist network-level speed- and flow-density relations, which are referred to as network fundamental diagrams (NFD).

In an urban network, NFD is highly related to signal settings. A simple choice is the trapezoidal flow-density relation shown in Fig. 3.5, where the flow-density relation is given by

$$q = Q(k) \equiv \min\{v_1 k, C, v_2(\kappa - k)\}. \tag{3.57}$$

Here k is the per-lane density in the road network, and q the flow-rate per lane. If the total lane-mileage is L, then Lq represents the processing rate of the vehicle-miles traveled with the unit of VMT per hour. Here the capacity C is determined by the saturation rate (capacity) given by the dashed triangular fundamental diagram shown in Fig. 3.5 and the effective green ratio of signals.

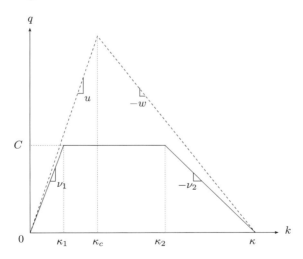

FIGURE 3.5 A trapezoidal network fundamental diagram.

Based on the trapezoidal fundamental diagram, traffic states can be separated into three types: under-saturated when $k < \kappa_1$, saturated when $k \in [\kappa_1, \kappa_2]$, and over-saturated when $k > \kappa_2$. Here κ_1 and κ_2 are two critical densities with $\kappa_1 \leq \kappa_c \leq \kappa_2$. In the transportation economics literature, the three types of states are respectively called uncongested, congested, and hyper-congested.

3.4 Bounded acceleration and higher-order constraints

Vehicles' acceleration rates are bounded when they are accelerating or decelerating, and the bounds depend on vehicles' mechanics, road conditions, weather conditions, and the speed:

$$-A^-(v(t,n), X(t,n), t, n) \leq a(t,n) \leq A^+(v(t,n), X(t,n), t, n). \quad (3.58)$$

A fundamental relation is the acceleration-speed relation during the acceleration process, when a vehicle is far from its leader. This can be considered second-order fundamental diagram, as it involves the second-order variables. In this case, the acceleration rate is function of the speed:

$$A^+ = A(x, v), \quad (3.59)$$

which may be location-dependent on an upgrade.

1. A base scenario is when there is no acceleration bound:

$$A(x, v) = \infty. \quad (3.60)$$

2. A simple choice is the constant bounded acceleration model:

$$A(x, v) = a_0 - \phi\Phi(x), \quad (3.61)$$

where a_0 is the maximum acceleration rate, ϕ the acceleration of gravity, and $\Phi(x)$ the decimal grade at x.

3. In the TWOPAS acceleration model,

$$A(x, v) = (a_0 - \phi\Phi(x))(1 - \frac{v}{u}). \quad (3.62)$$

4. In the Gipps acceleration model,

$$A(x, v) = (a_0 - \phi\Phi(x))(1 - \frac{v}{u})\sqrt{1 + 40\frac{v}{u}}. \quad (3.63)$$

Here the acceleration-speed relation has the following properties: (i) the acceleration rate should be non-negative; i.e., $A(v) \geq 0$ for $v \in [0, u]$; (ii) except the first one, the acceleration rate is bounded; i.e., $A(v) \leq a_0$; and (iii) the acceleration-speed relation is non-increasing; i.e., $A'(v) \leq 0$.

When a car is within the vicinity of a leader, its acceleration relate is a function of the car's speed, the spacing, and the speed difference. Such a relation is usually referred to as a car-following model and will be discussed in Part III.

In addition, the jerk is related to the comfort level of driving and also bounded.

Notes

Note 3.1. *Traffic flow models for ACC systems have been studied in (Hiraoka et al., 2005; Shladover et al., 2012).*

Note 3.2. *(Shalev-Shwartz et al., 2017) presented a very convincing argument on why we need a driving (including car-following and lane-changing) model based on the principles defined in this chapter. Basically, only such models are provably safe or mathematically guaranteed to be safe, given perfect sensing technology. In contrast, with data-driven approaches, one needs to test the driving model for about 30 billion miles, to guarantee one fatality every 10^9 hours; and such a test has to be re-done, even a single line of codes is changed.*

Note 3.3. *The number of lane changes induced by on-ramp vehicles and the distribution of lane changes across different lanes were theoretically and empirically studied in (Jin, 2013) and (Gan and Jin, 2013).*

Note 3.4. *(Yang et al., 2011) calibrated the jam spacing and time gap with the NGSIM data sets of vehicle trajectories on I-80 near Berkeley, CA. The website of the NGSIM project is at https://ops.fhwa.dot.gov/trafficanalysistools/ngsim.htm.*

Note 3.5. *Fig. 3.1 is from (Yan et al., 2018).*

Note 3.6. *The term of "fundamental diagram" was first introduced in (Haight, 1963).*

Note 3.7. *The Greenshields fundamental diagram was first reported in (Greenshields, 1935), where the flow-rate was called "the density in vehicles per hour". As the Greenshields fundamental diagram signals the beginning of the area of traffic flow theory, the Traffic Flow Theory committee of the Transportation Research Board started the Greenshields Prize in 2011.*

Note 3.8. *Fundamental diagrams of flow- and speed-density relations are also observed in flows of ants and pedestrians. See the fundamental diagram for the traffic of the Leaf-Cutting Ant, Atta cephalotes in (Burd et al., 2002) and pedestrians in (Hankin and Wright, 1958).*

Note 3.9. *Sonic, subsonic, and supersonic states were introduced to traffic flow in (LeVeque, 1992).*

Note 3.10. *The references on the triangular fundamental diagram are quite scarce. The triangular fundamental diagram was first used in (Munjal et al.,*

1971), Figure 1. *The authors did not justify the relations either empirically or theoretically, but instead attributed it to (Drake et al., 1967), probably due to a misunderstanding of hypothesis IV, which was a truncated Greenberg's speed-density relation. In (Haberman, 1977, Chapter 64), the triangular fundamental diagram was derived for steady states in the General Motors' linear car-following model, by truncating the maximum speed. The use of the triangular fundamental diagram was really populated by Newell (1993), in which the triangular fundamental diagram was used in the simplified kinematic wave model. In (Del Castillo and Benitez, 1995), it was shown that the triangular fundamental diagram can be a rough estimation of observations.*

Note 3.11. *In addition to the Greenshields and triangular fundamental diagrams, many different fundamental diagrams have been proposed and calibrated with data. The following are some examples of the speed-density relations:* $V(k) = u_0 \ln(\kappa/k)$ *(Greenberg, 1959),* $u[1 - \exp(\frac{w}{u}(1 - \kappa/k))]$ *(Newell, 1961),* $u \exp(-k/\kappa)$ *(Underwood, 1961),* $u \exp[-\frac{1}{2}(\frac{k}{\kappa})^2]$ *(Drake et al., 1967),* $u\left(1 - \frac{k}{\kappa}\right)^b$, $b > 1$ *(Pipes, 1967), and* $u\{1 - \exp[1 - \exp(\frac{w}{u}(\kappa/k - 1))]\}$ *(Del Castillo and Benitez, 1995).*

Note 3.12. *The triangular fundamental diagram can be approximated the following fundamental diagram:*

$$Q(k) = \begin{cases} uk(1 - \epsilon \frac{k}{k_1}), & 0 \leq k \leq k_1; \\ Q_1(k - k_1; u_1, w, k_2 - k_1) + q_1, & k_1 < k < k_2; \\ w(\kappa - k), & k_2 \leq k \leq \kappa, \end{cases}$$

where $k_1 = \frac{w\kappa}{u+w}(1 - \epsilon)$, $q_1 = \frac{uw\kappa}{u+w}(1 - \epsilon)^2$, $u_1 = u(1 - 2\epsilon)$, *and* $k_2 = \kappa - \frac{q_1}{w}$. *Here* $Q_1(k - k_1; u_1, w, k_2 - k_1)$ *can be Newell's exponential fundamental diagram (Newell, 1961) or the maximum sensitivity fundamental diagram in (Del Castillo and Benitez, 1995) with the free-flow speed* u_1, *shock wave speed* $-w$, *jam density* $k_2 - k_1$, *and density* $k - k_1$. *It can be shown that the new fundamental diagram has the following properties: (i)* $Q(k)$ *is differentiable for* $k \in [0, \kappa]$; *(ii)* $V(k)$ *strictly decreases; (iii)* $Q(k)$ *is concave; (iv)* $Q(k) \leq \min\{uk, w(\kappa - k)\}$; *(v)* $Q'(\kappa) = -w$; *(vi)* $V(0) = u$; *(vii)* $\lim_{\epsilon \to 0} Q(k) = \min\{uk, w(\kappa - k)\}$.

Note 3.13. *The Kerner-Konhauser fundamental diagram was proposed in (Kerner and Konhäuser, 1994) to study phantom jams.*

Note 3.14. *The fundamental diagram for night traffic was proposed in (LeVeque, 2001), in which the speed-density relation increases in uncongested traffic.*

Note 3.15. *Since 1960s, discontinuous, or even multi-valued with a reverse-lambda shape flow-density relations have been proposed in the literature (Edie, 1961; Drake et al., 1967; Koshi et al., 1983; Payne, 1984; Hall et al., 1992). However, a discontinuous fundamental diagram is challenged both theoretically* and empirically. Theoretically, a discontinuous flow-density relation is non-differentiable at the discontinuous point (usually the critical density) and leads to infinite characteristic wave speeds (Li and Zhang, 2013). Clearly this contradicts the fact that information travels at a finite speed along a traffic stream. Empirically, even though many studies confirm the existence of discontinuous fundamental diagrams inside a bottleneck area, e.g., Figure 4 of (Hall et al., 1992), Cassidy (1998) demonstrated that, in near-stationary states, bivariate fundamental diagrams are still continuous at a location upstream to a bottleneck with capacity drop, but densities in some ranges cannot be observed.

Note 3.16. *In (Godfrey, 1969), the network-level speed- and flow-density relations, i.e., the network fundamental diagram, were proposed and empirically calibrated for the town center road network in the city of Ipswich, England. The relations were verified by simulations in (Mahmassani et al., 1984; Gartner and Wagner, 2004). Such relations were theoretically assumed in (Vickrey, 1991, 2020) as a building block of Vickrey's bathtub model. The validity of the network fundamental diagram has been supported by more recent observations for other city or freeway networks (e.g. Geroliminis and Daganzo, 2008; Cassidy et al., 2011; Wang et al., 2015; Ambühl et al., 2017). As the traditional fundamental diagram, the network fundamental diagram is only meaningful on average (Buisson and Ladier, 2009; Cassidy et al., 2011). Theoretically, a trapezoidal flow-density relation was derived for a signalized network under stationary (periodic in both time and space) traffic conditions (Jin and Yu, 2015).*

Note 3.17. *The TWOPAS acceleration model was discussed in (Allen et al., 2000). However, it was written as $A(x,v) = a_0(1 - \frac{v}{u}) - \phi \Phi(x)$, which is not reasonable since $A(x,u) < 0$ for $\Phi(x) > 0$. The Gipps' acceleration model was developed in (Gipps, 1981), as a part of a car-following model. But it was written as $A(u) = 2.5 a_1 (1 - \frac{v}{u}) \sqrt{0.025 + \frac{v}{u}}$ without the grade.*

Problems

Problem 3.1. *Consider a semi-infinite hightway $0 \le x < \infty$ (with no entrances or exits other than at $x = 0$). Show that the number of vehicles on the road at time t is*

$$\Phi(0) + \int_{y=0}^{t} f(y) dy,$$

where $\Phi(0)$ is the number of vehicles on the road at $t = 0$, and $f(t)$ the boundary flux at $x = 0$ and t.

Problem 3.2. *Prove the conclusions in Theorem 3.3.1.*

Problem 3.3. *Prove that, in the Greenshields fundamental diagram, the speed-density relation is strictly decreasing, and the flow-density relation is concave.*

Problem 3.4. *What is the time gap in the Greenshields fundamental diagram, $q = uk(1 - k/\kappa)$?*

Problem 3.5. *Prove Theorem 3.3.2.*

Problem 3.6. *Prove that $q = Q(k)$ is a piecewise linear relation, if and only if $h = \Xi(\omega)$ is a piecewise linear relation. Note here that such relations may not be functions.*

Problem 3.7. *There is evidence that drivers tend to leave larger distances (clearances) at the same speed when driving in tunnels or on slopes. That is, the time gap is different at different locations. Derive the triangular fundamental diagram with the free-flow speed, jam density, and time gap. What are the critical density and capacity? In congested traffic, how can we calculate the density and speed from flow-rate?*

Problem 3.8. *Plot the speed- and flow-density relations with the calculated densities, speeds, and flow-rates in Problem 2.4. Fit the data with the triangular fundamental diagram and estimate the corresponding parameters.*

CHAPTER 4

Basic concepts

This chapter introduces some basic concepts related to steady states, stationary states, first-in-first-out, and unifiability.

With these concepts we are ready to solve the simple lead-vehicle problem and analyze the capacity reduction and capacity drop phenomena at various bottlenecks.

4.1 Steady states

In the trajectory coordinates, a traffic stream is in a *steady state* when all vehicles have the same speed and spacing. That is, in a steady state,

$$v(t, n) = v,$$
$$z(t, n) = z,$$
$$X(t, n) = vt - zn + X(0, 0).$$

Equivalently, in the flow coordinates, the density and flow-rate are both time- and location-independent:

$$k(t, x) = k = \frac{1}{z},$$
$$q(t, x) = \frac{v}{z},$$
$$N(t, x) = qt - kx + N(0, 0);$$

in the schedule coordinates, the headway and pace are constant:

$$h(n, x) = h = \frac{z}{v},$$
$$\omega(n, x) = \omega = \frac{1}{v},$$
$$T(n, x) = hn + \omega x + T(0, 0).$$

Thus, in steady states, the traffic surface is a plane, and all vehicle trajectories are parallel, equally placed lines, as illustrated in Fig. 4.1.

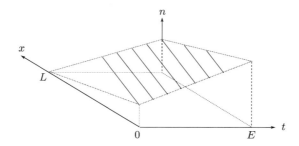

FIGURE 4.1 Traffic surface for a steady state.

A special steady state is when a road is empty. In this case, $k(t, x) = 0$, and $q(t, x) = 0$. Thus $N(t, x) = N(0, 0)$, which is a flat plane in the (t, x)-domain, but the speed is not well-defined and takes different values.

Another special steady state is when a road is jammed with stopped vehicles. In this case, $k(t, x) = \kappa$, and $q(t, x) = 0$, since $v(t, x) = 0$. Thus $N(t, x) = -\kappa x + N(0, 0)$, $X(t, n) = -\zeta n + X(0, 0)$, and $T(n, x)$ is not well-defined.

In general, the speed-density relation in the steady states should follow that in the fundamental diagram; i.e., $v = V(k)$ in steady states. Traffic flow models that violate this principle are physically meaningless.

4.2 The simple lead-vehicle problem

Consider a platoon of vehicles on a single-lane road, where the leader's speed is constant at v_2, and the initial spacings and speeds of all following vehicles are constant at z_1 and v_1, respectively. We call this a *simple lead-vehicle problem (SLVP)*; in a general lead-vehicle problem (LVP), the leader's speed and the followers' initial spacings and speeds may not be constant.

Here we assume that traffic is always in equilibrium with a non-increasing speed-density relation, $v = V(k)$, and a concave flow-density relation, $q = Q(k)$. The fundamental diagram does not have to be triangular or Greenshields. Therefore $v_1 = V(k_1)$, where $k_1 = \frac{1}{z_1}$ is the initial density of the followers. The initial location of vehicle n is $X(0, n) = -nz_1$.

Generally vehicular traffic is *anisotropic*; i.e., a follower's status does not impact the leader's choice in speed. Thus the leader maintains its speed at v_2, and its trajectory is $X(t, 0) = v_2 t$, if we label the leader as vehicle 0. Therefore the SLVP is equivalent to the following *Riemann problem*, in which the upstream and downstream platoons are initially steady with densities of k_1 and k_2, respectively. In the Riemann problem all downstream vehicles continue to travel at v_2, and the vehicle at $x = 0$ serves as the leader for the upstream platoon. But a follower needs to adapt its speed according to the leader's, and desires to be as fast as possible, but maintains a safety distance at the same time.

Using these simple principles, we can solve the SLVP with $v_1 > v_2$; i.e., the follower's initial speed is faster. In this case, a reasonable solution is that the followers attempt to drive at the higher speed v_1 as long as possible until they have to decelerate to the leader's speed. When a follower's speed is v_2, its spacing should be z_2, where $v_2 = V(\frac{1}{z_2})$. That is, a follower's state is $U_1 = (z_1, v_1)$ before decelerating and $U_2 = (z_2, v_2)$ after decelerating. If ignoring the decelerating process, all vehicles' trajectories can be found graphically, as shown in Fig. 4.2.

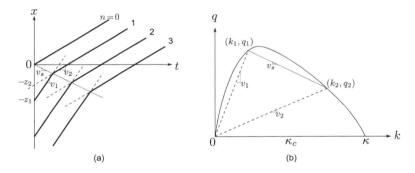

FIGURE 4.2 Vehicles' trajectories in a decelerating simple lead vehicle problem.

In Fig. 4.2(a), the dashed lines are the trajectories with a speed of either v_1 or v_2, and the thick piecewise lines are vehicles' trajectories. Linking all points when vehicles decelerate from v_1 to v_2, we have another line, which is referred to as a *shock wave*. Thus the shock wave is the interface between two traffic states, U_1 and U_2. From another viewpoint, a vehicle decelerates when its trajectory reaches the shock wave. The shock wave speed, v_s, is the slope of the line. Denote the point when the first vehicle reaches the shock wave by (t, x). Then from the figure we have the following equations:

$$x = v_s t,$$
$$x + z_2 = v_2 t,$$
$$x + z_1 = v_1 t.$$

Eliminating t and x from the equations, we have

$$v_s = \frac{z_1 v_2 - z_2 v_1}{z_1 - z_2} = \frac{k_2 v_2 - k_1 v_1}{k_2 - k_1} = \frac{q_2 - q_1}{k_2 - k_1}.$$

Thus the shock wave speed equals the slope of the secant line connecting (k_1, q_1) to (k_2, q_2) in the fundamental diagram, as shown in Fig. 4.2(b). Therefore, a shock wave forms when vehicles decelerate, or congestion (the downstream traffic state) propagates with a shock wave.

In the SLVP, if the leader's speed is faster; i.e., if $v_2 > v_1$, the solution is not so straightforward for a general fundamental diagram, since we cannot determine a follower's trajectory by connecting two trajectories in the upstream and downstream states as in the decelerating case.

However, for a triangular fundamental diagram, the SLVP can be solved by the above principle for the following scenarios: (i) $k_1, k_2 \leq \kappa_c$; (ii) $k_1, k_2 \geq \kappa_c$; (iii) $k_1 < \kappa_c < k_2$. But this principle cannot be applied when $k_1 > \kappa_c > k_2$. See Problem 4.2 for related problems.

4.3 Stationary states

4.3.1 Definition

In the flow coordinates, a traffic stream is in a *stationary state* when both density and flow-rate are time-independent, but may be location-dependent:

$$\frac{\partial k(t, x)}{\partial t} = 0,$$

$$\frac{\partial q(t, x)}{\partial t} = 0.$$

Further from the conservation equation, (3.7), we have

$$\frac{\partial q(t, x)}{\partial x} = 0.$$

Thus in a stationary state, the flow-rate is constant: $q(t, x) = q^*$. Note that this conclusion is correct for any geometry of a road, whether its number of lanes, curvature, or grade changes with x or not.

We denote the stationary density by $k^*(x)$. Hence the cumulative flow is given by

$$N(t, x) = N^*(x) + q^* t,$$

where $\frac{dN^*(x)}{dx} = -k^*(x)$ and $N^*(0) = N(0, 0)$. Thus, a steady state is a special stationary state.

The stationary speed may be location-dependent

$$v^*(x) = \frac{q^*}{k^*(x)},$$

and the stationary acceleration rate is

$$a^*(x) = \frac{\partial}{\partial t}v^*(x) + v^*(x)\frac{\partial}{\partial x}v^*(x) = \frac{\mathrm{d}\frac{1}{2}(v^*(x))^2}{\mathrm{d}x}.$$

Thus, in a stationary state, vehicles can accelerate or decelerate, but the acceleration rates only depend on the location, not the vehicles or time.

4.3.2 Equilibrium stationary state in a lane-drop/sag/tunnel zone

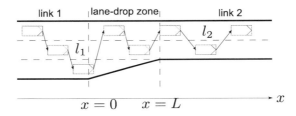

FIGURE 4.3 A lane-drop bottleneck.

For a continuous lane-drop zone, shown in Fig. 4.3, the numbers of upstream and downstream lanes are l_1 and l_2, respectively. The number of lanes linearly decrease inside the lane-drop zone, and the number of lanes is ($x \in [0, L]$)

$$l_0(x) = l_1 - \frac{\Delta l}{L}x,$$

where $\Delta l = l_1 - l_2$.

In the stationary state, we denote the constant flow-rate by q^*. Clearly the flow-rate cannot be greater than the downstream capacity; i.e., $q^* \leq C_2 \equiv l_2 C$, where C is the per-lane capacity. The upstream capacity is $C_1 = l_1 C$.

Here we assume that all lanes are identical and have the same triangular fundamental diagram. Consider two simple stationary states:

1. When the traffic state is UC at any point, the stationary states are trivial

$$\begin{aligned} v^*(x) &= u, \\ k^*(x) &= \frac{q^*}{u}, \\ a^*(x) &= 0. \end{aligned}$$

2. When the traffic state is OC at any point, the stationary states are

$$v^*(x) = \frac{q^*}{(l_1 - \frac{\Delta l}{L}x)q_0 - q^*}w,$$

$$k^*(x) = \frac{(l_1 - \frac{\Delta l}{L}x)q_0 - q^*}{w},$$

$$a^*(x) = \frac{\Delta l}{L \cdot ((l_1 - \frac{\Delta l}{L}x)q_0 - q^*)^3}(q^*w)^2 q_0.$$

In such a congested lane-drop zone, both the speed and acceleration rate increase in x, and the density decreases in x.

Fig. 4.4 shows the trajectories of four vehicles driving through the Kobotoke tunnel in Japan at different times after an upstream queue forms. The speeds and, therefore, the traffic states are relatively stationary from time to time inside the tunnel, whose entrance is at 40.75 km. In addition, vehicles accelerate away from the upstream queue. These observations are consistent with the stationary states inside a lane-drop zone.

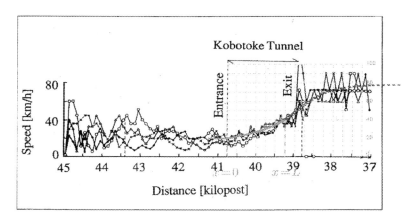

FIGURE 4.4 Stationary states in the Kobotoke tunnel in Japan.

4.3.3 Considering bounded acceleration

Thus the maximum speed and acceleration rate are achieved when vehicles get out of the lane-drop zone. In particular, when $u = 30$ m/s, $w = 5$ m/s, $\kappa = 1/7$ veh/m, $l_1 = 2$, $l_2 = 1$, and $L = 100$ m, then the maximum acceleration rate equals 63 m/s^2. Obviously it is too high and unrealistic.

To have realistic acceleration behavior, the acceleration rate of the stationary states should be bounded:

$$a^*(x) \leq A(v^*(x)).$$

When the lane-drop zone is uncongested, this condition is automatically satisfied. In the following we only consider the congested case. We define

$$\Upsilon(x;q^*) = a^*(x) - A(v^*(x))$$
$$= \frac{\Delta l}{L \cdot ((l_1 - \frac{\Delta l}{L}x)q_0 - q^*)^3}(q^*w)^2 q_0 - A\left(\frac{q^*}{(l_1 - \frac{\Delta l}{L}x)q_0 - q^*} w\right).$$

Thus the bounded acceleration condition is equivalent to $\Upsilon(x;q^*) \leq 0$. As the acceleration-speed relation, $A(v)$ is non-increasing, both $v^*(x)$ and $a^*(x)$ increase in x, $f(x;q^*)$ increases in x. Hence the bounded acceleration condition can be simply written as

$$\Upsilon(L;q^*) \leq 0,$$

where $\Upsilon(L;q^*) = \frac{\Delta l}{L \cdot (l_2 q_0 - q^*)^3}(q^*w)^2 q_0 - A\left(\frac{q^*}{l_2 q_0 - q^*}w\right)$. Furthermore, $\Upsilon(L;q^*)$ increases in q^*. We denote C_3 as the solution of $\Upsilon(L;C_3) = 0$. Then under the bounded acceleration condition, the stationary flow-rate in congested traffic has to be bounded:

$$q^* \leq C_3. \qquad (4.1)$$

The fundamental diagrams and stationary states in a lane-drop bottleneck are illustrated in Fig. 4.5. The figure confirms that vehicles accelerate inside the lane-drop zone.

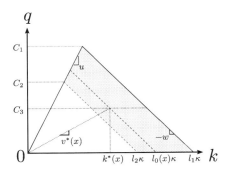

FIGURE 4.5 The fundamental diagrams and stationary states in a lane-drop bottleneck.

4.4 Bottlenecks on a road

On a road, there can be various bottlenecks, which restrict the passage of vehicles. These bottlenecks can be time-, location-, vehicle-, or traffic state-dependent.

4.4.1 Capacity reduction

In the triangular fundamental diagram, (3.42), the capacity is given by

$$C = \frac{u\kappa}{1 + u\kappa\tau} = \frac{1}{\frac{1}{u\kappa} + \tau}, \qquad (4.2)$$

which increases in the free-flow speed, u and the jam density, κ, but decreases in the time gap, τ. Thus on a road segment, where u and κ are reduced or τ increased, the capacity is reduced, and the road segment constitutes a bottleneck with the capacity reduction effect.

Bridges, school zones, variable speed limit zones, narrow roads, curvatures, mountainous roads, and dangerous road conditions caused by clement weather can result in smaller free-flow speed and thus constitute road bottlenecks.

A road segment with a smaller number of lanes, or different mixtures of vehicles with different lengths (e.g., cars and trucks) lead to different jam density κ. Thus such a road segment can be a bottleneck. A lane-drop bottleneck is a typical one.

Inside a tunnel or on an uphill road (sag), vehicles' responses may be slower and lead to larger time gaps. That is, vehicles tend to leave larger spacings at the same speed. Thus tunnels and sags are typical road bottlenecks. In Japan, tunnels and sags can reduce the capacity by 25%, from 2000 vphpl to 1500 vphpl.

In addition, traffic signals can also reduce the capacity and constitute bottlenecks. For example, if the ratio of the green time to the cycle length is $r < 1$ for an approach, the maximum throughput of the road equals rC, where C is the normal capacity.

Heterogeneity in individual driver-vehicle units can also have bottleneck effects. Trucks or other vehicles can have different speed-spacing relations, $v = W(z)$, and different acceleration-speed relations, $a = A(v)$. Due to the car-following (anisotropic) principle, vehicles have to slow down to follow the slower vehicle in the front, or switch a lane to overtake. In both cases, slower vehicles constitute moving bottlenecks.

Such capacity reduction effects can be considered the first-order bottleneck effects. To address them, roads need to designed and planned differently. On freeways, one can expand the road or improve the road conditions to increase the capacity; but such efforts usually entail substantial financial and environmental costs. On the arterial roads, one can increase the green time of one road to increase its capacity; but one has to decrease the green time on the competing roads.

4.4.2 More on lane-drop bottlenecks

For a road with l_1 lanes, an accident occurs and leads to a closure of Δl lanes. Let the number of open lanes be $l_2 = l_1 - \Delta l$. After a while, a portion of the upstream road becomes congested in an OC state. Assuming the traffic state is steady, and the maximum flow-rate equals $l_2 C$. From the multilane fundamental diagram in Section 3.3.7, we can estimate the upstream density and speed on the upstream queue:

$$k = \frac{l_1 q_0 - l_2 C}{w},$$
$$v = \frac{l_2 C}{l_1 q_0 - l_2 C} w.$$

For an example, let $u = 30$ m/s, $\kappa = 1/7$ v/m, $w = 5$ m/s, and $l_1 = 6$. For $\Delta l = 1, \cdots, 5$, the upstream speeds and densities are given in **Table** 4.1, in which the speeds are normalized against the free-flow speed, and the densities against the jam density per lane. We can see that lane closure can cause severe congestion: if just one lane is closed, the speed drops by more than half; if two lanes are closed, the speed drops to about one fifth; and if five lanes are closed, vehicles are almost stopped.

TABLE 4.1 The upstream speeds and densities after lane closure on a six-lane road.

Number of closed lanes	1	2	3	4	5
Normalized speed	0.42	0.22	0.13	0.07	0.03
Normalized density	1.71	2.57	3.43	4.29	5.14

When congestion starts at a bottleneck, sometimes it is beneficial to restrict the upstream demand. Variable speed limits (VSL) have been implemented upstream to a bottleneck to reduce the flow-rate. With a speed limit, the maximum flow-rate equals the capacity:

$$C = \frac{uw}{u+w} \kappa.$$

When $u = 30$ m/s, $\kappa = 1/7$ v/m, and $w = 5$ m/s, the capacity equals 2204 vphpl. If we want to reduce the flow-rate by 10% to 50%, the variable speed limits have to be reduced to 56%, 36%, 25%, 18%, and 13% of the free-flow speed, which are about 38, 25, 17, 12, and 8 mph. Therefore, the speed has to be substantially reduced to achieve modest restrictions in the flow-rate.

4.4.3 Capacity drop

At lane-drop, sag, or tunnel bottlenecks, it has been observed that the maximum flow-rate drops below the downstream capacity, when an upstream queue forms, even though there is no congestion on the downstream road. This is the so-called two-capacity or *capacity drop* phenomenon, which has the following three basic characteristics: (i) the capacity can be reached when the upstream road is uncongested, (ii) but the maximum flow-rate is substantially below this when the upstream road is congested, and (iii) the observed fundamental diagram on the downstream road is discontinuous, missing some congested states.

For a bottleneck with capacity drop, there are usually three capacities: the normal capacity of the upstream road, C_1, the reduced capacity that can be reached in uncongested traffic, C_2, and the dropped capacity in congested traffic, C_3. The ratio of capacity drop is defined by

$$\xi = \frac{C_2 - C_3}{C_2} = 1 - \frac{C_3}{C_2}. \tag{4.3}$$

The capacity drop ratio is in the order of 10%. For example, for sags and tunnels in Japan, $C_1 \approx 2000$ vphpl, $C_2 \approx 1500$ vphpl, and $C_3 \approx 1300$ vphpl. Thus the capacity drop ratio is about 13%.

Such a phenomenon has been a baffling feature of freeway traffic dynamics, since the capacity of a road network may drop substantially when it is most needed during the peak period. Many traffic control strategies, including variable speed limits and ramp metering, have been developed to prevent or delay the occurrence of capacity drop.

At signalized intersections, capacity drop can also occur with upstream queues. When the traffic light turns green, vehicles have to accelerate away from the upstream queue and cause the start-up lost time, which further reduces the flow-rate. Consider a two-phase signal, whose cycle length is 60 s. The normal capacity is $C_1 \approx 2000$ vphpl. The green time for one approach is 30 s, and the start-up lost time is 3 s. Then $C_2 \approx 1000$ vphpl, and $C_3 \approx 900$ vphpl. In this case, the capacity drop ratio $\xi = 10\%$. The cycle length and the offset can be adjusted to address the capacity drop effect of signals.

Capacity drop is traffic state-dependent, and can be considered second-order bottleneck effects of various bottlenecks. Compared with the first-order capacity reduction effect, the capacity drop effect is relatively easier to address.

In a network, capacity reduction and capacity drop can have cascading bottleneck effects associated with route choices. In a freeway network, capacity drop can lead to longer and more severe queues and therefore reduce the discharging flow-rate at upstream off-ramps. In a signalized road network, turning movements can lead to gridlock at a relatively low density.

4.5 First-in-first-out (FIFO)

Without loss of generality, we assume that vehicles of the same commodity follow the First-In-First-Out (FIFO) principle. That is, $X_m(t, n_1) > X_m(t, n_2)$ for $n_1 < n_2$.

We say that two commodities, e.g., 1 and 2, follow the FIFO principle, if for any n_1 and n_2, at any t

$$\min\{X_1(t, n_1) - X_2(t, n_2)\} \geq 0; \tag{4.4a}$$

i.e., vehicle n_1 of commodity 1 is always in the front of vehicle n_2 of commodity 2, or

$$\max\{X_1(t, n_1) - X_2(t, n_2)\} \leq 0; \tag{4.4b}$$

i.e., vehicle n_1 of commodity 1 is always behind vehicle n_2 of commodity 2. One can show that (4.4) is equivalent to saying that at any t and x

$$v_1(t, x) = v_2(t, x). \tag{4.5}$$

The proof is assigned as Problem 4.6.

Further a multi-commodity traffic stream is called FIFO if all commodities follow the FIFO principle among them; in this case,

$$v_m = v; \tag{4.6}$$

i.e., the commodity speed equals the total speed. In a FIFO traffic stream, the commodity density proportion equals the commodity flow-rate proportion; i.e., for $m = 1, \cdots, M$

$$p_m = \gamma_m.$$

Equivalently, in a FIFO traffic stream,

$$\eta_m = 1.$$

In a FIFO multi-commodity traffic stream, if both $N_t(t, x)$ and $N_x(t, x)$ are bounded, the cumulative flow $N(t, x)$ can be used as a vehicle's identity; i.e., if the location of vehicle n at t is $X(t, n)$, then

$$n = N(t, X(t, n)),$$

which is (2.4a).

4.5.1 FIFO multilane traffic

For an inhomogeneous road with different number of lanes at different locations, as shown in Fig. 4.3, we denote the number of lanes at location x by $l(x)$, which may not be an integer value as in the lane-drop zone. Such inhomogeneity can lead to traffic bottlenecks, where congestion initiates. The total primary variables are still denoted by $N(t, x)$, $X(t, n)$, and $T(n, x)$.

For simplicity, we assume that all lanes are balanced with the same density and flow-rate at the same location and time. As shown in Fig. 4.3, we assume that vehicles follow each other on different lanes. In this case, there is no need to differentiate lanes. In the flow coordinates, denote the per-lane density and flow-rate by $k(t, x)$ and $q(t, x)$ respectively, then the total density and flow-rate are $l(x)k(t, x) = -N_x(t, x)$ and $l(x)q(t, x) = N_t(t, x)$. In the trajectory coordinates, we denote the per-lane spacing by $z(t, n)$. Clearly, $z(t, n) \neq -X_n(t, n) = \frac{X(t, n - \Delta n) - X(t, n)}{\Delta n}$, which is the spacing between vehicles on different lanes. We introduce the cumulative lane-miles, $Z(x)$, as the integral of the number of lanes:

$$Z(x) = \int_{y=0}^{x} l(y) dy.$$

Then the per-lane spacing is written as

$$z(t, n) = \frac{Z(X(t, n - \Delta n)) - Z(X(t, n))}{\Delta n};$$

That is, the available spacing to vehicle n equals the cumulative lane-miles between it and its leader.

4.5.2 Non-FIFO traffic

In reality, vehicles may not follow the FIFO principle on a multilane road. Still we assume that there is a well-behaved total cumulative flow, $N(t, x)$, on which both $N_t(t, x)$ and $N_x(t, x)$ are bounded.

For vehicle i at time t, we denote its location by $X_i(t)$ and its order by $\phi_i(t)$, where

$$\phi_i(t) = N(t, X_i(t)). \tag{4.7}$$

For a FIFO traffic stream, $\phi_i(t)$ is independent of t. Hence $\phi'_i(t) = 0$, and

$$N_t(t, X_i(t)) + N_x(t, X_i(t)) X'_i(t) = 0,$$

which leads to $v_i(t) = X'_i(t) = q(t, X_i(t))/k(t, X_i(t)) = v(t, X_i(t))$. That is, in a FIFO traffic stream, vehicle's speed, $v_i(t)$, equals the total speed, $v(t, X_i(t))$.

But for a non-FIFO traffic stream, $\phi_i(t)$ may change with time. If vehicle i belongs to commodity m, then we have

$$X'_i(t) = v_m(t, X_i(t)),$$

and

$$\phi'_i(t) = N_t(t, X_i(t)) + N_x(t, X_i(t)) X'_i(t)$$
$$= q(t, X_i(t)) - k(t, X_i(t)) v_m(t, X_i(t))$$

$$= k(t, X_i(t))(v(t, X_i(t)) - v_m(t, X_i(t))).$$

Thus if vehicle i's speed is faster, its order decreases; otherwise, its order increases. Physically, $\phi_i'(t)$ represents the rate of traffic passing vehicle i.

Consider a special case when all commodity traffic streams are in steady states: $k_m(t,x) = k_m$ and $q_m(t,x) = q_m$. In this case the total traffic is also in a steady state: $k = \sum_{m=1}^M k_m$, and $q = \sum_{m=1}^M q_m$. The corresponding total and commodity speeds are $v = q/k$ and $v_m = q_m/k_m$. Assume that vehicle i belongs to commodity m, then

$$\phi_i'(t) = k(v - v_m),$$

which is constant. Hence $\phi_i(t) = \phi_i(0) + k(v - v_m)t$, which is linear in time. Therefore, the vehicle order changes linearly in time, when traffic is relatively steady.

4.6 First-in-first-out and unifiable equilibrium states

Multi-commodity fundamental diagrams have the following two properties:

- First-in-first-out (FIFO). A multi-commodity traffic flow is FIFO if all commodities' speeds are the same (Section 2.5). Thus, all commodities have the same speed-density relation according to (3.54):

$$V_1(k, \vec{p}) = \cdots = V_M(k, \vec{p}) = V(k, \vec{p}). \quad (4.8)$$

- Unifiable. A multi-commodity traffic flow unifiable if the total traffic speed is a function of the total traffic density; i.e., if (3.54) can be simplified as

$$v = V(k, \vec{p}) = V(k). \quad (4.9a)$$

In a unifiable multi-commodity traffic flow, there exists a simple fundamental diagram for the total flow-density relation:

$$q = Q(k) \equiv kV(k). \quad (4.9b)$$

But the commodity speed-density relation may not be the same:

$$v_m = \eta_m(k, \vec{p})V(k), \quad (4.9c)$$

where $\sum_{m=1}^M p_m \eta_m(k, \vec{p}) = 1$.

If multi-commodity fundamental diagrams are both FIFO and unifiable, the speed-density relation can be written as

$$V_1((k, \vec{p})) = \cdots = V_M((k, \vec{p})) = V(k). \quad (4.10)$$

Notes

Note 4.1. *Steady states are also called uniform traffic or constant states. The concept was introduced in (Chandler et al., 1958): "We assume that if such a (steady) state could be achieved, the separation distance between vehicles plus the car length would have a constant value and each vehicle would have the same velocity." In the reference it was also called a stable state. In this book, steady states may not be stable. In contrast, stationary states have been less studied. They were theoretically defined in (Jin, 2012c) and later studied for a network in (Jin, 2015a, 2017d). Empirically, a method to identify "near-stationary" states was presented in (Cassidy, 1998). Steady states may not exist on inhomogeneous roads, but stationary states can.*

Note 4.2. *The lead-vehicle problem has been studied ever since the first car-following models. For example, the steady state and its stability of a platoon following a leader was studied in (Chandler et al., 1958) and many follow-up studies. However, the term "lead vehicle problem" seems to be first used in (Del Castillo et al., 1994; Agogino et al., 1995).*

Note 4.3. *A stationary state along an acceleration wave on a homogeneous road may not be in equilibrium; an equilibrium state in a shock wave may not be stationary; a stationary and equilibrium state on an inhomogeneous road may be not steady; but a steady state is usually both equilibrium and stationary. The logical relationships among stationary, steady, and equilibrium states were discussed in (Yan et al., 2018). Illustrations of various states are also available in the reference.*

Note 4.4. *Sags and tunnels are critical bottlenecks in Japan. Their bottleneck effects, including both capacity reduction and capacity drop effects, were systematically studied in (Koshi, 1984, 1986; Koshi et al., 1992). Fig. 4.3 was from Figure 3 of (Koshi et al., 1992), reproduced in (Jin, 2018).*

Note 4.5. *Equilibrium stationary states in a lane-drop bottleneck were defined and analyzed in (Jin, 2017b,a). Equilibrium stationary states in a tunnel/sag bottleneck were defined and analyzed in (Jin, 2018).*

Note 4.6. *Since 1990s, the two-capacity or capacity drop phenomenon of active bottlenecks has been observed and verified at many bottleneck locations (Banks, 1990, 1991b; Hall and Agyemang-Duah, 1991). It has been observed at a merge bottleneck, tunnels, lane drops, curves, and upgrades (Cassidy and Bertini, 1999; Chung et al., 2007). Capacity drop also occurs at bottlenecks caused by work zones (Krammes and Lopez, 1994; Dixon et al., 1996; Jiang, 1999) as well as accidents/incidents (Smith et al., 2003).*

Note 4.7. *Variable speed limits (VSL) have been implemented to improve the throughput of a traffic system since 1960s (Greenberg and Daou, 1960). Refer to (Hegyi et al., 2005; Zhang et al., 2006; Papageorgiou et al., 2008; Carlson et* al., 2011, 2013) for recent theoretical, simulation, and empirical studies. Refer to (Papageorgiou et al., 2003) a review of traffic control strategies for both freeway and arterial networks.

Note 4.8. *A vehicle's order in a non-FIFO traffic stream was first introduced in (Rey et al., 2019). This concept is critical for estimating vehicles' trajectories when the FIFO principle is violated.*

Note 4.9. *The concept of unifiability was introduced in (Jin, 2017e). Construction of general unifiable multi-commodity fundamental diagrams was also presented.*

Note 4.10. *An equilibrium multi-commodity traffic state can be either FIFO or unifiable. In particular, the FIFO and unifiable states are also called 1-pipe, and non-FIFO, non-unifiable 2-pipe (Daganzo, 1997b). Generally, unifiable multi-commodity traffic flows have been implicitly assumed to follow the FIFO principle (Daganzo, 1995a; Lebacque, 1996). Several fundamental diagrams are FIFO but not unifiable: in (Zhang and Jin, 2002), different commodities have the same speed, but different contributions to the total speed, depending on their free-flow speeds; in (Jin, 2013), weaving and non-weaving vehicles have the same speed, but weaving vehicles have more contributions to the effective density and therefore the total speed.*

Many multi-commodity fundamental diagrams are neither FIFO nor unifiable: in (Daganzo, 1997b), different speed-density relations were proposed for 1- and 2-pipe regimes of two classes of vehicles on roads with two types of lanes; in (Benzoni-Gavage and Colombo, 2003), different commodities are assumed to have different free-flow speeds, and similar multi-commodity fundamental diagrams were presented (Wong and Wong, 2002; Burger and Kozakevicius, 2007; Bürger et al., 2008); in (Chanut and Buisson, 2003), different passenger-car equivalents are used to define total density for trucks and cars, different classes are assumed to have different speeds in uncongested traffic but the same speeds in congested traffic, and similar multi-class fundamental diagrams were also studied in (van Lint et al., 2008; Ngoduy, 2010). Very few unifiable, non-FIFO fundamental diagrams have been reported: in (Yan and Jin, 2017; Jin and Yan, 2019), a unifiable, non-FIFO multi-lane fundamental diagram was calibrated from PeMS data.

Problems

Problem 4.1. *Solve the simple lead vehicle problem with a normalized triangular fundamental diagram: $q = \min\{k, \frac{1}{4}(1-k)\}$. The downstream speed is $v_2 = \frac{1}{2}$, and the upstream density is $k_1 = 0.1$.*

Problem 4.2. *For a triangular fundamental diagram, $q = \min\{uk, w(\kappa - k)\}$, solve the SLVP for (i) $k_1, k_2 \leq \kappa_c$; (ii) $k_1, k_2 \geq \kappa_c$; and (iii) $k_1 < \kappa_c < k_2$. How about (iv) $k_1 > \kappa_c > k_2$? In particular, the queue discharge problem is when the* upstream is jammed, and the downstream empty. That is, $k_1 = \kappa$, $v_1 = 0$, $k_2 = 0$, and $v_2 = u$. For the SLVP, can we simply determine a follower's trajectory by connecting two trajectories in the upstream and downstream states as in the decelerating case?

Problem 4.3. On a 5-lane road, if one lane is closed, assuming the upstream part is congested but the downstream part not, what will be the speed in the upstream queue? How about 4-lane, 3-lane, and 2-lane roads?

Problem 4.4. For a continuous lane-drop zone, shown in Fig. 4.3, let $u = 30$ m/s, $w = 5$ m/s, $\kappa = 1/7$ veh/m, $l_1 = 2$, $l_2 = 1$, and $L = 100$ m. If the maximum acceleration rate is constant $a_0 = 2$ m/s^2. What is the maximum flow-rate in a congested lane-drop zone?

Problem 4.5. Consider a very long tunnel, where drivers' time gap equals 1.5 s outside the tunnel ($x < 0$), linearly increases to 2.1 s at $x = 1.5$ km, and stays at 2.1 s thereafter. The free-flow speed is 80 km/h, and the jam density is 140 veh/km. What is the maximum congested flow-rate between 0 and 1.5 km, such that vehicles' acceleration rates are bounded by the TWOPAS model with $a_0 = 0.6$ m/s^2?

Problem 4.6. Prove that (4.4) is equivalent to (4.5). That is, the two definitions of FIFO are the same.

Problem 4.7. Devise a scheme to obtain equivalent FIFO trajectories from non-FIFO ones. As a hint, two traffic streams can be considered equivalent if they have the same average density, speed, and flow-rate in a spatial-temporal domain.

PART II

First-order models

Making sense of anything means making models that can predict outcomes and accommodate observations. Truth is a model. - Neil Gershenfeld

CHAPTER 5

The Lighthill-Whitham-Richards (LWR) model

The following steps are usually taken to model a traffic system at the macroscopic level:

1. Identify a network with one or more bottlenecks that impose congestion or other problems.
2. Define relevant variables as in Chapter 2.
3. Introduce basic behavioral principles, such as the fundamental diagrams, as in Chapter 3.
4. Derive dynamic equations.
5. Discuss analytical solutions under simple conditions and introduce basic concepts as in Chapter 4.
6. Develop numerical solution methods under general initial and boundary conditions, which will be discussed in Chapters 6 and 8.
7. Calibrate and validate the models with empirical data from PeMS, NGSIM, and other datasets.

The seminal Lighthill-Whitham-Richards (LWR) model applies when traffic states can change with time and location but are always in equilibrium, where the flow-rate and speed are functions of the density. As the fundamental diagram, the LWR model describes the average traffic dynamics. The original LWR model only applies to single-lane, single-commodity traffic, but it has been extended to more complex traffic systems.

This chapter contains the following eight sections. Section 5.1 derives the original LWR model and discusses some of its basic properties. Section 5.2 presents extensions of the LWR model for more complicated traffic systems. Section 5.3 solves the LWR model under either under-critical or over-critical initial conditions and introduces the linear transport equation. Section 5.4 discusses simple solutions of the LWR model with general fundamental diagrams and introduces the concept of characteristic waves. Section 5.5 solves the Riemann problem with shock or rarefaction waves and explains the role of entropy conditions Section 5.6 discusses the stationary states and boundary fluxes in Riemann solutions. Section 5.7 solves the LWR model for inhomogeneous roads. Section 5.8 applies the LWR model to solve an example with a moving bottleneck.

5.1 Model derivation

In the flow coordinates the LWR model can be derived from the following three rules:

(R1) Constitutive law: $q = kv$;
(R2) Conservation law: $\frac{\partial k}{\partial t} + \frac{\partial q}{\partial x} = 0$;
(R3) Fundamental diagram: $v = V(k)$.

R1 and R3 lead to $q = Q(k) \equiv kV(k)$. The flow-density relation and R2 lead to the LWR model:

$$k_t + Q(k)_x = 0, \qquad (5.1)$$

which is a partial differential equation or, more specifically, a hyperbolic conservation law.

5.1.1 With the Greenshields fundamental diagram

With the Greenshields fundamental diagram, the LWR model can be written as

$$\frac{\partial k}{\partial t} + \frac{\partial uk(1 - \frac{k}{\kappa})}{\partial x} = 0.$$

Consider a normalized fundamental diagram with $u = 1$ and $\kappa = 1$, the LWR model can be simplified as

$$\frac{\partial k}{\partial t} + \frac{\partial k(1-k)}{\partial x} = 0.$$

Let $y = \frac{1}{2}k$, we further have

$$\frac{\partial y}{\partial t} + y\frac{\partial y}{\partial x} = 0,$$

which is the inviscid Burgers equation.

Thus, the LWR model with the Greenshields fundamental diagram is equivalent to the Burgers equation; and the LWR model with a general fundamental diagram is called a scalar hyperbolic conservation law, which has been used to describe the dynamics of water, cosmological, and other waves. Many of the mathematical theories were developed to understand these physical phenomena.

With the triangular fundamental diagram, the LWR model can be written as

$$\frac{\partial k}{\partial t} + \frac{\partial \min\{uk, w(\kappa - k)\}}{\partial x} = 0. \tag{5.2}$$

Under general traffic conditions, this special version is more challenging mathematically, as the flow-density relation is non-differentiable. However, as the triangular fundamental diagram is more consistent with empirical observations, this model is more meaningful for traffic flow. In addition, as shown in Section 5.3, if traffic is either UC or OC, the model is still quite simple mathematically. Based on this observation, in recent decades, many theories unique to this model have been developed in the traffic flow theory field.

5.1.2 Equivalent formulations in other coordinates

In the trajectory coordinates, the LWR model is equivalent to the following hyperbolic conservation law:

$$z_t + W(z)_n = 0. \tag{5.3}$$

In the schedule coordinates, the LWR model is equivalent to the following hyperbolic conservation law:

$$\omega_n - \Xi(\omega)_x = 0. \tag{5.4}$$

Here the speed-spacing and headway-pace relations are defined in Section 3.3.5.

5.1.3 Initial and boundary conditions

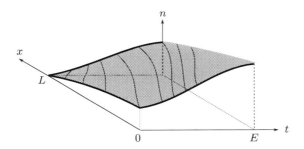

FIGURE 5.1 Initial-boundary value problem on the t-x-n surface.

5. The Lighthill-Whitham-Richards (LWR) model

The LWR model describes the formation, propagation, and dissipation of congestion on a homogeneous road. It uses the initial and boundary conditions to predict the future traffic states. For example, for the 3-D surface as shown in Fig. 5.1, the LWR model can solve the whole 3-D surface from the initial cumulative flow at $t = 0$, denoted by $N_0(x) = N(0, x)$, and the boundary cumulative flows at $x = 0$ and $x = L$, denoted by $F(t) = N(t, 0)$ and $G(t) = N(t, L)$ respectively. In the figure, the initial and boundary values are highlighted by the thick curves, and the 3-D surface that can be solved from the LWR model is shaded.

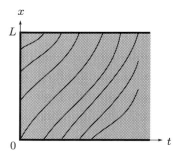

FIGURE 5.2 The initial-boundary value problem in the (t, x) space.

In the (t, x) space, the initial-boundary value problem is demonstrated in Fig. 5.2, in which the initial and boundary values are given on the thick lines, and the LWR model can be solved to obtain the values in the shaded region.

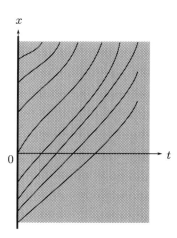

FIGURE 5.3 The initial value problem in the (t, x) space.

In contrast, the initial value problem in the (t, x) space is demonstrated in Fig. 5.3, in which the initial values are given on the thick line, and the LWR model is solved to obtain the values in the shaded region.

5.2 Extensions

The LWR model can be extended to describe traffic dynamics in other traffic systems. In particular, the extension can be done with respect to one or more of the three rules.

Inhomogeneous roads

For an inhomogeneous road, where the flow-density relation is location-dependent, $q = Q(x, k)$, the LWR model is

$$\frac{\partial k}{\partial t} + \frac{\partial Q(x, k)}{\partial x} = 0. \tag{5.5}$$

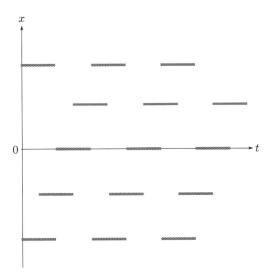

FIGURE 5.4 Signal settings on a signalized street in the (t, x) plane.

For a signalized street without significant turning-in and turning-out movements, the effective red intervals (red thick bars) and green intervals (between the red thick bars) at different intersections in the (t, x) plane are illustrated in Fig. 5.4. If the set of the red intervals is denoted by $\mathcal{B}$, then the signal setting can be represented by the following indicator function:

$$B(t, x) = \begin{cases} 0, & (t, x) \in \mathcal{B}; \\ 1, & (t, x) \notin \mathcal{B}. \end{cases} \tag{5.6}$$

That is, if there is a signal at x and the signal indication is red at t, then $B(t,x) = 0$; otherwise, if there is no signal at x, or the signal indication is green at (t,x), then $B(t,x) = 1$. Clearly, when $B(t,x) = 0$, no vehicles can pass the location; otherwise, traffic flow dynamics can be described by the LWR model. Hence, the LWR model for the signalized street can be written as

$$\frac{\partial k}{\partial t} + \frac{\partial}{\partial x} B(t,x) Q(k) = 0. \tag{5.7}$$

For a multilane road, where the number of lanes is location-dependent, $l(x)$, the LWR model is

$$\frac{\partial k}{\partial t} + \frac{\partial k V\left(\frac{k}{l(x)}\right)}{\partial x} = 0, \tag{5.8}$$

where $v = V(k)$ is the speed-density relation on each lane.

For a multilane road with location-dependent lane-changing intensity, $c(x)$, the LWR model is

$$\frac{\partial k}{\partial t} + \frac{\partial k V\left(\frac{k}{\tilde{l}(x)}\right)}{\partial x} = 0, \tag{5.9}$$

where the effective number of lanes is $\tilde{l}(x) = l(x)/(1 + c(x))$.

Multi-commodity traffic

If a multi-commodity traffic flow is both FIFO and unifiable, the total and commodity speed-density relations are the same, $v = V(k)$, and the density of commodity m is $k_m = p_m k$ ($m = 1, \cdots, M$). The LWR model is

$$\frac{\partial k}{\partial t} + \frac{\partial k V(k)}{\partial x} = 0, \tag{5.10a}$$

$$\frac{\partial k_m}{\partial t} + \frac{\partial k_m V(k)}{\partial x} = 0, \tag{5.10b}$$

where the second equation is equivalent to

$$\frac{\partial p_m k}{\partial t} + \frac{\partial p_m k V(k)}{\partial x} = 0, \tag{5.11}$$

or equivalently,

$$\frac{\partial p_m}{\partial t} + V(k) \frac{\partial p_m}{\partial x} = 0. \tag{5.12}$$

5.2 Extensions

That is, the density proportion travels along vehicles, since $\frac{dp_m}{dt} = \frac{\partial p_m}{\partial t} + v\frac{\partial p_m}{\partial x} = 0$. Equivalently, in the trajectory coordinate, $\frac{\partial}{\partial t} p_m(t, n) = 0$. Here only M equations are independent, due to $\sum_{m=1}^{M} p_m = 1$.

Such FIFO and unifiable multi-commodity LWR model can be used to describe traffic dynamics on a network with homogeneous links. For link $b \in \mathcal{B}$, the location is denoted by x_b, the traffic flow variables have the subscript b, and the speed-density relation by $v_b = V_b(k_b)$. Then the LWR model can be written as

$$\frac{\partial k_b}{\partial t} + \frac{\partial k_b V_b(k_b)}{\partial x_b} = 0, \tag{5.13a}$$

$$\frac{\partial k_{b,m}}{\partial t} + \frac{\partial k_{b,m} V_b(k_b)}{\partial x_b} = 0, \tag{5.13b}$$

where $k_{b,m}$ is the density of commodity m on link b.

If a multi-commodity traffic flow is FIFO but may not be unifiable, the total and commodity speed-density relations are the same, $v = V(\vec{k})$, and the LWR model is

$$\frac{\partial k}{\partial t} + \frac{\partial k V(\vec{k})}{\partial x} = 0, \tag{5.14a}$$

$$\frac{\partial k_m}{\partial t} + \frac{\partial k_m V(\vec{k})}{\partial x} = 0, \tag{5.14b}$$

where the second equation is equivalent to

$$\frac{\partial p_m}{\partial t} + V(\vec{k})\frac{\partial p_m}{\partial x} = 0. \tag{5.15}$$

If a multi-commodity traffic flow is unifiable, the total speed-density relation is $v = V(k)$, but the commodity speed-density relation is $v_m = \gamma_m(\vec{k})V(k)$, where $\sum_{m=1}^{M} p_m \gamma_m(\vec{k}) = 1$. The LWR model can be written as

$$\frac{\partial k}{\partial t} + \frac{\partial k V(k)}{\partial x} = 0, \tag{5.16a}$$

$$\frac{\partial k_m}{\partial t} + \frac{\partial k_m \gamma_m(\vec{k}) V(k)}{\partial x} = 0. \tag{5.16b}$$

For a multi-commodity traffic flow, which is neither FIFO nor unifiable, the LWR model is

$$\frac{\partial k}{\partial t} + \frac{\partial k V(\vec{k})}{\partial x} = 0, \tag{5.17a}$$

$$\frac{\partial k_m}{\partial t} + \frac{\partial k_m \gamma_m(\vec{k}) V(\vec{k})}{\partial x} = 0. \tag{5.17b}$$

The original LWR model, (5.1), applies for traffic on a homogeneous single-lane road or total traffic on a homogeneous multilane road with unifiable fundamental diagrams.

5.3 The initial value problem with the triangular fundamental diagram and linear transport equation

This section discusses the solutions of the LWR model with the triangular fundamental diagram under under-critical or over-critical initial conditions:

$$k(0, x) = k_0(x), \quad x \in (-\infty, \infty). \tag{5.18}$$

Refer to Fig. 5.3 for an illustration.

For the triangular fundamental diagram, the characteristic wave speed is piecewise constant:

$$\lambda(k) = \begin{cases} u, & 0 \le k < \kappa_c; \\ -w, & \kappa_c < k \le \kappa. \end{cases}$$

At the critical density, κ_c, $\lambda(k)$ can be considered a multi-valued or set-valued: $\lambda(\kappa_c) \in [-w, u]$.

5.3.1 Under-critical initial conditions

If the initial state is UC; i.e., if $k_0(x) \le \kappa_c$, the traffic state at any later time should be UC. The LWR model can be simplified as

$$\frac{\partial k}{\partial t} + u \frac{\partial k}{\partial x} = 0.$$

This is a linear transport equation, whose solution is

$$k(t, x) = k_0(x - ut).$$

Imagine an observer starting at $(0, x_0)$ in the (t, x) plane and traveling at a constant speed of u. Then the density along the observer's trajectory is always constant at $k_0(x_0)$. This is illustrated in Fig. 5.5(a).

Since there is no congestion, vehicles' speeds are constant at u: $v(t, x) = V(k(t, x)) = u$. We denote $q_0(x) = Q(k_0(x)) = u k_0(x)$. Hence $q(t, x) = Q(k(t, x)) = q_0(x - ut)$. Then the 3-D traffic surface is

$$N(t, x) = N_0(x - ut),$$

where $N_0(x) = N(0, x)$ is the initial cumulative flow. This is consistent with the observation that vehicles travel at a constant speed, and the cumulative flow remains constant along a vehicle's trajectory in the trajectory coordinates: $X(t, n) = X(0, n) + ut$, where $N_0(X(0, n)) = n$. In the schedule coordinates, $T(n, x) = \frac{x}{u} - \frac{X(0,n)}{u}$.

Locally, if we limit the time-step size to τ, then we have the following results in this case:

$$N(t, x) = N(t - \tau, x - u\tau), \quad (5.19a)$$
$$X(t, n) = X(t - \tau, n) + u\tau, \quad (5.19b)$$
$$T(n, x) = T(n, x - u\tau) + \tau. \quad (5.19c)$$

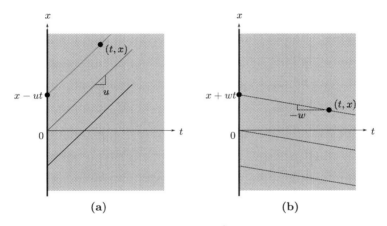

FIGURE 5.5 Solutions of the LWR model with the triangular fundamental diagram under initial conditions: (a) Under-critical; (b) Over-critical.

5.3.2 Over-critical initial conditions

If the initial condition is OC; i.e., if $k_0(x) \geq \kappa_c$, the traffic state at any later time should be OC. The LWR model can be simplified as

$$\frac{\partial k}{\partial t} - w \frac{\partial k}{\partial x} = 0,$$

which is also a linear transport equation and solved by

$$k(t, x) = k_0(x + wt).$$

Imagine an observer starting at $(0, x_0)$ in the (t, x) plane and traveling at a constant speed of $-w$. Then the density along the observer's trajectory is always constant at $k_0(x_0)$. This is illustrated in Fig. 5.5(b).

The flow-rate is $q(t, x) = Q(k(t, x)) = q_0(x + wt) = \frac{1}{\tau} - wk_0(x + wt)$, and the speed is $v(t, x) = \frac{1}{\tau k_0(x+wt)} - w$. The 3-D traffic surface is

$$N(t, x) = N_0(x + wt) + \frac{1}{\tau} t.$$

In the trajectory coordinates, vehicles' trajectories are

$$X(t, n) = X(0, n - \frac{1}{\tau}t) - wt;$$

and in the schedule coordinates, $T(n, x)$ satisfies

$$x = X(0, n - \frac{1}{\tau}T(n, x)) - wT(n, x).$$

From the definition of the time gap for vehicle n at x, $\tau(n, x) = T(n, x - \zeta) - T(n - 1, x)$, we have

$$\begin{aligned}
x - \zeta &= X(0, n - \frac{1}{\tau}T(n, x - \zeta)) - wT(n, x - \zeta) \\
&= X(0, n - \frac{1}{\tau}T(n - 1, x) - \frac{1}{\tau}\tau(n, x)) - wT(n - 1, x) - w\tau(n, x).
\end{aligned}$$

Since $x = X(0, n - 1 - \frac{1}{\tau}T(n - 1, x)) - wT(n - 1, x)$, the solution of the time gap is

$$\tau(n, x) = \tau.$$

That is, the time gap in congested traffic with the triangular fundamental diagram is always constant and equals τ. This is why τ is called the time gap.

Locally, if we limit the time-step size to τ, then we have the following results in this case:

$$\begin{aligned}
N(t, x) &= N(t - \tau, x + w\tau) + 1, & (5.20a) \\
X(t, n) &= X(t - \tau, n - 1) - w\tau, & (5.20b) \\
T(n, x) &= T(n - 1, x + w\tau) + \tau. & (5.20c)
\end{aligned}$$

5.3.3 Mixed under- and over-critical initial conditions

For the triangular fundamental diagram, if the initial traffic states are mixed with both SUC and SOC states, there is no simple closed-form solutions to the LWR model. We have to resort to more general techniques developed for the hyperbolic conservation laws.

However, locally we can combine (5.19) and (5.20) to obtain the following approximate, iterative solutions in the three coordinates:

$$\begin{aligned}
N(t, x) &= \min\{N(t - \tau, x - u\tau), N(t - \tau, x + w\tau) + 1\}, & (5.21a) \\
X(t, n) &= \min\{X(t - \tau, n) + u\tau, X(t - \tau, n - 1) - w\tau\}, & (5.21b) \\
T(n, x) &= \max\{T(n, x - u\tau) + \tau, T(n - 1, x + w\tau) + \tau\}. & (5.21c)
\end{aligned}$$

To obtain more accurate solutions, we can use a smaller time-step size and refine the above equations accordingly.

(5.21a) also applies to the initial-boundary value problems for the LWR model with the triangular fundamental diagram, which will be discussed in Chapter 7.

(5.21b) is Newell's simplified car-following model and will be discussed in Chapter 9.

5.4 General fundamental diagram and characteristic wave

For general fundamental diagrams, closed-form solutions are possible under very simple initial conditions.

The LWR model can be linearized into a quasi-linear form:

$$\frac{\partial k}{\partial t} + \lambda(k)\frac{\partial k}{\partial x} = 0, \quad (5.22)$$

which is similar to the linear transport equation, except with a state-dependent speed, $\lambda(k)$. Here $\lambda(k)$ is called the characteristic wave speed.

5.4.1 Steady solutions

For a general fundamental diagram, the simplest possible solutions are the steady ones, for which the initial condition is

$$k(0, x) = k_0, \quad x \in (-\infty, \infty). \quad (5.23)$$

Clearly the solution is always steady:

$$k(t, x) = k_0, \quad x \in (-\infty, \infty), t \in [0, \infty). \quad (5.24)$$

This can be easily verified by substituting the solution into the LWR model. The speed is $v(t, x) = V(k_0)$, and the flow-rate $q(t, x) = Q(k_0)$.

The 3-D traffic surface is a plane. In the flow coordinates, it can be written as

$$N(t, x) = Q(k_0)t - k_0 x + N(0, 0).$$

In particular, if $k_0 = 0$, $Q(k_0) = 0$, and $N(t, x) = N(0, 0)$, which is a horizontal plane; if $k_0 = \kappa$, $Q(k_0) = 0$, and $N(t, x) = -\kappa x + N(0, 0)$, which is also time-independent.

5.4.2 Nearly steady solutions and characteristic wave

The initial density is nearly constant, but with a small perturbation,

$$k_0(x) = k_0 + \epsilon \phi(x),$$

where ϵ is a very small number. Physically, small perturbations can be caused by a slight acceleration or deceleration process of a vehicle or the entrance or exit of a vehicle.

Intuitively, the density at any time should also be nearly constant,

$$k(t, x) = k_0 + \epsilon k_1(t, x),$$

where $k_1(t, x)$ is unknown and needs to be solved.

Substituting $k(t, x)$ into the LWR model, we have

$$\frac{\partial}{\partial t}[k_0 + \epsilon k_1(t, x)] + \lambda(k_0 + \epsilon k_1(t, x))\frac{\partial}{\partial x}[k_0 + \epsilon k_1(t, x)] = 0,$$

which leads to

$$\frac{\partial k_1(t, x)}{\partial t} + \lambda(k_0 + \epsilon k_1(t, x))\frac{\partial k_1(t, x)}{\partial x} = 0.$$

Since ϵ is much smaller than k_0, we can approximate $\lambda(k_0 + \epsilon k_1(t, x))$ by $\lambda(k_0)$, and the equation for $k_1(t, x)$ can be simplified as

$$\frac{\partial k_1(t, x)}{\partial t} + \lambda(k_0)\frac{\partial k_1(t, x)}{\partial x} = 0,$$

which is a linear transport equation. The initial condition for $k_1(t, x)$ is $k_1(0, x) = \phi(x)$. Thus $k_1(t, x) = \phi(x - \lambda(k_0)t)$, and the LWR model is solved by

$$k(t, x) = k_0 + \epsilon \phi(x - \lambda(k_0)t). \tag{5.25}$$

According to (5.25), such small perturbations travel at a speed of $\lambda(k_0)$. We can see that (i) the magnitude of the perturbation does not change, and the LWR model is stable; (ii) but the perturbation moves at a speed of $\lambda(k_0)$.

We refer to such a propagation wave of small perturbations at a constant density as a characteristic wave, as it characterizes the corresponding density. Note that a characteristic wave's trajectory is usually not the same as a vehicle's trajectory, since the former can travel backward.

When $Q(k)$ is unimodal, the characteristic wave speed is positive for $k < k_c$ and negative for $k > k_c$. That is, in SUC traffic, small perturbations propagate forward; but in SOC traffic, small perturbations propagate backward.

More importantly, the characteristic wave propagates the information regarding the traffic density. That is, along a characteristic wave emanating from any point (t_0, x_0), the density is constant. Let $k(t_0, x_0) = k_0$. Then along the characteristic wave emanating from the point,

$$x = x_0 + \lambda(k_0)(t - t_0).$$

The density along the wave is $k(t, x_0 + \lambda(k_0)(t - t_0))$, which satisfies the LWR model:

$$\frac{\partial k(t, x_0 + \lambda(k_0)(t - t_0))}{\partial t} + \lambda(k(t, x_0 + \lambda(k_0)(t - t_0)))\frac{\partial k(t, x_0 + \lambda(k_0)(t - t_0))}{\partial x} = 0.$$

The total derivative of the density along the wave is

$$\frac{d}{dt}k(t, x_0 + \lambda(k_0)(t - t_0)) = \frac{\partial k(t, x_0 + \lambda(k_0)(t - t_0))}{\partial t} + \lambda(k_0)\frac{\partial k(t, x_0 + \lambda(k_0)(t - t_0))}{\partial x}.$$

Thus $k(t, x_0 + \lambda(k_0)(t - t_0)) = k_0$ is the solution. That is, the traffic density is constant along a characteristic wave.

Along the characteristic wave, $x = x_0 + \lambda(k_0)(t - t_0)$, we have

$$\frac{d}{dt}N(t, x) = N_t(t, x) + N_x(t, x)\frac{dx}{dt} = q(t, x) - k(t, x)\lambda(k(t, x))$$
$$= q_0 - k_0\lambda(k_0) = -k_0^2 V'(k_0),$$

which is also constant. Thus

$$N(t, x_0 + \lambda(k_0)(t - t_0)) = N(t_0, x_0) - k_0^2 V'(k_0)(t - t_0).$$

In particular, for the triangular fundamental diagram, $V'(k_0) = 0$ for $k_0 \leq \kappa_c$ and $k_0^2 V'(k_0) = -w\kappa$. The above solution is consistent with those in the preceding section.

5.5 Solutions to the Riemann problem, shock and rarefaction waves, and entropy condition

Still for the original LWR model with a concave fundamental diagram, we solve the Riemann problem under the following jump initial condition:

$$k_0(x) = \begin{cases} k_1, & x < 0; \\ k_2, & x > 0. \end{cases} \quad (5.26)$$

Initially, there are two platoons with constant densities that meet at the boundary at $x = 0$. Correspondingly, the initial speeds are $v_1 = V(k_1)$ and $v_2 = V(k_2)$.

There are two scenarios: (i) $k_1 < k_2$ and $v_1 \geq v_2$, when the upstream platoon is less congested and faster; (ii) $k_1 > k_2$, when the upstream platoon is more congested and slower. An extreme example for the first scenario is when the traffic light turns red. In this case, the stop line is at $x = 0$, the upstream platoon is moving with a density of k_1, but the downstream density is effectively the jam density. An extreme example for the second scenario is when the traffic light turns green. In this case, the upstream density is the jam density, and the downstream density is zero. This problem is called the queue discharge problem.

The Riemann problem is equivalent to the simple lead-vehicle problem studied in Section 4.2, where the leader's speed is constant at v_2, and the upstream platoon's spacing is $z_1 = \frac{1}{k_1}$. But here we solve the problem for both scenarios, not just for $k_1 < k_2$.

5.5.1 Shock wave

When $k_1 < k_2$, the characteristic wave speeds $\lambda(k_1) \geq \lambda(k_2)$ for a concave fundamental diagram. As shown in Fig. 5.6(a), the upstream characteristic waves travel faster than the downstream ones, and they cross each other after a while. At the cross point, the cumulative number of vehicles is continuous, but the density can be either k_1 or k_2, since the density is constant along a characteristic wave. In this case, a shock wave appears at the interface between the upstream and downstream states. The shock wave speed is denoted by v_s. From the figure, we have

$$x = v_s t = x_2 + \lambda(k_2)t = x_1 + \lambda(k_1)t.$$

Since the traffic state along a characteristic wave is constant, we have

$$N(t, x) = N(0, x_2) + (q_2 - k_2\lambda(k_2))t = N(0, x_1) + (q_1 - k_1\lambda(k_1))t.$$

Further from the initial condition, we have

$$N(0, x_1) = N(0, 0) - x_1 k_1,$$
$$N(0, x_2) = N(0, 0) - x_2 k_2.$$

Note that $x_1 < 0 < x_2$. From these equations, we obtain the shock wave speed

$$v_s = \frac{q_1 - q_2}{k_1 - k_2}, \tag{5.27}$$

which is the slope of the secant line in Fig. 5.6(b). This is consistent with the conclusion in Section 4.2. Thus the solution of the Riemann problem is

$$k(t, x) = \begin{cases} k_1, & x < v_s t; \\ k_2, & x > v_s t. \end{cases} \tag{5.28}$$

There is a discontinuity along the shock wave. One feature of the LWR model is that it can have such discontinuous shock waves as its solutions. Moreover, even if the initial condition is continuous, such discontinuous shock waves can still develop.

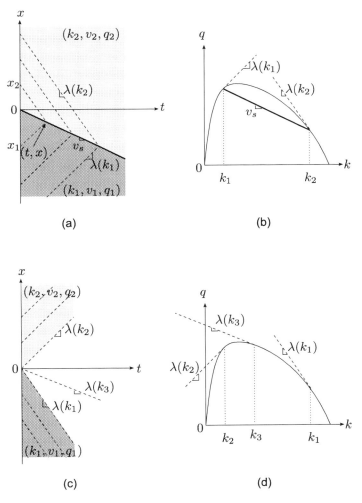

FIGURE 5.6 Solutions of the Riemann problem: (a)-(b) A shock wave; (c)-(d) A rarefaction wave. The dashed lines represent the characteristic waves.

5.5.2 Rarefaction wave

In contrast, when $k_1 > k_2$, the upstream characteristic wave speed is slower: $\lambda(k_1) \leq \lambda(k_2)$. In this case, the Riemann problem is solved by a rarefaction wave, which can be written as

$$k(t,x) = \begin{cases} k_1, & x < \lambda(k_1)t; \\ k_3, & \lambda(k_1)t \leq x \leq \lambda(k_2)t; \\ k_2, & x > \lambda(k_2)t, \end{cases} \tag{5.29}$$

where the intermediate value $k_c(t,x)$ satisfies $\lambda(k_3) = \frac{x}{t}$ at (t,x) for $\lambda(k_1)t \leq x \leq \lambda(k_2)t$. That is, along a characteristic wave emanating from the origin, the traffic density is constant. The acceleration along the rarefaction wave is

$$a(t,x) = v_t + vv_x = V'(k)(k_t + V(k)k_x) = -(V'(k))^2 kk_x.$$

Since $\lambda(k) = \frac{x}{t}$, we have $k_x = \frac{1}{t\phi''(k)}$, and

$$a(t,x) = -\frac{(V'(k))^2 k}{t\phi''(k)},$$

which is non-negative for a concave flow-density relation, and becomes infinite when $t = 0$ or when $\phi''(k) = 0$ in the triangular fundamental diagram. That is, vehicles accelerate in a rarefaction wave, but the acceleration rate can be infinite.

5.5.3 Entropy condition

Thus, the Riemann problem is solved by a shock wave when the upstream density is smaller and a rarefaction wave when the upstream density is greater. Equivalently, a shock wave forms when vehicles decelerate; and a rarefaction wave forms when vehicles accelerate. This rule is called the *entropy condition*, which helps to pick out unique, physical solutions.

Thus the LWR model is defined from the following five rules:

R1. Constitutive law: $q = kv$.
R2. Conservation law: $\frac{\partial k}{\partial t} + \frac{\partial q}{\partial x} = 0$.
R3. Fundamental diagram: $v = V(k)$.
R4. Shock wave solutions: $\frac{\partial k}{\partial t}$ and $\frac{\partial q}{\partial x}$ are not well-defined at a shock wave interface.
R5. Entropy condition: deceleration leads to a shock wave, and acceleration leads to a rarefaction wave.

Here R1, R2, and R4 apply to other continuum fluids, but R3 and R5 are vehicular traffic specific. In particular, R3 describes the traffic characteristics under steady conditions, and R5 describes the traffic characteristics under dynamic conditions.

The entropy condition cannot guarantee that vehicles' acceleration or deceleration rates are reasonable. In a shock wave, vehicles' deceleration rate is infinite, and in a rarefaction wave, vehicles' initial acceleration rate is also infinite. To ensure more realistic features, additional entropy conditions and fundamental diagrams need to be introduced.

The LWR model is also called the kinematic wave model, since it describes the evolution of traffic dynamics as a combination of characteristic, shock, and rarefaction waves. These waves are resulted from the movements of vehicles, not of vehicles themselves.

5.5.4 Riemann solutions with the triangular fundamental diagram

For the triangular fundamental diagram, $\lambda(k)$ is constant at u for $k < \kappa_c$ or $-w$ for $k > \kappa_c$, but multi-valued for $k = \kappa_c$. The Riemann solutions can be simplified as follows.

When $k_1 < k_2 \leq \kappa_c$, the Riemann problem is solved by a shock wave, whose speed is u. When $k_2 < k_1 \leq \kappa_c$, the solution is a rarefaction wave, but with only one characteristic wave speed of u. Thus, there is a single interface between the two initial densities:

$$k(t,x) = k_0(x - ut) = \begin{cases} k_1, & x < ut; \\ k_2, & x > ut. \end{cases} \tag{5.30}$$

This is consistent with the result in Section 5.3.1.

When $k_2 > k_1 \geq \kappa_c$, the Riemann problem is solved by a shock wave, whose speed is $-w$. When $k_1 < k_2 \geq \kappa_c$, the solution is a rarefaction wave, but with only one characteristic wave speed of $-w$. Thus, there is a single interface between the two initial densities:

$$k(t,x) = k_0(x + wt) = \begin{cases} k_1, & x < -wt; \\ k_2, & x > -wt. \end{cases} \tag{5.31}$$

This is consistent with the result in Section 5.3.2.

But when $k_1 < \kappa_c < k_2$, the Riemann problem is solved by a shock wave with a speed of

$$v_s = \frac{uk_1 - w(\kappa - k_2)}{k_1 - k_2}, \tag{5.32}$$

which can be positive, zero, or negative. Such a "transonic" shock wave is illustrated in Fig. 5.7.

When $k_1 > \kappa_c > k_2$, the Riemann problem is solved by a rarefaction wave, with the intermediate value always at κ_c, since $\lambda(\kappa_c) \in [-w, u]$. Such a "transonic" rarefaction wave is illustrated in Fig. 5.7.

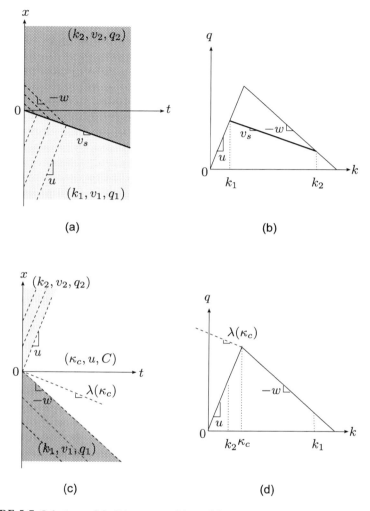

FIGURE 5.7 Solutions of the Riemann problem of the LWR model with the triangular fundamental diagram: (a)-(b) A transonic shock wave; (c)-(d) A transonic rarefaction wave. The dashed lines represent the characteristic waves.

5.6 Stationary states and boundary fluxes in Riemann solutions

In the Riemann solutions, along any line $x = \beta t$, the density is constant, and the results are called self-similar. In particular, at the boundary $x = 0$, we denote

$$k_1^* = \lim_{\beta \to 0^-} k(t, \beta t),$$

5.6 Stationary states

$$k_2^* = \lim_{\beta \to 0^+} k(t, \beta t).$$

Equivalently, at any $x < 0$, $\lim_{t \to +\infty} k(t, x) = k_1^*$; and at any $x > 0$, $\lim_{t \to +\infty} k(t, x) = k_2^*$. That is, k_1^* and k_2^* eventually spread over the upstream and downstream links respectively. We call them stationary states on the upstream and downstream links.

We have the following eight types of Riemann solutions for a concave flow-density relation:

- There are two cases when both links are initially under-critical.

  1. When $k_1 < k_2 \leq \kappa_c$, the Riemann problem is solved by a shock wave, whose speed $v_s > 0$. The stationary densities are $k_1^* = k_2^* = k_1$. For the triangular fundamental diagram, $v_s = u$.
  2. When $k_2 < k_1 \leq \kappa_c$, the Riemann problem is solved by a rarefaction wave, whose characteristic wave speeds are between $\lambda(k_1)$ and $\lambda(k_2)$. The stationary densities are $k_1^* = k_2^* = k_1$. For the triangular fundamental diagram, the rarefaction wave degenerates into a contact wave, whose width equals zero, since $\lambda(k_1) = \lambda(k_2) = u$.

- There are two cases when both links are initial over-critical.

  3. When $k_2 > k_1 \geq \kappa_c$, the Riemann problem is solved by a shock wave, whose speed $v_s < 0$. The stationary densities are $k_1^* = k_2^* = k_2$. For the triangular fundamental diagram, $v_s = -w$.
  4. When $k_1 > k_2 \geq \kappa_c$, the Riemann problem is solved by a rarefaction wave, whose characteristic wave speeds are between $\lambda(k_1)$ and $\lambda(k_2)$. The stationary densities are $k_1^* = k_2^* = k_2$. For the triangular fundamental diagram, the rarefaction wave degenerates into a contact wave, whose width equals zero, since $\lambda(k_1) = \lambda(k_2) = -w$.

- When the upstream link is strictly under-critical and the downstream link is strictly over-critical; i.e., when $k_1 < \kappa_c < k_2$, the Riemann problem is solved by a shock wave, whose speed is $v_s = \frac{q_1 - q_2}{k_1 - k_2}$. We denote the image density of k_1 by $P(k_1)$, where $k_1 > \kappa_c$ and $Q(P(k_1)) = Q(k_1)$. There are three cases, depending on the direction of the shock wave speed.

  5. When $k_2 < P(k_1)$, $q_2 > q_1$, and the shock wave speed is positive: $v_s > 0$. The stationary densities are $k_1^* = k_2^* = k_1$.
  6. When $k_2 > P(k_1)$, $q_2 < q_1$, and the shock wave speed is negative: $v_s < 0$. The stationary densities are $k_1^* = k_2^* = k_2$.
  7. When $k_2 = P(k_1)$, $q_2 = q_1$, and the shock wave speed is zero: $v_s = 0$. The stationary densities are different for the upstream and downstream links: $k_1^* = k_1$, and $k_2^* = k_2$.

  8. When the upstream link is strictly over-critical and the downstream link is strictly under-critical; i.e., when $k_1 > \kappa_c > k_2$, the Riemann problem

is solved by a transonic rarefaction wave, whose characteristic wave speeds are between $\lambda(k_1) < 0$ and $\lambda(k_2) > 0$. The stationary densities are $k_1^* = k_2^* = \kappa_c$. For the triangular fundamental diagram, $k(t,x) = \kappa_c$ for $\lambda(k_1)t < x < \lambda(k_2)t$.

Except in the last case, the stationary states are the same as the upstream or downstream initial states. In the last case, the stationary densities are the critical densities. Even though the stationary densities are different in Case 7 with a zero-speed shock wave, their flow-rates are the same: $Q(k_1^*) = Q(k_2^*) = q_1 = q_2$. We denote the boundary flux by $q(t,0)$, then in all cases

$$q(t,0) = Q(k_1^*) = Q(k_2^*). \tag{5.33}$$

5.7 Inhomogeneous LWR model

We solve the Riemann problem for two scenarios of the inhomogeneous LWR model, (5.5), with the triangular fundamental diagram.

5.7.1 Location-dependent speed limits

With location-dependent speed limits, the flow-density relation is written as $q = Q(u(x), k) = \min\{u(x)k, w(\kappa - k)\}$. The LWR model is

$$\frac{\partial}{\partial t} u = 0,$$

$$\frac{\partial}{\partial t} k + \frac{\partial}{\partial x} Q(u(x), k) = 0.$$

This is a system of two hyperbolic conservation laws, for which $U = \begin{bmatrix} u \\ k \end{bmatrix}$ is the state variable. The system can be written as

$$\frac{\partial U}{\partial t} + \frac{\partial}{\partial x} \Phi(U) = 0, \tag{5.34}$$

where $\Phi(U) = \begin{bmatrix} 0 \\ Q(u,k) \end{bmatrix}$. The Jacobian matrix is

$$B = \begin{bmatrix} 0 & 0 \\ \frac{\partial}{\partial u} Q(u,k) & \frac{\partial}{\partial k} Q(u,k) \end{bmatrix},$$

and (5.34) can be written in the following quasi-linear form:

$$\frac{\partial U}{\partial t} + B \frac{\partial U}{\partial x} = 0.$$

5.7 Inhomogeneous LWR model

The eigenvalues of B are the two characteristic wave speeds: $\lambda_0(U) = 0$ and $\lambda_1(U) = Q_k(u, k)$. The right-eigenvectors for the two characteristic wave speeds are

$$r_0 = \begin{bmatrix} -Q_k(u,k) \\ Q_u(u,k) \end{bmatrix},$$

$$r_1 = \begin{bmatrix} 0 \\ 1 \end{bmatrix},$$

where $Br_0 = \lambda_0(U)r_0$ and $Br_1 = \lambda_1(U)r_1$. The corresponding Riemann invariants are $\varphi_0(u, k)$ and $\varphi_1(u, k)$, which are defined by $[\frac{\partial}{\partial u}\varphi_i(u, k), \frac{\partial}{\partial k}\varphi_i(u, k)] \cdot r_i = 0$ for $i = 0, 1$. Thus the two Riemann invariants are $\varphi_0(u, k) = Q(u, k)$, and $\varphi_1(u, k) = u$. That is, along a standing wave, the flow-rate $Q(u, k)$ is constant; and along a 1-wave, the speed limit u is constant.

The Riemann problem has the following initial condition:

$$(u(x), k(0, x)) = \begin{cases} (u_1, k_1), & x < 0; \\ (u_2, k_2), & x > 0. \end{cases}$$

Associated with $\lambda_0(U) = 0$ is the 0-wave, also called the *standing wave*, as it stands at the boundary $x = 0$. Associated with $\lambda_1(U)$ is the 1-wave, which is either a shock or rarefaction wave. The standing wave is a new type of kinematic wave caused by the inhomogeneity.

For the homogeneous LWR model, the Riemann problem is solved by at most one wave, which can be a shock or rarefaction wave; the wave connects the upstream and downstream initial states. In contrast, for the inhomogeneous LWR model, the Riemann problem can be solved by at most three waves: a shock or rarefaction wave on each of the links, and a standing wave at the boundary. In particular, if we denote the stationary densities on the upstream and downstream links by k_1^* and k_2^*, respectively. Then k_1 and k_1^* are connected by a 1-wave on the upstream link, k_2^* and k_2 are connected by a 1-wave on the downstream link, and k_1^* and k_2^* are connected by the standing wave.

To solve the LWR model, we still apply the entropy condition for the homogeneous LWR model; i.e., (R5) the 1-wave is a shock wave when vehicles decelerate and a rarefaction wave when vehicles accelerate. In particular, the 1-wave on the upstream (downstream) link is a shock wave when $k_1 < k_1^*$ ($k_2^* < k_2$), a rarefaction wave when $k_1 > k_1^*$ ($k_2^* > k_2$), and non-existent when $k_1 = k_1^*$ ($k_2^* = k_2$). However, this entropy condition alone is insufficient to pick out unique, physical solutions. Additional entropy conditions need to be introduced to pick out physically meaningful waves:

R5'. The 1-wave's speed is non-positive on the upstream link, and non-negative on the downstream link.

R5''. The two stationary states have the same criticality. That is, the standing wave cannot connect SOC and SUC states.

5. The Lighthill-Whitham-Richards (LWR) model

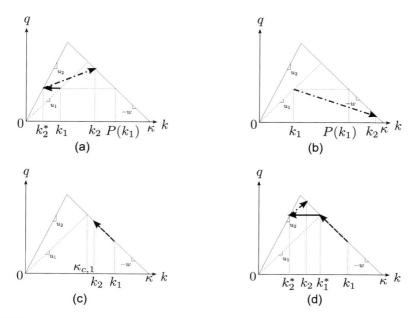

FIGURE 5.8 Solutions to the Riemann problem for the inhomogeneous LWR model with location-dependent speed limits.

With the three entropy conditions, (R5), (R5′), and (R5″), the Riemann problem has the following four types of solutions when $u_1 < u_2$. In this case, the region upstream to $x = 0$ is the VSL zone with a reduced speed limit, u_1, and the downstream region is the normal zone. The Riemann problem when $u_1 > u_2$ is assigned as Problem 5.4.

1. When $k_1 \le \kappa_{c,1}$ and $k_2 < P(k_1)$; i.e., when the upstream link is initially uncongested, and the downstream link's initial density is smaller than the image density of k_1, as shown in Fig. 5.8(a), the upstream link's stationary density $k_1^* = k_1$, and there is no wave on the upstream link; the downstream link's stationary density k_2^* is uncongested and given by $Q(u_2, k_2^*) = q_1$, and on the downstream link there is a forward-traveling shock wave when $k_2 > k_2^*$ (the dash-dotted line with an arrow in the figure), no wave when $k_2 = k_2^*$, or a forward-traveling rarefaction wave when $k_2 < k_2^*$. In addition, there is a standing wave connecting k_1 to k_2^* (the solid line with an arrow). The boundary flux $q(t, 0) = q_1 = Q(u_1, k_1^*) = Q(u_2, k_2^*)$.
2. When $k_1 \le \kappa_{c,1}$ and $k_2 \ge P(k_1)$, as shown in Fig. 5.8(b), the upstream link's stationary density $k_1^* = k_2$, and there is a backward-traveling shock wave when $k_2 > P(k_1)$ (the dash-dotted line with an arrow in the figure), or a zero-speed shock wave when $k_2 = P(k_1)$; the downstream

link's stationary density $k_2^* = k_2$, and there is no wave on the link. The boundary flux $q(t, 0) = q_2 = Q(u_1, k_1^*) = Q(u_2, k_2^*)$.

3. When $k_1 > \kappa_{c,1}$ and $k_2 \geq \kappa_{c,1}$; i.e., when the upstream link is initially SOC, and the downstream link's initial density is not smaller than the upstream critical density, as shown in Fig. 5.8(c), the upstream link's stationary density $k_1^* = k_2$, and there is a backward-traveling shock wave when $k_2 > k_1$, no wave when $k_2 = k_1$, or a backward-traveling rarefaction wave when $k_2 < k_1$ (the dashed line with an arrow in the figure); the downstream link's stationary density $k_2^* = k_2$, and there is no wave on the link. The boundary flux $q(t, 0) = q_2 = Q(u_1, k_1^*) = Q(u_2, k_2^*)$.

4. When $k_1 > \kappa_{c,1}$ and $k_2 < \kappa_{c,1}$; i.e., when the upstream link is initially SOC, and the downstream link's initial density is smaller than the upstream critical density, as shown in Fig. 5.8(d), the upstream link's stationary density $k_1^* = \kappa_{c,1}$, and there is a backward-traveling rarefaction wave on the link (the dashed line with an arrow in the figure); the downstream link's stationary density k_2^* is uncongested and given by $Q(u_2, k_2^*) = Q(u_1, \kappa_{c,1})$, and on the downstream link there is a forward-traveling shock wave when $k_2 > k_2^*$ (the dash-dotted line with an arrow in the figure), no wave when $k_2 = k_2^*$, or a forward-traveling rarefaction wave when $k_2 < k_2^*$. In addition, there is a standing wave connecting k_1^* to k_2^* (the solid line with an arrow). The boundary flux $q(t, 0) = Q(u_1, \kappa_{c,1}) = Q(u_1, k_1^*) = Q(u_2, k_2^*)$, which is the upstream link's capacity.

We can verify that the three entropy conditions are satisfied.

5.7.2 Location-dependent number of lanes

With location-dependent number of lanes, $l(x)$, the flow-density relation $q = Q(l(x), k) = \min\{uk, l(x)q_0 - wk\}$, and the LWR model can be written as

$$\frac{\partial}{\partial t} l = 0,$$

$$\frac{\partial}{\partial t} k + \frac{\partial}{\partial x} Q(l(x), k) = 0.$$

This is a system of two hyperbolic conservation laws, for which $U = \begin{bmatrix} l \\ k \end{bmatrix}$ is the state variable. The two characteristic wave speeds: $\lambda_0(U) = 0$ and $\lambda_1(U) = Q_k(l, k)$.

The Riemann problem has the following initial condition:

$$(l(x), k(0, x)) = \begin{cases} (l_1, k_1), & x < 0; \\ (l_2, k_2), & x > 0. \end{cases}$$

5. The Lighthill-Whitham-Richards (LWR) model

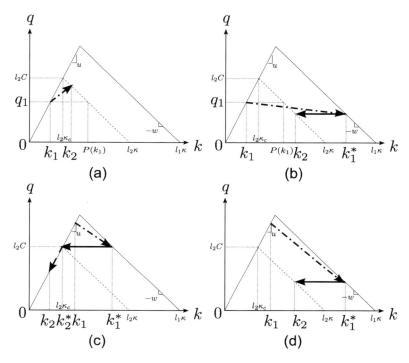

FIGURE 5.9 Solutions to the Riemann problem for the inhomogeneous LWR model with location-dependent number of lanes.

It is solved by a combination of 0- and 1-waves. Under the three entropy conditions, the Riemann problem for $l_2 > l_1$ can be solved in the following. Thus the number of lanes drops at $x = 0$, and this corresponds to a discontinuous lane-drop bottleneck in Fig. 4.3, where the width of the lane-drop zone is reduced to zero. The Riemann problem for a lane-increase case is assigned as a homework problem Problem 5.5. Here C, κ, and κ_c are the per-lane capacity, jam density, and critical density, respectively.

1. When $k_1 \leq l_2\kappa_c$ and $k_2 < P(k_1)$, as shown in Fig. 5.9(a), the upstream link's stationary density $k_1^* = k_1$, and there is no wave on the link; the downstream link's stationary density $k_2^* = k_1$, and there is a forward-traveling shock wave (the dash-dotted line with an arrow in the figure) when $k_2 > k_1$, no wave when $k_2 = k_1$, or a forward-traveling rarefaction wave when $k_2 < k_1$. The boundary flux $q(t, 0) = q_1 = Q(l_1, k_1^*) = Q(l_2, k_2^*)$.
2. When $k_1 \leq l_2\kappa_c$ and $k_2 \geq P(k_1)$, as shown in Fig. 5.9(b), the upstream link's stationary density k_1^* is congested and defined by $Q(l_1, k_1^*) = q_2$, and there is a backward-traveling shock wave (the dash-dotted line

with an arrow in the figure) when $k_2 > P(k_1)$, or a zero-speed shock wave when $k_2 = P(k_1)$; the downstream link's stationary density $k_2^* = k_2$, and there is no wave on the link. In addition, there is a standing wave connecting k_1^* to k_2 (the solid line with an arrow). The boundary flux $q(t, 0) = q_2 = Q(l_1, k_1^*) = Q(l_2, k_2^*)$.

3. When $k_1 > l_2\kappa_c > k_2$, as shown in Fig. 5.9(c), the upstream link's stationary density k_1^* is congested and defined by $Q(l_1, k_1^*) = l_2C$, and there is a backward-traveling shock wave (the dash-dotted line with an arrow in the figure) when $k_1 < k_1^*$, no wave when $k_1 = k_1^*$, or a backward-traveling rarefaction wave when $k_1 > k_1^*$; the downstream link's stationary density $k_2^* = l_2\kappa_c$, and there is a forward-traveling rarefaction wave on the link (the dashed line with an arrow in the figure). In addition, there is a standing wave connecting k_1^* to k_2^* (the solid line with an arrow). The boundary flux $q(t, 0) = l_2C = Q(l_1, k_1^*) = Q(l_2, k_2^*)$.

4. When $k_1 > l_2\kappa_c$ and $k_2 \geq l_2\kappa_c$, as shown in Fig. 5.9(d), the upstream link's stationary density k_1^* is congested and defined by $Q(l_1, k_1^*) = q_2$, and there is a backward-traveling shock wave (the dash-dotted line with an arrow in the figure) when $k_1 < k_1^*$, no wave when $k_1 = k_1^*$, or a backward-traveling rarefaction wave when $k_1 > k_1^*$; the downstream link's stationary density $k_2^* = k_2$, and there is no wave on the link. In addition, there is a standing wave connecting k_1^* to k_2 (the solid line with an arrow). The boundary flux $q(t, 0) = q_2 = Q(l_1, k_1^*) = Q(l_2, k_2^*)$.

5.8 An example with a moving bottleneck

In this section we apply the kinematic wave theory to analyze traffic dynamics on a single-lane road with an on-ramp and an off-ramp that are two miles apart, as illustrated in Fig. 5.10(a). The fundamental diagram is shown in Fig. 5.10(b), in which the free-flow speed $u = 60$ mph, the jam density $\kappa = 150$ vpm, the capacity $C = 1800$ vph, the critical density $\kappa_c = 30$ vpm, and the shock wave speed in congested traffic $-w = -15$ mph.

Initially (for $t < 0$), the traffic state on the road is steady with a density $k_1 = 28$ vpm and a speed of 60 mph, which leads to $q_1 = 1680$ vph. But at $t = 0$, a slow truck enters the road from the on-ramp with a speed of $v = 30$ mph.

As long as the truck joins the traffic, it splits the original traffic stream into two parts, with the downstream part not impacted and still traveling at the free-flow speed. But the upstream part is slowed down. For simplicity, we omit the difference between the truck and other vehicles in characteristics other than the speed. Then the traffic upstream to the truck enters a state of $(k_2, q_2) = (50, 1500)$ with $v_2 = 30$ mph, as shown in Fig. 5.10(b). This new state is slower than the original state, and a queue forms inside the state. A shock wave forms between the queue, whose

100   5. The Lighthill-Whitham-Richards (LWR) model

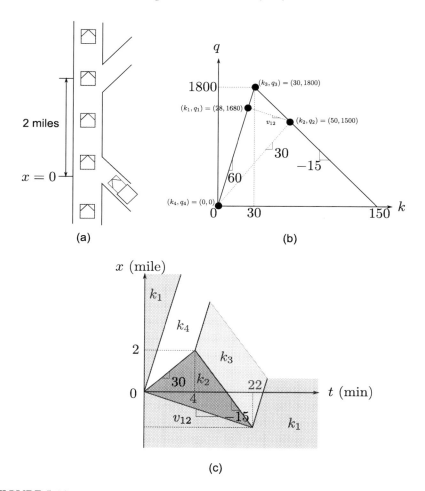

FIGURE 5.10 Kinematic wave analysis with a slow truck.

density is k_2, and the upstream traffic at k_1 at the speed of

$$v_{12} = \frac{q_1 - q_2}{k_1 - k_2} = -8.18 \text{ mph}.$$

Thus, at $t = 0$, the traffic stream is split into four regions as illustrated in Fig. 5.10(c), whose densities are from downstream to upstream k_1, $k_4 = 0$ (a void in front of the truck), k_2, and k_1. Here k_1 and k_4 are separated by the trajectory of the vehicle right in front of the truck, whose speed is 60 mph. k_4 and k_2 are separated by the truck's trajectory whose speed is 30 mph. k_2 and k_3 are separated by the shock wave whose speed is -8.18 mph. Thus, the shock wave travels upstream. For the queue, its downstream boundary (the queue head) travels at a speed of 30 mph, its upstream boundary (the queue tail) travels at a speed of -8.18 mph. Hence, the queue size grows in a speed of 38.18 mph, as can be seen in Fig. 5.10(c).

At 4 min, the truck exits the road from the off-ramp. At the off-ramp location, the upstream traffic density is k_2, and the downstream traffic density is $k_4 = 0$. The LWR model is then solved by a transonic rarefaction wave. With the triangular fundamental diagram, as shown in Section 5.5.4, a new, intermediate state emerges with the critical density $k_3 = \kappa_c$. The wave between k_3 and k_4 travels at the free-flow speed $v_{34} = 60$ mph. The wave between k_2 and k_3 travels at $v_{23} = -15$ mph. The new state and the corresponding waves are illustrated in Fig. 5.10(c). Such waves correspond to the process when the blocked vehicles accelerate away from the queue, since vehicles inside the intermediate state at k_3 travel at the free-flow speed.

The wave between k_2 and k_3 also travels upstream, and its speed is faster than the shock wave between k_1 and k_2. Therefore, the queue starts to shrink after the truck leaves the road, and the maximum queue size occurs at 4 min and equals $38.18 \cdot 4/60 = 2.55$ miles.

We assume that the wave between k_2 and k_3 catches up the shock wave between k_1 and k_2 at t^*. Then, we have

$$v_{12} \cdot t^* = 2 + (-15) \cdot (t^* - 4/60),$$

which leads to $t^* = 26.4$ min. Thus, the queue disappears at 26.4 min, which is long after the truck leaves the road. The last queued vehicle appears at -3.6 miles, which is 3.6 miles upstream to the on-ramp.

At the time and location $(t, x) = (26.4 \text{ min}, -3.6 \text{ miles})$ where the queue disappears, the upstream density is k_1, and the downstream density is $k_3 = \kappa_c > k_1$. Thus, a new shock wave forms with a speed of $v_{13} = 60$ mph. After that, the road has four densities, which are from downstream to upstream k_1, k_4, k_3, and k_1. These densities are all separated by waves traveling at the free-flow speed. That is, the traffic state is always under-critical, and vehicles travel at the free-flow speed. This can be seen from Fig. 5.10(c).

Notes

Note 5.1. *The Burgers equation was introduced by JM Burgers (Burgers, 1940, 1948) and systematically solved by (Hopf, 1950).*

Note 5.2. *The LWR model was proposed by (Lighthill and Whitham, 1955) as an extension of the kinematic wave theory of flood movement and independently by (Richards, 1956).*

Note 5.3. *The LWR model with the triangular fundamental was systematically studied by Gordon Newell and the Berkeley school of traffic flow theory since*

(Newell, 1993). (5.21b) is Newell's simplified car-following model (G.F. Newell, 2002; Daganzo, 2006). (5.21) is similar to but different from the discrete equations presented in Section 5.3 of (Laval and Leclercq, 2013).

Note 5.4. *The entropy condition used in this chapter is due to (Ansorge, 1990). This entropy condition is physically meaningful for traffic flow. For fluid dynamics, the Lax or Oleinik entropy conditions have been widely used (Lax, 1972).*

Note 5.5. *The Riemann problem of the LWR model was solved in seven cases, without explicitly solving the one with a zero-speed shock wave, in (Lebacque, 1996).*

Note 5.6. *The term, "transonic rarefaction wave", for the Riemann solutions of type 8 was introduced in (LeVeque, 1992). This solution is quite unique and will be discussed in Chapter 6.*

Note 5.7. *The Riemann problem for several multi-commodity LWR models was solved in (Daganzo, 1997b) for a non-unifiable and non-FIFO model, (Zhang and Jin, 2002) and (Jin, 2013) for a non-unifiable and FIFO model, and (Jin, 2017e) for a unifiable and non-FIFO model. Additional entropy conditions were introduced implicitly or explicitly for these studies.*

Note 5.8. *The additional entropy condition R5" was introduced in (Isaacson and Temple, 1992) for solving resonant nonlinear systems. The inhomogeneous LWR model is a special case of resonant nonlinear systems and was solved by following (Isaacson and Temple, 1992) in (Jin and Zhang, 2003a; Jin, 2010a). In Section 5.7, by explicitly introducing the stationary states on both links and the additional entropy condition R5', the Riemann problem for the inhomogeneous LWR model can be solved in a more straightforward manner. The "generalized Riemann problem" for the inhomogeneous LWR model was solved in (Lebacque, 1996) for 18 cases.*

Note 5.9. *The example in Section 5.8 was adapted from an example devised by Prof. Wilfred Recker at UC Irvine for a graduate-level class, CEE 229A: Traffic Operations and Control.*

Problems

Problem 5.1. *Solve the LWR model with a normalized triangular fundamental diagram, $Q(k) = \min\{k, \frac{1}{4}(1-k)\}$, under the following initial condition: $k_0(x) = 0.3 + 0.1\sin(\pi x)$. Use Jupyter notebook to plot the solutions for $x \in [-1, 1]$:*

1. $k(t, x)$ at $t = 0$ and $t = 1$.
2. 3-D plot of $k(t, x)$ for $t \in [0, 1]$.
3. Contour plot of $k(t, x)$ for $t \in [0, 1]$.

Problem 5.2. *For the Greenshields fundamental diagram, $q = uk(1 - \frac{k}{\kappa})$, what is the solution of the Riemann problem when $k_1 = \kappa$ and $k_2 = 0$? How about the triangular fundamental diagram?*

Problem 5.3. *Solve the LWR model under the initial condition:*

$$k(0, x) = \begin{cases} 0.1, & x < 0; \\ 1, & x > 0, \end{cases}$$

with a normalized triangular fundamental diagram: $q = \min\{k, \frac{1}{4}(1-k)\}$.

Problem 5.4. *Solve the Riemann problem for the inhomogeneous LWR model with location-dependent speed limits, where $u_1 > u_2$; i.e., the upstream speed limit is larger than the downstream one.*

Problem 5.5. *Solve the Riemann problem for the inhomogeneous LWR model with location-dependent number of lanes, where $l_1 < l_2$.*

Problem 5.6. *Solve the Riemann problem for the inhomogeneous LWR model with location-dependent time gaps.*

Problem 5.7. *For the example in Section 5.8, if the truck's speed is 45 mph, draw the waves in the space-time diagram, and answer the following questions.*

1. When will the truck leave the off-ramp?
2. What is the maximum queue length?
3. When will the queue disappear?

CHAPTER 6

The Cell Transmission Model (CTM)

In Chapter 5, the LWR model is analytically solved for special fundamental diagrams (the triangular fundamental diagram) and/or special initial conditions, especially for the Riemann problem. Under general initial and boundary conditions with general fundamental diagrams, however, we have to resolve to approximate, numerical solutions. Such numerical solution methods are similar to experiments, which can lead to further insights under general conditions. Analytical and numerical simulations supplement each other and can propel their development: numerical solutions of the Riemann problem should be consistent with the analytical ones, and numerical studies on more complicated scenarios can guide the development of theories.

This chapter focuses on the celebrated Cell Transmission Model (CTM). By introducing the demand and supply of a cell, the CTM is consistent with the Godunov scheme for the LWR model on a single road. More importantly, the CTM can be readily extended for multi-commodity traffic in a road network, with well-defined junction models.

6.1 Numerical methods for solving the LWR model

In numerical methods for solving the LWR model, a time interval $[0, E]$ is divided into J time steps with a time-step size of Δt, and a road segment $[0, L]$ is split into I cells with a length of Δx. The (t, x) domain is discretized as illustrated in Fig. 6.1. In particular, cell i's boundaries are at $(i-1)\Delta x$ and $i\Delta x$, and its center at $(i - \frac{1}{2})\Delta x$.

Denote k_i^j as the average density inside cell i at $j\Delta t$, f_i^j as the average in-flux of cell i at $(i-1)\Delta x$ between $j\Delta t$ and $(j+1)\Delta t$, and g_i^j as the average out-flux of cell i at $i\Delta x$ between $j\Delta t$ and $(j+1)\Delta t$. The flow-rate $q_i^j = Q(k_i^j)$. Then from the conservation law, we can update the density

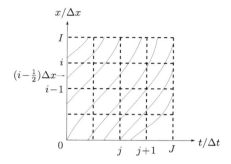

FIGURE 6.1 Discretization of the (t, x) domain.

k_i^{j+1} by $(i = 1, \cdots, I, j = 0, \cdots, J-1)$

$$k_i^{j+1} = k_i^j + \frac{\Delta t}{\Delta x}(f_i^j - g_i^j), \tag{6.1}$$

which is the discrete version of (3.7). The variables and the discrete conservation equation are illustrated in Fig. 6.2. In Fig. 6.2(a), the arrows show the directions for increasing cumulative flows, as can be confirmed in Fig. 6.2(b).

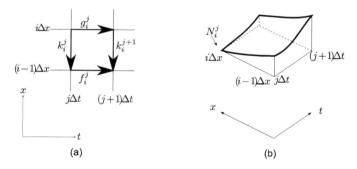

FIGURE 6.2 An illustration of the discrete conservation equation.

The initial densities k_i^0 are given by the initial conditions, and the boundary fluxes f_1^j and g_I^j are given by the boundary conditions. Numerical methods will attempt to calculate k_i^j for $j = 1, \cdots, J$ and $i = 1, \cdots, I$. Note that on a road, the out-flux of cell i, g_i^j, equals the in-flux of cell $i+1$, f_{i+1}^j. Thus, at each time step, there are $I+1$ boundary fluxes, among which the internal fluxes f_i^j ($i = 1, \cdots, I$) need to be calculated.

Different methods differ in their calculations of the internal fluxes passing the cell boundaries, f_i^j. In addition to the conservation law, a well-defined method should also satisfy the first-order principles defined in Chapter 3.

Definition 6.1.1. *A numerical method for the LWR model is called (physically) well-defined if the densities are always non-negative and not greater than the jam density. That is, if $k_i^j \in [0, \kappa]$, $k_i^{j+1} \in [0, \kappa]$ for a well-defined numerical method.* That k_i^{j+1} should be non-negative is a straightforward requirement. If $k_i^{j+1} > \kappa$, then the corresponding spacing is smaller than the jam spacing, and vehicles collide into each other. Thus, physically, a numerical method is well-defined if and only if the traffic stream is collision-free.

6.1.1 Finite difference methods

In a backward difference method, $f_i^j = g_{i-1}^j = Q(k_{i-1}^j) = q_{i-1}^j$, and $g_i^j = f_{i+1}^j = Q(k_i^j) = q_i^j$; i.e., the boundary flux from cell i to cell $i+1$ equals the upstream cell's flow-rate. The density is then updated as

$$\begin{aligned} k_i^{j+1} &= k_i^j + \frac{\Delta t}{\Delta x}(Q(k_{i-1}^j) - Q(k_i^j)) \\ &= k_i^j + \frac{\Delta t}{\Delta x}(q_{i-1}^j - q_i^j). \end{aligned}$$

In this method, the derivative $\frac{\partial q}{\partial x}$ is approximated by the backward difference, $\frac{q_i^j - q_{i-1}^j}{\Delta x}$. This method assumes that the congestion information propagates from the upstream cell to the downstream cell. Intuitively, this is correct when there is no congestion; but under congested conditions, it is incorrect with queue spillback, when the congestion information propagates backward. Thus the method is not physically well-defined. This can be verified according to Definition 6.1.1. Assume that cell i is jammed at time-step j; i.e., $k_i^j = \kappa$, but cell $i-1$ is not with a density $k_{i-1}^j \in (0, \kappa)$. Thus $Q(k_i^j) = 0$, and $Q(k_{i-1}^j) > 0$. In this case, $k_i^{j+1} > k_i^j = \kappa$, which is not well-defined.

In a forward difference method, $g_i^j = Q(k_{i+1}^j) = q_{i+1}^j$; i.e., the boundary from cell i to cell $i+1$ equals the downstream cell's flow-rate. The density is then updated as

$$\begin{aligned} k_i^{j+1} &= k_i^j + \frac{\Delta t}{\Delta x}(Q(k_i^j) - Q(k_{i+1}^j)) \\ &= k_i^j + \frac{\Delta t}{\Delta x}(q_i^j - q_{i+1}^j). \end{aligned} \quad (6.2)$$

In this method, the derivative $\frac{\partial q}{\partial x}$ is approximated by the forward difference $\frac{q_{i+1}^j - q_i^j}{\Delta x}$. This method assumes that the congestion information propagates from the downstream cell to the upstream cell. This is correct with congestion, but incorrect under uncongested traffic conditions. It can be shown that this method is not well-defined either, according to Definition 6.1.1.

If using a central difference to approximate $\frac{\partial q}{\partial x} \approx \frac{q_{i+1}^j - q_{i-1}^j}{2\Delta x}$, then the LWR model can be numerically solved by

$$k_i^{j+1} = k_i^j + \frac{\Delta t}{2\Delta x}(q_{i-1}^j - q_{i+1}^j)$$
$$= k_i^j + \frac{\Delta t}{2\Delta x}(Q(k_{i-1}^j) - Q(k_{i+1}^j)).$$

Again this method is not well-defined according to Definition 6.1.1.

If we let $f_i^j = g_{i-1}^j = \frac{1}{2}(q_{i-1}^j + q_i^j) + \frac{\Delta x}{2\Delta t}(k_{i-1}^j - k_i^j)$, this leads to the Lax-Friedrichs method

$$k_i^{j+1} = k_i^j +$$
$$\frac{\Delta t}{\Delta x}[\frac{1}{2}(q_{i-1}^j + q_i^j) + \frac{\Delta x}{2\Delta t}(k_{i-1}^j - k_i^j) - \frac{1}{2}(q_i^j + q_{i+1}^j) -$$
$$\frac{\Delta x}{2\Delta t}(k_i^j - k_{i+1}^j)]$$
$$= \frac{1}{2}(k_{i-1}^j + k_{i+1}^j) + \frac{\Delta t}{2\Delta x}(q_{i-1}^j - q_{i+1}^j), \quad (6.3)$$

which is not well-defined according to Definition 6.1.1.

6.1.2 The Godunov method

In the Godunov method, the boundary flux, g_i^j, is set to the boundary flux through $i\Delta x$ for the Riemann problem under the following initial conditions:

$$k(0, i\Delta x) = \begin{cases} k_i^j, & x < i\Delta x; \\ k_{i+1}^j, & x > i\Delta x. \end{cases}$$

For the homogeneous LWR model, the eight types of Riemann solutions and the corresponding boundary fluxes are discussed in Section 5.6. The boundary flux has the following solutions: (i) in cases 1, 2, 5

$$f_{i+1}^j = g_i^j = q(t, i\Delta x) = \begin{cases} q_i^j, & \text{in cases 1, 2, 5, 7;} \\ q_{i+1}^j, & \text{in cases 3, 4, 6, 7;} \\ C = Q(\kappa_c), & \text{in case 8.} \end{cases}$$

In particular, the Godunov flux can be written as

$$g_i^j = \begin{cases} \min_{k_i^j \leq k \leq k_{i+1}^j} Q(k), & k_i^j \leq k_{i+1}^j; \\ \max_{k_{i+1}^j \leq k \leq k_i^j} Q(k), & k_i^j > k_{i+1}^j. \end{cases} \quad (6.4)$$

That is, one does not have to completely solve the Riemann problem to obtain the boundary flux. In addition, (6.4) applies even if the fundamental diagram is non-concave or non-unimodal. However, this formula does not apply when the upstream and downstream cells have different fundamental diagrams on an inhomogeneous road, or when there are multiple entering and exiting links at a network junction.

In the Godunov method, the congestion information can propagate forward, backward, or in both directions, depending on the traffic states in both cells. This method is physically meaningful. However, before proving that is well-defined according to Definition 6.1.1, we introduce a simpler and equivalent way to calculate the boundary flux, which leads to the Cell Transmission Model.

6.2 The Cell Transmission Model

The *Cell Transmission Model (CTM)* is a numerical method to solve the LWR model. It is equivalent to the Godunov method for simple road traffic flows. The CTM has been extended for more complicated traffic systems, for which the CTM may not be equivalent to the Godunov method. In the CTM, traffic densities are still updated with (6.1), but the in- and out-fluxes are calculated in two steps.

6.2.1 Demand and supply

In the CTM, two new variables, demand ($d(t,x)$) and supply ($s(t,x)$), are introduced, in addition to the density ($k(t,x)$), speed ($v(t,x)$), and flow-rate ($q(t,x)$). The unit of demand and supply is the same as that of the flow-rate. Thus rigorously they should be called demand-rate and supply-rate.

Given a flow-density relation, $q = Q(k)$, we can define demand- and supply-density relations:

$$d = D(k) \equiv Q(\min\{k, \kappa_c\}) = \begin{cases} Q(k), & k \leq \kappa_c; \\ C, & k > \kappa_c; \end{cases} \quad (6.5a)$$

$$s = S(k) \equiv Q(\max\{k, \kappa_c\}) = \begin{cases} C, & k \leq \kappa_c; \\ Q(k), & k > \kappa_c. \end{cases} \quad (6.5b)$$

The demand and supply functions can be written as:

$$D(k) = \int_0^k \max\{Q'(y), 0\} dy,$$

$$S(k) = C + \int_0^k \min\{Q'(y), 0\} dy.$$

As shown in Fig. 6.3(a), the demand function is the increasing part of the fundamental diagram, and the supply function the decreasing part.

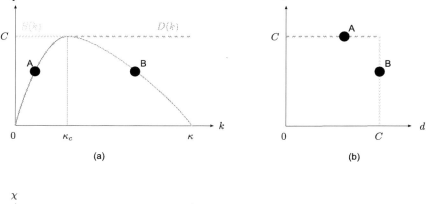

FIGURE 6.3 (a) Demand- and supply-density relations; (b) Demand-supply space; (c) Congestion-density relation.

Physically, the demand is the flow-rate that an upstream platoon can send, assuming the downstream road is empty (or uncongested). That is, we can solve the Riemann problem under the following initial condition:

$$k(0, x) = \begin{cases} k, & x < 0; \\ 0, & x > 0. \end{cases}$$

6.2 The Cell Transmission Model

Then the boundary flux $q(t, 0) = D(k)$ for any k. Following Section 5.6, if $k \leq \kappa_c$, we have type 2 solutions: $D(k) = Q(k)$; if $k > \kappa_c$, we have type 8 solution: $D(k) = C$. Thus the demand is also called the sending flow-rate.

Similarly, the supply is the flow-rate that a downstream platoon can receive, assuming the upstream road is jammed (or congested). This can also be verified by solving a corresponding Riemann problem. Thus the supply is also called the receiving flow-rate.

For the triangular fundamental diagram, the demand and supply functions can be written as

$$D(k) = \min\{uk, C\} = u \cdot \min\{k, \kappa_c\},$$
$$S(k) = \min\{C, w(\kappa - k)\} = w(\kappa - \max\{k, \kappa_c\}).$$

The demand and supply functions have the following properties:

1. When $k \leq \kappa_c$ in uncongested traffic, $D(k) \leq S(k) = C$; when $k \geq \kappa_c$ in congested traffic, $S(k) \leq D(k) = C$.
2. $\min\{D(k), S(k)\} = Q(k)$, and $\max\{D(k), S(k)\} = C$.

The pair of demand and supply, (d, s), can be used as a state variable to represent the traffic condition. The fundamental diagram in the (k, q) space corresponds to two line segments in the (d, s) space, as illustrated in Fig. 6.3(b).

Define the congestion level by

$$\chi = \frac{d}{s} = \frac{D(k)}{S(k)}. \tag{6.6}$$

$\chi \geq 0$. It equals zero when $k = 0$, 1 when $k = \kappa_c$, and ∞ when $k = \kappa$. Traffic is SUC, C, or SOC when $\chi <, =, > 1$. For the triangular fundamental diagram,

$$\chi = \frac{u \min\{k, \kappa_c\}}{w(\kappa - \max\{k, \kappa_c\})}.$$

Since χ increases in k, we can define the following density-congestion function

$$k = K(\chi) = K\left(\frac{d}{s}\right). \tag{6.7}$$

The congestion-density relation is illustrated in Fig. 6.3(c).

Theorem 6.2.1. *For a concave flow-density relation, $q = Q(k)$, the demand and supply functions are upper-bounded:*

$$D(k) \leq \min\{k, \kappa_c\} \cdot \lambda(0) \leq k \cdot \lambda(0), \tag{6.8}$$

$$S(k) \leq -(\kappa - \max\{k, \kappa_c\}) \cdot \lambda(\kappa) \leq -(\kappa - k) \cdot \lambda(\kappa). \tag{6.9}$$

For the triangular fundamental diagram, the bounds are straightforward:

$$\begin{aligned} D(k) &= u\min\{k, \kappa_c\} \leq uk, \\ S(k) &= w(\kappa - \max\{k, \kappa_c\}) \leq w(\kappa - k). \end{aligned}$$

This theorem is highly related to Theorem 3.3.2. The proof is a homework problem Problem 6.4.

For cell i at time step j, we denote its demand and supply by d_i^j and s_i^j, respectively. Thus

$$d_i^j = D(k_i^j), \tag{6.10a}$$
$$s_i^j = S(k_i^j). \tag{6.10b}$$

Note that here we assume that the fundamental diagram and, therefore, the demand and supply functions are location-dependent.

6.2.2 Boundary flux function

From the physical meaning of the demand and supply, the boundary flux between cells i and $i+1$ cannot exceed cell i's demand and cell $i+1$'s supply; i.e.,

$$\begin{aligned} g_i^j &\leq d_i^j, \\ g_i^j &\leq s_{i+1}^j. \end{aligned}$$

That is, the boundary flux is constrained by the upstream cell's demand and the downstream cell's supply.

Further it is reasonable to assume that, without any other bottlenecks, the boundary flux is maximized:

$$\max g_i^j. \tag{6.11}$$

Then the boundary flux can be solved:

$$g_i^j = f_{i+1}^j = \min\{d_i^j, s_{i+1}^j\}. \tag{6.12}$$

It is straightforward to show that (6.12) is consistent with (6.4) for a unimodal fundamental diagram. That is, this is another formula for the Godunov flux. This formula uses the new variables, demand and supply, which give the bounds of boundary fluxes, as well as the maximization principle, (6.11). Both the variables, constraints, and maximization principle can be extended to an inhomogeneous road and a network junction, including merges, diverges, and more general junctions. Hereafter, we call (6.12) as the supply-demand flux function.

6.2.3 Boundary conditions

On a road segment, we can use (6.12) to calculate all internal boundaries' fluxes for $i = 1, \cdots, \frac{L}{\Delta x} - 1$. At the external boundaries at $x = 0$ and $x = L$, boundary conditions are needed to calculate the fluxes. To apply the boundary condition, we introduce a dummy cell 0 at the upstream boundary and a dummy cell $I + 1$ at the downstream boundary. Cell 0's demand at time step j is denoted by d_0^j, and cell $I + 1$'s supply by s_{I+1}^j.

There can be three types of boundary conditions:

1. Under Dirichlet boundary conditions, both d_0^j and s_{I+1}^j are given exogenously. The upstream demand depends on drivers' choice behaviors in routes and departure times. The downstream supply depends on the congestion situation on the downstream destination.
2. Under Neumann boundary conditions, the derivatives in the upstream demand and downstream supply are zero; i.e., $d_0^j = d_1^j$, and $s_{I+1}^j = s_I^j$. In this case, congestion patterns initiate inside the road and propagate outwards.
3. Under periodic boundary conditions, the road segment becomes a ring road, and vehicles leaving from the downstream boundary enter the upstream boundary. In this case, cell I overlaps the upstream dummy cell 0, and cell 1 overlaps the downstream dummy cell $I + 1$. Hence $d_0^j = d_I^j$, and $s_{I+1}^j = s_1^j$.

6.2.4 The CTM

With the boundary and initial conditions, the CTM can be written as

$$k_i^{j+1} = k_i^j + \frac{\Delta t}{\Delta x}(\min\{d_{i-1}^j, s_i^j\} - \min\{d_i^j, s_{i+1}^j\}). \quad (6.13)$$

Therefore, the Cell Transmission Model can be used to solve the link initial-boundary value problem (LIBVP) with three different types of boundary conditions.

For the Cell Transmission Model to be well-defined, or collision-free, according to Definition 6.1.1, the cell size Δx and the time-step size Δt need to be carefully chosen.

Theorem 6.2.2. *The CTM is collision-free if Δx and Δt satisfy the following conditions:*

$$\frac{\Delta t}{\Delta x} \leq \min\{\min_{k \in [0, \kappa_c]} \frac{1}{V(k)}, \min_{k \in [\kappa_c, \kappa]} \frac{\kappa - k}{Q(k)}\}. \quad (6.14)$$

Proof. We assume that $k_i^j \in [0, \kappa]$ at jth time step. From (6.13), we have

$$k_i^j - \frac{\Delta t}{\Delta x} d_i^j \leq k_i^{j+1} \leq k_i^j + \frac{\Delta t}{\Delta x} s_i^j,$$

where the left equal sign occurs when both cells $i-1$ and $i+1$ are empty; i.e., when s_{i+1}^j is very large and $d_{i-1}^j = 0$, and the right equal sign occurs when both cells $i-1$ and $i+1$ are jammed; i.e., when $s_{i+1}^j = 0$, and d_{i-1}^j is very large.

Thus $k_i^{j+1} \in [0, \kappa]$ if and only if for any k_i^j

$$\frac{\Delta t}{\Delta x} \leq \frac{k_i^j}{Q\left(\min\{\kappa_c, k_i^j\}\right)},$$

$$\frac{\Delta t}{\Delta x} \leq \frac{\kappa - k_i^j}{Q\left(\max\{\kappa_c, k_i^j\}\right)}.$$

Therefore the condition for the multilane CTM to be forward-traveling and collision-free is when

$$\frac{\Delta t}{\Delta x} \leq \min_{k \in [0,\kappa]} \{\frac{k}{Q(\min\{\kappa_c, k\})}, \frac{\kappa - k}{Q(\max\{\kappa_c, k\})}\},$$

which leads to (6.14). □

Theorem 6.2.3. *The collision-free condition, (6.14), is equivalent to the CFL (Courant-Friedrichs-Lewy) condition,*

$$\frac{\Delta t}{\Delta x} \leq \min_{k \in [0,\kappa]} \frac{1}{|Q'(k)|}, \quad (6.15)$$

when (i) the speed-density relation is non-increasing; i.e., (3.35) is satisfied; and (ii) the flow-density relation is concave; i.e., (3.36), or equivalently, (3.40), is satisfied.

Proof. We first prove that (6.14) is equivalent to

$$\frac{\Delta t}{\Delta x} \leq \min\{\frac{1}{V(0)}, -\frac{1}{Q'(\kappa)}\}.$$

1. Since $V'(k) \leq 0$, we have $V(k) \leq V(0)$. Thus

$$\min_{k \in [0,\kappa_c]} \frac{1}{V(k)} = \frac{1}{V(0)}.$$

2. From (3.40) we have $(\kappa - k)(kV''(k) + 2V'(k)) \leq 0$ for $k \in [0, \kappa]$; thus $(\kappa - k)kV'(k) + \kappa V(k)$ is non-increasing in k, since its derivative is $(\kappa - k)(kV''(k) + 2V'(k))$. Hence

$$(\kappa - k)kV'(k) + \kappa V(k) \geq (\kappa - \kappa)\kappa V'(\kappa) + \kappa V(\kappa) = 0.$$

6.2 The Cell Transmission Model

Further, since

$$\frac{d}{dk}\frac{Q(k)}{\kappa-k} = \frac{Q'(k)(\kappa-k)+Q(k)}{(\kappa-k)^2} = \frac{(\kappa-k)kV'(k)+\kappa V(k)}{(\kappa-k)^2} \geq 0,$$

$\frac{Q(k)}{\kappa-k}$ is non-decreasing, and

$$0 \leq \frac{Q(k)}{\kappa-k} \leq \frac{Q(k)}{\kappa-k}\Big|_{k=\kappa} = -Q'(\kappa).$$

Thus

$$\min_{k \in [\kappa_c, \kappa]} \frac{\kappa-k}{Q(k)} = -\frac{1}{Q'(\kappa)}.$$

From (3.36) we can see that $Q'(k)$ is non-increasing. In addition, $Q'(0) = V(0) > 0$, and $Q'(\kappa) = \kappa V'(\kappa) < 0$, since the flow-density relation is unimodal. Thus

$$\min_{k \in [0,\kappa]} \frac{1}{|Q'(k)|} = \min\{\frac{1}{V(0)}, -\frac{1}{Q'(\kappa)}\}.$$

Therefore (6.15) is also equivalent to

$$\frac{\Delta t}{\Delta x} \leq \min\{\frac{1}{V(0)}, -\frac{1}{Q'(\kappa)}\}.$$

Hence the collision-free condition is equivalent to the CFL condition for a concave fundamental diagram. □

Note that, for non-concave fundamental diagrams, the two conditions may not be equivalent. For example, for a non-concave fundamental diagram in (Kerner and Konhäuser, 1994), (3.48), the speed-density relation is decreasing, but the flow-density relation is non-concave. In this case, the CFL condition is

$$\frac{\Delta t}{\Delta x} \leq \frac{1}{V(0)} = \frac{1}{27.83},$$

and the collision-free condition is the same. But a non-concave fundamental diagram in (LeVeque, 2001), (3.49), the CFL condition is $\frac{\Delta t}{\Delta x} \leq \frac{1}{3}$, but the collision-free condition is $\frac{\Delta t}{\Delta x} \leq \frac{1}{6}$. Thus the collision-free condition is more restrictive.

Compared with the CFL condition, the CTM collision-free condition is more general and physically meaningful.

6.2.5 Numerical accuracy and computational cost

As a numerical method, the CTM only provides approximate solutions to the LWR model. The accuracy depends on the choice of Δt and Δx.

For the Greenshields or triangular fundamental diagrams, we can define the CFL number as $u \frac{\Delta t}{\Delta x}$, which cannot be greater than 1, as shown in Theorem 6.2.3. Generally, the larger the CFL number, the more accurate the CTM is. In addition, given a CFL number, the smaller the cell size, the more accurate the CTM is.

Therefore, the best CFL number is 1, and $\Delta x = u\Delta t$. However, for the same road length L and simulation time duration E, the smaller the cell size, the larger numbers of cells and time steps we have, and the longer computational time it takes. As the computational cost is proportional to the number of cells multiplied by the number of time steps, the CTM's computational cost is proportional to $\frac{1}{\Delta x^2}$ for a given CFL number.

6.3 Stationary states on a link

The stationary states defined in Section 4.3 can be extended for those in the I cells. That is, if $k_i^j = k_i$ is time-independent for $i = 1, \cdots, I$ and $j = 0, \cdots, J$, then the traffic state on the link is stationary. Thus $d_i^j = d_i$ and $s_i^j = s_i$ are also time-independent. Further from (6.12), g_i^j is time-independent for $i = 1, \cdots, I-1$. From (6.1), we have $f_i^j = g_i^j$ for $i = 1, \cdots, I$; i.e., the boundary fluxes are location-independent: $f_1^j = g_1^j = f_2^j = \cdots = g_I^j$. Thus the boundary fluxes are constant: $f_1^j = \cdots = g_I^j = q^*$, and in stationary states, for $i = 1, \cdots, I+1$,

$$\min\{d_{i-1}^j, s_i^j\} = q^*. \tag{6.16}$$

Theorem 6.3.1. *In a stationary state, there exists no transonic rarefaction wave; i.e., it is impossible to have $k_i > \kappa_c > k_{i+1}$ for $i = 1, \cdots, I-1$.*

Proof. If there exists an $i = 1, \cdots, I-1$, such that $k_i > \kappa_c > k_{i+1}$. Then $d_i = s_{i+1} = C$, but $d_{i+1} < C$. Thus

$$\min\{d_i, s_{i+1}\} = C = q^*,$$

but $q^* = \min\{d_{i+1}, s_{i+2}^j\} < C$, which is impossible. □

From the above theorem, there are the following three possibilities:

1. All cells are under-critical; i.e., $k_i \leq \kappa_c$. Thus from (6.16), $s_i = C$, and $d_i = q^*$ for $i = 1, \cdots, I$; the congestion level $\chi = \frac{q^*}{C} \leq 1$, and $k_i = K(\frac{q^*}{C})$. Furthermore, the boundary conditions have to satisfy $d_0^j = q^*$, and

$s_{I+1}^j \geq q^*$, which does not have to constant. In this case, the upstream demand, d_0^j, is not greater than the downstream supply, s_{I+1}^j.

2. All cells are over-critical; i.e., $k_i \geq \kappa_c$. Thus from (6.16), $d_i = C$, and $s_i = q^*$ for $i = 1, \cdots, I$; the congestion level $\chi = \frac{C}{q^*} \geq 1$, and $k_i = K(\frac{C}{q^*})$. Furthermore, the boundary conditions have to satisfy $d_0^j \geq q^*$, which does not have to constant, and $s_{I+1}^j = q^*$. In this case, the downstream supply, s_{I+1}^j, is not greater than the upstream demand, d_0^j.

3. The upstream cells ($i = 1, \cdots, I_0$) are under-critical, and the downstream cells ($i = I_0 + 1, \cdots, I$) are over-critical; here $I_0 < I$. Thus from (6.16), $d_i = q^*$ and $s_i = C$ for $i = 1, \cdots, I_0 - 1$, and $d_i = C$ and $S_i = q^*$ for $i = I_0 + 2, \cdots, I$. But for cells I_0 and $I_0 + 1$, we only know that $s_{I_0} = C$, $d_{I_0+1} = C$, and $\min\{d_{I_0}, s_{I_0+1}\} = q^*$, which can have multiple solutions: $d_{I_0} = q^*$ and $s_{I_0+1} \geq q^*$, or $d_{I_0} \geq q^*$ and $s_{I_0+q} = q^*$. The densities are therefore: $k_i = K(\frac{q^*}{C})$ for $i = 1, \cdots, I_0 - 1$, and $k_i = K(\frac{C}{q^*})$ for $i = I_0 + 2, \cdots, I$; $k_{I_0} = K(\frac{q^*}{C})$ and $k_{I_0+1} \in [\kappa_c, K(\frac{C}{q^*})]$, or $k_{I_0} \in [K(\frac{q^*}{C}), \kappa_c]$ and $k_{I_0+1} = K(\frac{C}{q^*})$. Furthermore, the boundary conditions have to satisfy $d_0^j = q^*$, and $s_{I+1}^j = q^*$. In this case, the downstream supply, s_{I+1}^j, equals the upstream demand, d_0^j.

In the third case, there is a transitional state in either cell I_0 or cell $I_0 + 1$, whose density is between the upstream and downstream densities. Therefore, if the cell length decreases to 0, the stationary state on the link can be written as

$$k^*(x) = H(yL - \epsilon - x)K(\frac{q^*}{C}) + (1 - H(yL - x))K(\frac{C}{q^*})$$
$$+ (1 - H(yL - \epsilon - x))H(yL - x)k_0,$$

where $y \in [0, 1]$ is the uncongested fraction of the road, $H(\cdot)$ is the Heaviside function, ϵ is an infinitesimal number (can be considered the limit of Δx), and $k_0 \in [K(\frac{q^*}{C}), K(\frac{C}{q^*})]$ is a transitional state. When $y = 0$, all cells are congested; when $y = 1$, all cells are uncongested; when $y \in (0, 1)$, some upstream cells are uncongested, but downstream cells are congested.

6.4 Numerical solutions to the Riemann problem

The Cell Transmission Model simulates traffic dynamics on a link in the following steps:

1. Given k_i^j for $i = 1, \cdots, I$ at jth time-step.

2. Compute the demand and supply of cell i at jth time-step, d_i^j and s_i^j, from (6.5a) and (6.5b), respectively.
3. Given one of the three types boundary conditions: d_0^j and s_{I+1}^j.
4. Compute the in- and out-fluxes of cell i: $f_i^j = \min\{d_{i-1}^j, s_i^j\}$ and $g_i^j = \min\{d_i^j, s_{i+1}^j\}$.
5. Update the density: $k_i^{j+1} = k_i^j + \frac{\Delta t}{\Delta x}(f_i^j - g_i^j)$.
6. Return to Step 2 for $j+1$th time-step.

In the Riemann problem, the road is of infinite length. Thus it can be considered an infinite-road traffic problem. But it can be solved on a road of a finite length under the Neumann boundary condition, since the waves start from the jump point and propagate outwards.

6.4.1 Shock wave

For a normalized Greenshields fundamental diagram, $Q(k) = k(1-k)$, we first solve the Riemann problem under the following initial conditions:

$$k(0, x) = \begin{cases} 0.4, & x < 0; \\ 0.7, & x > 0. \end{cases}$$

Theoretically this is solved by a shock wave, whose speed is $v_s = -0.1$, as illustrated in Fig. 6.4(d).

We choose a road section $[-100, 50]$ with a simulation time interval of $[0, 400]$. We split the road into $I = 15$ cells with $\Delta x = 10$ and divide the time interval into $J = 50$ steps with $\Delta t = 8$. For the Greenshields fundamental diagram, the CFL condition, (6.15), and the collision-free condition, (6.14), are equivalent and both satisfied.

The initial conditions are $k_1^0 = \cdots k_{10}^0 = 0.4$, $k_{11}^0 = \cdots = k_{15}^0 = 0.7$. The Neumann boundary conditions are $d_0^j = d_1^j$, and $s_{16}^j = s_{15}^j$. The numerical results are shown in Fig. 6.4. In Fig. 6.4(a), the density curves are still discontinuous at later times, but the jump points travel backwards, along with the shock wave speed. In Fig. 6.4(b), the interface between the two initial states has a constant width and travels backward at the speed of $v_s = -0.1$. Fig. 6.4(c) shows the 3-D plot of $k(t, x)$, which again confirms the existence of a shock wave. The results are consistent with the analytical solution illustrated in Fig. 6.4(d).

6.4.2 Rarefaction wave

Next we solve the Riemann problem under the following initial conditions:

$$k(0, x) = \begin{cases} 0.6, & x < 0; \\ 0.4, & x > 0. \end{cases}$$

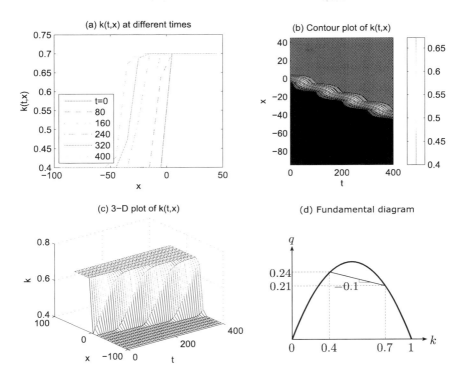

FIGURE 6.4 Numerical solutions to the Riemann problem: A shock wave.

Theoretically this is solved by a transonic rarefaction wave, whose characteristic wave speeds vary from -0.2 to 0.2, as illustrated in Fig. 6.5(d).

We choose a road section $[-100, 100]$ with a simulation time interval of $[0, 400]$. We split the road into $I = 20$ cells with $\Delta x = 10$ and divide the time interval into $J = 50$ steps with $\Delta t = 8$. The initial conditions are $k_1^0 = \cdots k_{10}^0 = 0.6$, $k_{11}^0 = \cdots = k_{20}^0 = 0.4$. The Neumann boundary conditions are $d_0^j = d_1^j$, and $s_{21}^j = s_{20}^j$. The numerical results are shown in Fig. 6.5. In Fig. 6.5(a), the density at $x = 0$ remains constant at 0.5, which is the critical density. This is because the characteristic wave speed at the critical density is zero. But other values of density keep propagating outwards, determined by their corresponding characteristic wave speeds. These form the rarefaction wave of a fan shape, as can be seen in Fig. 6.5(b). The discontinuity in the initial density is smeared out along the time, as can also be verified in Fig. 6.5(c). The results are consistent with the analytical solutions illustrated in Fig. 6.5(d).

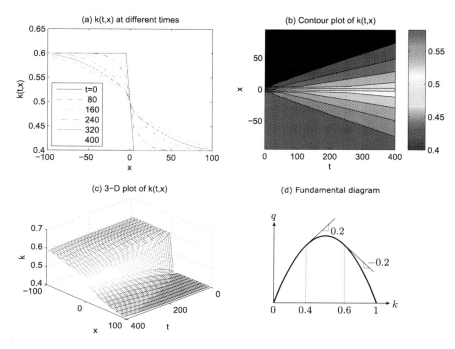

FIGURE 6.5 Numerical solutions to the Riemann problem: A rarefaction wave.

6.5 Generalized CTM for link traffic

The CTM can be generalized to model dynamics for different types of roads and traffic streams. For some traffic systems where the LWR model can be formulated, the CTM can help to verify the existing theory (e.g., for inhomogeneous roads) or guide the development of new theory (e.g., for unifiable multi-commodity traffic). For other systems (e.g., at a signalized intersection) where the higher-order effects caused by bounded acceleration cannot be ignored, the CTM could be extended to capture such effects.

6.5.1 Inhomogeneous roads

For an inhomogeneous road with location-dependent road and traffic characteristics, including the number of lanes, lane-changing intensities, speed limits, or time gaps, the flow-density relation is location-dependent: $q = Q(x, k)$, whose critical density is location-dependent and denoted by $\kappa_c(x)$. Thus the demand and supply functions are also location-dependent:

$$D(x, k(t, x)) = Q(x, \min\{k(t, x), \kappa_c(x)\}), \tag{6.17a}$$
$$S(x, k(t, x)) = Q(x, \max\{k(t, x), \kappa_c(x)\}). \tag{6.17b}$$

In the Cell Transmission Model, a simple way to treat an inhomogeneous road is to assume that each cell is homogeneous with the same road and traffic characteristics. That is, the characteristics are assumed to be piece-wise constant. Thus for cell i at time step j, the demand and supply are

$$d_i^j = D(x_i, k_i^j), \quad (6.18a)$$
$$s_i^j = S(x_i, k_i^j). \quad (6.18b)$$

The boundary flux can still be calculated from (6.12). However, if the road and traffic characteristics are continuously changes, it may be more accurate to approximate them by a piece-wise linear function. An example is the number of lanes inside a continuous lane-drop zone gradually decreases in Fig. 4.3.

For an inhomogeneous road, the collision-free condition, (6.14), is also location-dependent. The time-step size should be the same for all cells, but the cell sizes can be different.

For some inhomogeneous roads, the LWR model can be analytically solved, as discussed in Section 5.7. In this case, the numerical solutions can be used to verify the existing theory.

6.5.2 Multi-commodity models

For a multi-commodity traffic flow in cell i at time step j, the total density, speed, flow-rate, in- and out-fluxes are denoted by k_i^j, v_i^j, q_i^j, f_i^j, and g_i^j, respectively. For commodity m, its density, speed, flow-rate, in- and out-fluxes are denoted by $k_{i,m}^j$, $v_{i,m}^j$, $q_{i,m}^j$, $f_{i,m}^j$, and $g_{i,m}^j$. Clearly,

$$k_i^j = \sum_{m=1}^{M} k_{i,m}^j,$$
$$f_i^j = \sum_{m=1}^{M} f_{i,m}^j,$$
$$g_i^j = \sum_{m=1}^{M} g_{i,m}^j.$$

If the commodity flows are conserved, their densities can be updated similarly to (6.1):

$$k_{i,m}^{j+1} = k_{i,m}^j + \frac{\Delta t}{\Delta x}(f_{i,m}^j - g_{i,m}^j).$$

We denote the commodity density and flow-rate proportions by $p_{i,m}^j = \frac{k_{i,m}^j}{k_i^j}$ and $\gamma_{i,m}^j = \frac{q_{i,m}^j}{q_i^j}$.

For unifiable multi-commodity traffic, whose LWR model is (5.10), or (5.16), the total traffic is governed by the LWR model, and the traditional Cell Transmission Model can be directly applied to update the total density. That is, the total demand and supply, d_i^j and s_i^j, can be computed by (6.10) for a homogeneous road or by (6.18) for an inhomogeneous road. The total in- and out-fluxes are calculated by (6.12) under proper boundary conditions. Further, if the multi-commodity traffic flow is FIFO, the density proportion always propagates forward; thus the commodity in- and out-fluxes are proportional to the commodity density proportions:

$$g_{i,m}^j = f_{i+1,m}^j = g_i^j \cdot p_{i,m}^j.$$

But in a general unifiable multi-commodity traffic flow, which may not be FIFO, the flow-rate proportion travels forward, and the commodity in- and out-fluxes are proportional to the commodity flow-rate proportions:

$$g_{i,m}^j = f_{i+1,m}^j = g_i^j \cdot \gamma_{i,m}^j.$$

In non-unifiable, FIFO multi-commodity traffic, the commodity and total flow-density relation are $q_m = p_m k V(k, \vec{p})$ and $q = Q(k, \vec{p}) = k V(k, \vec{p})$. If $Q(k, \vec{p})$ is still unimodal at any $\vec{p}$, its critical density is denoted by $\kappa_c(\vec{p})$. Commodity density proportions travel forward, and the upstream vehicles attempt to follow the downstream vehicles. Thus the total demand in cell i is defined by

$$d_i^j = Q(\min\{k_i^j, \kappa_c(\vec{p}_i^j)\}, \vec{p}_i^j),$$

where $\vec{p}_i^j$ is the vector of commodity density proportions in cell i at time step j. However, the total supply in cell $i+1$ depends on the commodity density proportions in cell i:

$$s_{i+1}^j = Q(\max\{\tilde{k}_{i+1}^j, \kappa_c(\vec{p}_i^j)\}, \vec{p}_i^j),$$

where $\tilde{k}_{i+1}^j$ is the maximum density, y, that satisfies $V(y, \vec{p}_i^j) = v_{i+1}^j = V(k_{i+1}^j, \vec{p}_{i+1}^j)$. Then the total in- and out-fluxes are calculated by (6.12) under proper boundary conditions, and the commodity in- and out-fluxes are proportional to the commodity density proportions:

$$g_{i,m}^j = f_{i+1,m}^j = g_i^j \cdot p_{i,m}^j. \tag{6.19}$$

There has been no general CTM for non-FIFO, non-unifiable multi-commodity traffic.

Definition 6.1.1 needs to be extended for a well-defined multi-commodity Cell Transmission Model.

Definition 6.5.1. *A multi-commodity Cell Transmission Model is (physically) well-defined if the total and commodity densities are always non-negative, and the total density is not greater than the jam density. That is, in a well-defined Cell Transmission Model, if $k_i^j \in [0, \kappa]$, $k_{i,m}^j \geq 0$, and $\sum_{m=1}^{M} k_{i,m}^j = k_i^j$, then $k_i^{j+1} \in [0, \kappa]$, $k_{i,m}^{j+1} \geq 0$, and $\sum_{m=1}^{M} k_{i,m}^{j+1} = k_i^{j+1}$. This can be considered as the generalized definition of collision-free multi-commodity traffic.*

The collision-free condition, (6.14), needs to be revised for multi-commodity traffic. Problem 6.9 is a homework assignment for unifiable multi-commodity traffic. This commodity-based condition leads to reasonable choices of Δt and Δx for multi-commodity CTM.

6.6 Junction models

This section extends the CTM for network traffic flow. This is achieved by the junction models that calculate the fluxes through the junction. Such models are built on the following rules:

- **Maximum total flux**. Vehicles cooperate with each other to maximize the total flux through the junction.
- **Bounded fluxes**. The in-flux to a downstream link is bounded by the supply. The out-flux from an upstream link is bounded by the demand.
- **Diverging rules**. When the FIFO principle is observed for diverging traffic, the commodity out-fluxes from an upstream link are proportional to the commodity density proportions. If the FIFO principles are violated, the commodity out-fluxes are proportional to the commodity flow-rate proportions.
- **Merging rules**. When the fair principle is observed for merging traffic, the distribution of a downstream road's capacity to an upstream link is proportional to the upstream link's demand. Otherwise, it is determined by the upstream link's priority.

Hence, a junction model can be considered the solution to the above optimization problem, in which the total flux is maximized subject to constraints in demands and supplies as well as merging and diverging rules.

For a general junction illustrated in Fig. 6.6, there are I upstream links, and J downstream links. At time t, the demand of upstream link i ($i = 1, \cdots, I$) is denoted by d_i (with t dropped), and the supply of the downstream link j ($j = 1, \cdots, J$) by s_j. The out- and in-fluxed are denoted by g_i and f_j, respectively. We assume that vehicles on link i can travel to

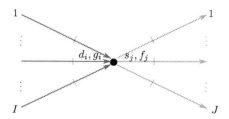

FIGURE 6.6 An illustration of a general junction.

any downstream link j without turning prohibitions. Thus, vehicles can be divided into J commodities on each upstream link, and we denote vehicles from link i to link j by $i \to j$. The commodity flow-rate proportion is denoted by $\gamma_{i \to j}$, and the commodity in- and out-fluxes by $f_{i \to j}$, $g_{i \to j}$, respectively. We denote the priority of link i by β_i. Then the optimization problem can be written as

$$\max q = \sum_{i=1}^{I} g_i, \tag{6.20}$$

where q is the total flux, subject to

$$g_i \leq d_i, \tag{6.21a}$$
$$f_j \leq s_j, \tag{6.21b}$$
$$g_{i \to j} = g_i \gamma_{i \to j}, \tag{6.21c}$$
$$f_{i \to j} = g_{i \to j}, \tag{6.21d}$$
$$f_j = \sum_{i=1}^{I} f_{i \to j}, \tag{6.21e}$$
$$g_i = \frac{d_i}{\sum_{\alpha=1}^{I} d_\alpha} q. \tag{6.21f}$$

For simplicity, here we only consider the fair merging rule in (6.21f), in which the out-flux of link i is proportional to its demand. It is easy to show that the conservation law is satisfied at the junction; i.e.,

$$\sum_{i=1}^{I} g_i = \sum_{j=1}^{J} f_j. \tag{6.22}$$

This is assigned in Problem 6.11. If there exists a closed-form solution to the above optimization problem, then a junction model can be written as

$$(\vec{\mathbf{f}}, \vec{\mathbf{g}}) = \Phi(\vec{\mathbf{d}}, \vec{\mathbf{s}}, \vec{\gamma}, \vec{\beta}), \tag{6.23}$$

where $\bar{\mathbf{f}} = (f_1, f_2, \cdots, f_J)$ and the other vectors are the sets of the corresponding variables. This section introduces some of such basic junction models.

6.6.1 Diverge models

For a diverge with only one upstream link ($I = 1$) and multiple downstream links ($J > 1$), the optimization problem can be simplified as

$$\max q = g_1, \qquad (6.24)$$

subject to

$$g_1 \leq d_1, \qquad (6.25a)$$
$$f_j \leq s_j, \qquad (6.25b)$$
$$g_{1 \to j} = g_1 \gamma_{1 \to j}, \qquad (6.25c)$$
$$f_j = g_{1 \to j}. \qquad (6.25d)$$

The last three constraints in (6.25b)-(6.25d) lead to

$$g_1 \gamma_{1 \to j} \leq s_j.$$

Thus, we have

$$g_1 \leq \min_{j=1}^{J} \frac{s_j}{\gamma_{1 \to j}}.$$

Combining the first constraint in (6.25a), we have

$$g_1 \leq \min\{d_1, \min_{j=1}^{J} \frac{s_j}{\gamma_{1 \to j}}\}.$$

Therefore, the solution of the optimization problem is straightforward at

$$q = g_1 = \min\{d_1, \min_{j=1}^{J} \frac{s_j}{\gamma_{1 \to j}}\}, \qquad (6.26a)$$
$$f_j = g_1 \gamma_{1 \to j}, \qquad (6.26b)$$

which is the closed-form diverge model.

When vehicles follow the FIFO rule, $\gamma_{1 \to j}$ can be replaced by the commodity density proportion $p_{1 \to j}$, and the above diverge model is also called FIFO.

When $\gamma_{i \to j} > 0$ for all i and j, then $q = 0$ for any $s_j = 0$. That is, if one downstream link is totally jammed, it prevents vehicles from entering any downstream links. This is the extreme case for queue spill-back. This is true if vehicles entering the jammed link use all lanes; otherwise, if vehicles entering the jammed link only use a portion of the lanes, such a phenomenon can be avoided.

6.6.2 Merge models

For a merge junction with multiple upstream links ($I > 1$) and only one downstream link ($J = 1$), the optimization problem can be simplified as

$$\max q = \sum_{i=1}^{I} g_i, \quad (6.27)$$

subject to

$$g_i \leq d_i, \quad (6.28a)$$
$$f_1 \leq s_1, \quad (6.28b)$$
$$f_1 = \sum_{i=1}^{I} g_i, \quad (6.28c)$$
$$g_i = \frac{d_i}{\sum_{\alpha=1}^{I} d_\alpha} q. \quad (6.28d)$$

From the first three constraints in (6.28), we can have $f_1 = q \leq \min\{\sum_{i=1}^{I} d_i, s_1\}$. Thus, the optimal total flux is

$$q = \min\{\sum_{i=1}^{I} d_i, s_1\}, \quad (6.29)$$

and the out-flux of link i can be calculated from (6.28d). In particular,

$$g_i = \min\{d_i, \frac{d_i}{\sum_{\alpha=1}^{I} d_\alpha} s_1\}. \quad (6.30)$$

Thus, the effective supply of link i is proportional to its demand. That is, the downstream supply is distributed to each upstream link according to its demand. This is a "fair" distribution scheme, and it is why this a fair merging rule.

When all upstream links are congested, their demands equal their capacities, which are proportional to their numbers of lanes for the same road conditions. In this case, the out-flux of each link is proportional to its number of lanes. This has been verified for freeway merges, where the upstream links are all freeways. But at a merge between a mainline freeway and an on-ramp, the out-flux of the upstream links may not be proportional to their numbers of lanes or capacities, since vehicles from the on-ramp may push mainline freeway's vehicles away from the on-ramp. That is, the on-ramp vehicles have higher priorities in this case. But the model in this section has to be revised for such merges.

6.6.3 General junction models

For a general junction with multiple upstream and downstream links, from (6.21a) and (6.21f), we have $q \leq \sum_{\alpha=1}^{I} d_\alpha$; i.e., the total flux is not greater than the total upstream demand.

From (6.21c-f), we have

$$f_j = \frac{\sum_{i=1}^{I} d_i \gamma_{i \to j}}{\sum_{i=1}^{I} d_i} q.$$

Then from (6.21b), we have (the dummy variable α is replaced by i)

$$q \leq s_j \frac{\sum_{i=1}^{I} d_i}{\sum_{i=1}^{I} d_i \gamma_{i \to j}}.$$

Thus, the maximum total flux equals (the dummy variable α is replaced by i)

$$q = \min\{\sum_{i=1}^{I} d_i, \min_{j=1}^{J} s_j \frac{\sum_{i=1}^{I} d_i}{\sum_{i=1}^{I} d_i \gamma_{i \to j}}\}. \tag{6.31}$$

Then the out- and in-fluxes of each link can be calculated from (6.21c-f).

The general junction models in (6.31) and (6.29) are different from each other in the downstream supply functions: the supply in the former is the minimum value by considering all downstream links' supplies. The supply in (6.31) is different from that in (6.26b), as the turning proportion to downstream link j is effectively $\frac{\sum_{i=1}^{I} d_i \gamma_{i \to j}}{}\sum_{i=1}^{I} d_i$, which is a weighted average of each upstream link's turning proportion.

Notes

Note 6.1. *Refer to (LeVeque, 1992, 2002) for detailed discussions on traditional numerical methods for solving the hyperbolic conservation laws. In both books, the LWR model was used as an example of scalar hyperbolic conservation laws. The Lax-Friedrichs method in (6.3) was adopted in (Federal Highway Administration, 2004, Chapter 5).*

Note 6.2. *The Godunov flux, (6.4), was presented in (Osher, 1984). The Godunov method was developed for numerically solving problems in fluid dynamics* in (Godunov, 1959). However, it was not well known in the transportation field before 1990's. For example, it was not included in (Federal Highway Administration, 2004) or cited in (Daganzo, 1994, 1995a). In (Bui et al., 1992), the Godunov flux, (6.4), was used to solve the LWR model. The Godunov method was cited in (Leo and Pretty, 1992) but not used to solve the LWR model. Godunov's work and LeVeque's book were cited in (Daganzo, 1995b). The relationship between the Godunov method and the Cell Transmission Model was clarified in (Lebacque, 1996).

Note 6.3. *The terms, demand and supply, and their physical meanings were introduced in (Lebacque, 1996). They were called sending and receiving flows in (Daganzo, 1995a,b). The consistency between the boundary flux, (6.12), and the Godunov flux was established in (Lebacque, 1996) for both homogeneous and inhomogeneous LWR models. Such demand and supply functions were introduced in the mathematics literature in 1980s (Engquist and Osher, 1980a,b).*

Note 6.4. *The supply-demand flux function for the LWR model was proposed for a triangular or trapezoidal fundamental diagram in (Daganzo, 1995a), and for a general fundamental diagram in (Daganzo, 1995b). The same formula for the Burgers equation was presented in (van Leer, 1984). However, as shown in Chapter 8, (Daganzo, 1995a) was the first to extend this to calculate boundary fluxes through merges and diverges.*

Note 6.5. *The CFL condition was proposed in (Courant et al., 1928). It is necessary for the stability and convergence for a well-defined numerical method. Thus, it is a mathematical and numerical concept. In contrast, the collision-free condition is physical concept.*

Note 6.6. *The Cell Transmission Model was presented for unifiable and FIFO multi-commodity traffic in (Lebacque, 1996), for unifiable multi-commodity traffic in (Jin, 2017e), and for FIFO multi-commodity lane-changing traffic in (Jin, 2013). The equation for calculating the boundary fluxes for FIFO multi-commodity traffic flow, (6.19), was derived in (Papageorgiou, 1990; Daganzo, 1995a; Lebacque, 1996).*

Note 6.7. *A Cell Transmission Model for non-unifiable, non-FIFO traffic was presented in (Jin and Wada, 2018) for priority vehicles and special lanes. The kinematic wave theory for such a system was presented in (Daganzo, 1997b). In (Daganzo et al., 1997), the Incremental Transfer (IT) principle was used to derive another Cell Transmission Model for the system. But the theory and the CTM may not be consistent for general fundamental diagrams.*

Note 6.8. *The Cell Transmission Model has been extended for air traffic (Sun and Bayen, 2008), pedestrian traffic (Asano et al., 2007), and many other traffic systems.*

Note 6.9. *The collision-free condition for unifiable multi-commodity traffic with a concave total fundamental diagram was derived in (Jin, 2017e).*

Note 6.10. *The optimization formulation of the junction model was first presented in the seminal paper (Daganzo, 1995a), which presents a priority-based merge model and a FIFO diverge model. This is a groundbreaking idea, as it is the first well-defined extension of the LWR model for network traffic flow, even though earlier attempts exist in the literature, e.g., (Lebacque, 1984).*

Note 6.11. *The fair merging rule was first presented in (Jin and Zhang, 2003b). It was later independently presented in (Laval and Daganzo, 2006). Empirically it was verified for freeway merges in (Bar-Gera and Ahn, 2010). As pointed out in (Lebacque and Khoshyaran, 2005), the fair merge model in (6.29) violates the invariance principle. But based on a new kinematic wave theory developed in (Jin et al., 2009), it was shown in (Jin, 2010c) that its continuous version is equivalent to an invariant merge model first proposed in (Ni and Leonard, 2005). Invariant priority-based merge model first proposed by (Daganzo, 1995a) was also presented in (Jin, 2010c).*

Note 6.12. *In a series of papers (Jin et al., 2009; Jin, 2010c, 2012b, 2017c), the CTM was elevated into a new network kinematic wave theory by adopting the mathematical framework in (Holden and Risebro, 1995) but using the junction models in the CTM as entropy conditions. The existence and uniqueness of the Riemann solutions were proved in these papers. In addition, the closed-form solution of the boundary flux through a general junction was obtained for fair merging and FIFO diverging rules. In addition to (Holden and Risebro, 1995), (Coclite et al., 2005) presented another mathematical theory of network traffic flow. But the merging and diverging rules in such mathematical theories may not be as realistic as those employed in the CTM.*

Note 6.13. *The first closed-form model for a general junction with fair merging and FIFO diverging rules was presented in (Jin and Zhang, 2004). It was later independently obtained in (Bliemer, 2007). Its invariant form was obtained in (Jin, 2012b) and proved in (Jin, 2017b). But the closed-form junction models for more general merging and diverging rules are still elusive. There have been many algorithmic models for general junctions, even when some turning movements are prohibited. See (Tampère et al., 2011; Flötteröd and Rohde, 2011; Jabari, 2016) for examples.*

Note 6.14. *The CTM has been applied to analyze traffic dynamics in various networks. In (Daganzo, 1996), it was shown that a beltway network can converge to gridlock. In (Jin, 2003, 2009), it was shown that stationary states in a diverge-merge network can be unstable. In (Jin, 2015a, 2017d), the existence and stability of traffic dynamics in general road networks were systematically studied.*

Problems

Problem 6.1. *Construct examples to demonstrate that the forward difference method, (6.2), and the central difference method, (6.3), are not well-defined, according to Definition 6.1.1.*

Problem 6.2. *Verify that (6.4) is the Godunov flux for a homogeneous LWR model with a concave fundamental diagram.*

Problem 6.3. *Solve the Riemann problem for the LWR model and verify that the supply is the flow-rate that a downstream platoon can receive, assuming the upstream road is jammed (or congested).*

Problem 6.4. *Prove Theorem 6.2.1.*

Problem 6.5. *Verify that (6.12) is equivalent to (6.4) for a homogeneous road. Also verify that (6.12) gives the Godunov flux at an inhomogeneous road.*

Problem 6.6. *Prove that $K\left(\frac{1}{\chi}\right) = P(K(\chi))$ for a congestion level $\chi \geq 0$.*

Problem 6.7. *Solve the Riemann problem for the Cell Transmission Model with a normalized Greenshields fundamental diagram, $Q(k) = k(1-k)$, under the following initial conditions:*

$$k(0, x) = \begin{cases} 0.4, & x < 0; \\ 0.7, & x > 0. \end{cases}$$

Choose a road section $[-100, 50]$ with a simulation time interval of $[0, 400]$; split the road into $I = 30$ cells with $\Delta x = 5$ and divide the time interval into $J = 100$ steps with $\Delta t = 4$. Plot the solutions of $k(t, x)$ at different times, its contour plot, and the 3-D plot. Compare the results with those in the example.

Problem 6.8. *Solve the Riemann problem for the Cell Transmission Model with a normalized triangular fundamental diagram, $Q(k) = \min\{k, \frac{1}{4}(1-k)\}$, under the following initial conditions:*

$$k(0, x) = \begin{cases} 1, & x < 0; \\ 0.1, & x > 0. \end{cases}$$

Choose a road section $[-100, 50]$ with a simulation time interval of $[0, 400]$; split the road into $I = 30$ cells with $\Delta x = 5$ and divide the time interval into $J = 100$ steps with $\Delta t = 4$. Plot the solutions of $k(t, x)$ at different times, its contour plot, and the 3-D plot. Compare the solutions with the transonic rarefaction wave solutions for the Greenshields fundamental diagram.

Problem 6.9. *Derive the collision-free condition for unifiable multi-commodity traffic flow.*

Problem 6.10. *For a road from $x = -1000$ m to $x = 1000$ m, there is a discontinuous lane-drop at $x = 0$. The numbers of lanes on the upstream and downstream links are $l_1 = 2$ and $l_2 = 1$, respectively. We assume that all lanes have the same triangular fundamental diagram with $u = 30$ m/s, $w = 5$ m/s, and $\kappa = 1/7$ veh/m. Assume that the capacity drop ratio is $\varsigma = 26.29\%$. Divide the road into 200 cells with the cell length of $\Delta x = 10$ m and set the time-step size $\Delta t = 0.3$ s. Solve the Cell Transmission Model during [0, 2000] s for the following scenario:*

1. *Initially the network is empty;*
2. *There is no queue at the downstream boundary; i.e., the supply at the downstream boundary equals $l_2 C$.*
3. *The upstream demand first increases over the downstream capacity and then decreases during $t = 0$ and 1980 s, and the demand from the upstream boundary at time step j is given by*

$$d_0^j = \max\{0, 1.2 l_2 C \cdot \min\{(j - \frac{1}{2})\Delta t/900, 1, 2.2 - (j - \frac{1}{2})\Delta t/900\}\}.$$

Plot and discuss the results.

Problem 6.11. *Prove the conservation law in (6.22).*

CHAPTER 7

Newell's simplified kinematic wave model

The theories and numerical methods in Chapters 5 and 6 apply to a broad range of traffic systems, fundamental diagrams, and initial and boundary conditions. The dependent variable is traffic density. This chapter introduces Newell's simplified kinematic wave model, which only applies to the triangular fundamental diagram and special initial and boundary conditions for a homogeneous road segment. The dependent variable is the cumulative flow, and it is still in the flow coordinates. For analytical, numerical, and empirical studies, Newell's simplified kinematic wave model is much simpler than the general LWR model and the Cell Transmission Model. Even though the model is limited, it has been successfully extended for network traffic as the Link Transmission Model, which will be introduced in the following chapter. Thus, the latter inherits much of the simplicity.

Before getting to Newell's simplified model, we first introduce in Section 7.1 some mathematical theories for general Hamilton-Jacobi equations, as the LWR model can be transformed to one of such partial differential equations. Then in Section 7.2 we derive Newell's simplified kinematic wave model and discuss its properties. In Section 7.3 we apply Newell's simplified kinematic wave model to discuss the initiation, propagation, and dissipation of a queue on a road segment.

7.1 The Hamilton-Jacobi equations and the Hopf-Lax formula for the LWR model

In this section we introduce and analyze the equivalent Hamilton-Jacobi equations for the LWR model for single-commodity traffic on a homogeneous road discussed in Section 5.1.

7.1.1 The four Hamilton-Jacobi equations equivalent to the LWR model

In the flow coordinates, $q = N_t$, and $k = -N_x$. The flow-density relation on a homogeneous road, $q = Q(k)$, leads to the following partial differential equation:

$$N_t = Q(-N_x), \qquad (7.1)$$

where the cumulative flow, $N(t, x)$, is the unknown variable. As R2 (conservation law) in Section 5.1 are embedded in the definitions of the variables, (7.1) is derived from R1 and R3.

Similarly in the trajectory coordinates, we obtain the following equations:

$$X_t = W(-X_n), \qquad (7.2)$$
$$X_n = -W^{-1}(X_t). \qquad (7.3)$$

In the schedule coordinates, we have

$$T_n = \Xi(T_x) \qquad (7.4)$$

The four equations are all Hamilton-Jacobi equations equivalent to the LWR model. The difference is in the dependent variables: in the Hamilton-Jacobi equations the dependent variables are the primary variables; but in the LWR models the dependent variables are the secondary variables.

7.1.2 The variational principle

Let's consider the LWR model with a time- and location-dependent fundamental diagram (e.g., on an inhomogeneous road or with time-dependent signals):

$$k_t + Q(t, x, k)_x = 0, \qquad (7.5)$$

and the corresponding Hamilton-Jacobi equation is

$$N_t - Q(t, x, -N_x) = 0. \qquad (7.6)$$

The characteristic ordinary differential equations for the LWR model can be written as:

$$\dot{x} = Q_k(t, x, k), \qquad (7.7a)$$
$$\dot{k} = -Q_x(t, x, k), \qquad (7.7b)$$
$$\dot{N} = Q(t, x, k) - k Q_k(t, x, k), \qquad (7.7c)$$
$$q = Q(t, x, k). \qquad (7.7d)$$

7.1 Hamilton-Jacobi equations

In (7.7), the first equation defines the characteristic curve $(t, x(t))$ in the time-space domain; the second equation, which is derived from the first equation and (7.5), determines the change in traffic density k along the curve; the third equation determines the cumulative flow N along the characteristic curve; and the fourth equation determines the flux q. Therefore, from the first two equations we can solve k and x at any time $t > r$ without knowing N or q, given the initial $x(r)$ and $k(r, x(r))$; then with given the initial $N(r, x(r))$ we can solve $N(t, x)$ for $t > r$ from the third equation, and $q(t, x)$ can always be calculated from the fourth equation. Note that the solutions of the characteristic equations are continuous, and the trajectory $(t, x(t))$ starting from different initial point $(r, x(r))$ may cross each other. Therefore, an additional principle is needed to pick out unique solutions of $k(t, x)$ when multiple solutions of $k(t, x)$ are obtained on multiple trajectories of the characteristic equations.

Extending the Legendre transformation of the flow-density relation, defined in (3.39), we define

$$L(t, x, \dot{x}) = \sup_{b \in [0, \kappa(t,x)]} Q(t, x, b) - \dot{x} \cdot b,$$

where $\kappa(t, x)$ is the jam density at (t, x). Physically, the Legendre transformation equals the maximum rate of flow passing an observer traveling at a speed of $\dot{x}$. When $Q_{bb}(t, x, b) < 0$, the optimal $b^* = k$ satisfies (7.7a). Since $Q_k(t, xk)$ decreases in k, k is uniquely determined by $\dot{x}$ from (7.7a). Therefore, along the characteristic curve in (7.7a),

$$L(t, x, \dot{x}) = Q(t, x, k) - \dot{x} \cdot k, \qquad (7.8)$$

where $k = Q_k^{-1}(t, x, \dot{x})$. That is, the maximum passing flow-rate occurs if the observer travels at the characteristic wave speed. From the above equation and (7.7a) we have

$$\frac{\partial L(t, x, \dot{x})}{\partial \dot{x}} = Q_k(t, x, k) \frac{\partial k}{\partial \dot{x}} - k - \dot{x} \frac{\partial k}{\partial \dot{x}} = -k,$$

and

$$\frac{\partial L(t, x, \dot{x})}{\partial x} = Q_x(t, x, k) + Q_k(t, x, k) \frac{\partial k}{\partial x} - \dot{x} \frac{\partial k}{\partial x} = Q_x(t, x, k).$$

Thus from (7.7b) we have

$$-\frac{d}{dt} \frac{\partial L(t, x, \dot{x})}{\partial \dot{x}} + \frac{\partial L(t, x, \dot{x})}{\partial x} = 0, \qquad (7.9)$$

which is the Euler-Lagrange equation.

Further from the calculus of variations, we notice that $L(t, x, \dot{x})$ is a Lagrangian, and $\dot{x}(t)$ minimizes the work from $y = x(r)$ to $x(t)$, $\int_r^t L(t, x, \dot{x}) dt$, which equals the number of vehicles passing an observer traveling along the trajectory of $x(t)$. Since $\dot{N} = L(t, x, \dot{x})$, we have

$$N(t, x) = N(r, y) + \min_{\dot{x} \in [Q_k(t,x,\kappa), Q_k(t,x,0)]} \int_r^t L(t, x, \dot{x}) dt.$$

Thus the characteristic path yields the minimum work among all valid paths. Furthermore, since $N(r, y)$ should also minimize the work from an earlier point when the cumulative flow is zero, then we have (Here $\partial\Omega$ is the boundary where $N(t, x)$ is given)

$$N(t, x) = \min_{(r,y) \in \partial\Omega, \dot{x} \in [Q_k(t,x,\kappa), Q_k(t,x,0)]} N(r, y) + \int_r^t L(t, x, \dot{x}) dt. \tag{7.10}$$

Therefore, when the cumulative flow $N(t, x)$ is known on the boundary of the spatial-temporal domain Ω, then all values inside the domain can be calculated by minimizing the values of $N(r, y) + \int_r^t L(t, x, \dot{x}) dt$ along all valid paths from all boundary points.

(7.10) is a variational principle for the Hamilton-Jacobi equation, (7.1), since $N(t, x)$ is the optimal value subject to variations in the initial data at (r, y) and the path from the initial point to (t, x). The variational principle still works when two characteristic curves cross each other. Fig. 7.1 illustrates the principle in the space-time domain.

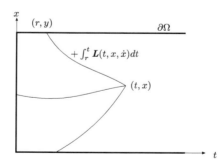

FIGURE 7.1 Illustration of the variational principle.

7.1.3 The Hopf-Lax formula

When the fundamental diagram is both time- and location-independent; i.e., when $q = Q(k)$, (7.7b) leads to $\dot{k} = 0$. That is, k is constant along a characteristic curve, and the characteristic curve is a line with a constant slope

of
$$b = \frac{x-y}{t-r} \tag{7.11}$$

between $Q_k(\kappa)$ and $Q_k(0)$. In this case, (7.10) can be simplified into the following Hopf-Lax formula:

$$N(t,x) = \min_{(r,y)\in\partial\Omega} N(r,y) + (t-r)L\left(\frac{x-y}{t-r}\right), \tag{7.12}$$

where $L(b)$ is the Legendre transformation of the fundamental diagram defined in (3.39), and $\partial\Omega(t,x) = \{(r,y)|(r,y)\in\partial\Omega, b = \frac{x-y}{t-r} \in [Q_k(\kappa), Q_k(0)], t > r\}$ is the subset of boundary points that contribute to $N(t,x)$.

For the triangular fundamental diagram, the Legendre transformation is given by (3.44) and the Hopf-Lax formula is simply written as

$$N(t,x) = \min_{(r,y)\in\partial\Omega(t,x)} B(r,y;t,x), \tag{7.13a}$$

where $\partial\Omega(t,x) = \{(r,y)|(r,y)\in\partial\Omega, b = \frac{x-y}{t-r} \in [-w,u], t > r\}$, and

$$\begin{aligned} B(r,y;t,x) &= N(r,y) + (t-r)L\left(\frac{x-y}{t-r}\right) \\ &= N(r,y) + (t-r)C - (x-y)\kappa_c. \end{aligned} \tag{7.13b}$$

We have the following special cases for $B(r,y;t,x)$:

1. When $b = 0$, $L(0) = C$, and $B(r,y;t,x) = N(r,y) + (t-r)C$. That is, at a fixed location, the cumulative flow is increased by the product of the time interval multiplied and the capacity.
2. When $b = u$, $L(u) = 0$, and $B(r,y;t,x) = N(r,y)$. That is, along a free-flow traveling vehicle, the cumulative flow remains constant.
3. When $u = -w$, $L(-w) = w\kappa = \frac{1}{\tau}$, and $B(r,y;t,x) = N(r,y) + (t-r)w\kappa = N(r,y) - (x-y)\kappa$. That is, along a back-traveling shock wave in congested traffic, the cumulative flow is increased by the product of the traveling distance and the jam density.

Furthermore, for any valid $u \in [-w,u]$ we can decompose the vector $(r,y) \to (t,x)$ $(t > r)$ into two vectors with an intermediate point (x_1,t_1) $(r \leq t_1 \leq t)$, such that $\frac{x_1-y}{t_1-r} = u$, $\frac{x-x_1}{t-t_1} = -w$, and $B(r,y;t,x) = N(r,y) - (x-x_1)\kappa$.

Assume that $N(r,y)$ is given along a road segment between x_1 and $x_2 > x_1$ at time s; i.e., $N(r,y)$ is known along $\partial\Omega_1 = \{(r,y)|x_1 \leq y \leq x_2\}$. Then for (t,x) inside a cone defined by $t - r \geq \frac{x_2-x_1}{u+w}$ and $x_2 - (t-r)w \leq x \leq x_1 + (t-r)u$, $\partial\Omega_1$ is a subset of $\partial\Omega(t,x)$. We refer to the Hopf-Lax formula on the partial domain, $\partial\Omega_1$, as a partial Hopf-Lax formula. In the following we present the simplified partial Hopf-Lax formula for some special cases.

Lemma 7.1.1. *(i) If initially traffic is uncongested; i.e., if $k(r, y) = -\frac{\partial N(r,y)}{\partial y} \leq \kappa_c$ for $y \in [x_1, x_2]$, then*

$$\min_{(r,y) \in \partial \Omega_1} B(r, y; t, x) = B(r, x_1; t, x), \tag{7.14}$$

which is determined by the upstream end point; (ii) If initially traffic is congested; i.e., if $k(r, y) > \kappa_c$ for $y \in [x_1, x_2]$, then

$$\min_{(r,y) \in \partial \Omega_1} B(r, y; t, x) = B(r, x_2; t, x), \tag{7.15}$$

which is determined by the downstream end point.

Proof. From (7.13b), we have $\frac{\partial B(r,y;t,x)}{\partial y} = \frac{\partial N(r,y)}{\partial y} + \kappa_c$. Thus $B(r, y; t, x)$ increases in y, and (7.14) is true, when $-\frac{\partial N(r,y)}{\partial y} \leq \kappa_c$. Thus $B(r, y; t, x)$ decreases in y, and (7.15) is true, when $-\frac{\partial N(r,y)}{\partial y} > \kappa_c$. □

From Lemma 7.1.1 we have the following corollary.

Corollary 7.1.2. *If the initial density satisfies*

$$k(r, y) \leq \kappa_c, \text{ for } y \in [x_1, x_3] \quad \text{and} \quad k(r, y) > \kappa_c, \text{ for } y \in (x_3, x_2] \tag{7.16}$$

where $x_1 \leq x_3 \leq x_2$; i.e., if the upstream section is uncongested, and the downstream section congested, then

$$\min_{(r,y) \in \partial \Omega_1} B(r, y; t, x) = \min \{ B(r, x_1; t, x), B(r, x_2; t, x) \}, \tag{7.17}$$

which is determined by the two end points.

Note (7.16) is the sufficient, but not necessary condition, for (7.17) to hold. Also note that the initial condition in (7.16) can be quite broad: traffic conditions can be uncongested ($x_3 = x_2$) or congested ($x_3 = x_1$) on the whole road segment, or uncongested in the upstream section and congested in the downstream section. From the traditional kinematic wave theory, we can see that rarefaction and shock waves can arise from the initial conditions; but (7.16) excludes congested upstream and uncongested downstream initial conditions, when transonic rarefaction waves can arise. See Fig. 7.2(a) for an illustration of the simplified partial Hopf-Lax formula in this special case.

Assume that $N(r, y)$ is given at y during a time interval $[t_1, t_2]$; i.e., $N(r, y)$ is known along $\partial \Omega_2 = \{(r, y) | t_1 \leq r \leq t_2\}$. Then for (t, x) inside a cone defined by $t > t_2 > t_1$ and $y - (t - t_2)w \leq x \leq y + (t - t_2)u$, $\partial \Omega_2$ is a subset of $\partial \Omega(t, x)$.

7.1 Hamilton-Jacobi equations

Lemma 7.1.3. *When $N(r, y)$ is given at y between t_1 and $t_2 > t_1$, we have*

$$\min_{(r,y)\in\partial\Omega_2} B(r, y; t, x) = B(t_2, y; t, x). \quad (7.18)$$

That is, the earlier boundary data is irrelevant.

Proof. From (7.13b), we have $\frac{\partial B(r,y;t,x)}{\partial r} = \frac{\partial N(r,y)}{\partial r} - C \leq 0$. Thus $B(r, y; t, x)$ decreases in r, and (7.18) is true. □

See Fig. 7.2(b) for an illustration of the simplified partial Hopf-Lax formula in this case.

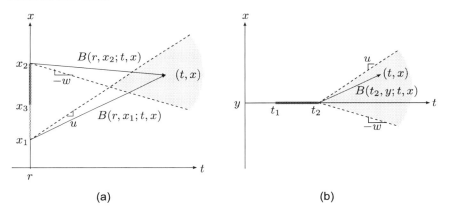

FIGURE 7.2 Illustration of two partial Hopf-Lax formulas with given $N(r, y)$: (a) at a time r; (b) at a location y.

7.1.4 The Riemann problem

In the Riemann problem for the original LWR model, the initial condition is given by (5.26). For the Hamilton-Jacobi equation, (7.1), the corresponding initial condition is given by

$$N_0(x) = \begin{cases} -k_1 x, & x < 0; \\ -k_2 x, & x \geq 0. \end{cases} \quad (7.19)$$

Here we solve $N(t, x)$ ($t > 0$) for the triangular fundamental diagram. Here

$$\partial\Omega(t, x) = \{(0, y) | x - ut \leq y \leq x + wt\}.$$

When $k_1, k_2 \leq \kappa_c$, the initial traffic is uncongested inside $\partial\Omega(t, x)$. From Lemma 7.1.1 we have

$$N(t, x) = B(0, x - ut; t, x) = N_0(x - ut)$$

$$= \begin{cases} -k_1(x - ut), & x < ut; \\ -k_2(x - ut), & x \geq ut. \end{cases}$$

In this case, all vehicles travel at the free-flow speed, and the cumulative flows are constant along the trajectories. The discontinuity in the density also travels along the vehicle at $x = 0$; i.e., the density jumps at $x = ut$.

When $k_1, k_2 > \kappa_c$, the initial traffic is congested inside $\partial\Omega(t, x)$. From Lemma 7.1.1 we have

$$\begin{aligned} N(t, x) &= B(0, x + wt; t, x) = N_0(x + wt) + w\kappa t \\ &= w\kappa t + \begin{cases} -k_1(x + wt), & x < -wt; \\ -k_2(x + wt), & x \geq -wt. \end{cases} \end{aligned}$$

In this case, the discontinuity in the density travels along with $x = -wt$.

When $k_1 < \kappa_c < k_2$, there are the following three sub-cases:

1. When $x \geq ut$, the initial traffic is congested inside $\partial\Omega(t, x)$. From Lemma 7.1.1 we have

$$N(t, x) = B(0, x + wt; t, x) = N_0(x + wt) + w\kappa t = -k_2(x + wt) + w\kappa t.$$

2. When $x \leq -wt$, the initial traffic is uncongested inside $\partial\Omega(t, x)$. From Lemma 7.1.1 we have

$$N(t, x) = B(0, x - ut; t, x) = N_0(x - ut) = -k_1(x - ut).$$

3. When $-wt < x < ut$, the initial traffic is uncongested for $x - ut < y < 0$ and congested for $0 < y < x + wt$ inside $\partial\Omega(t, x)$. From Corollary 7.1.2 we have

$$\begin{aligned} N(t, x) &= \min\{B(0, x - ut; t, x), B(0, x + wt; t, x)\} \\ &= \min\{-k_2(x + wt) + w\kappa t, -k_1(x - ut)\} \\ &= \begin{cases} -k_2(x + wt) + w\kappa t, & x > v_s t; \\ -k_1(x - ut), & x < v_s t, \end{cases} \end{aligned}$$

where $x = v_s t$ solves $-k_2(x + wt) + w\kappa t = -k_1(x - ut)$. Thus

$$v_s = \frac{q_2 - q_1}{k_2 - k_1} \in (-w, u),$$

where $q_1 = uk_1$ and $q_2 = w(\kappa - k_2)$ are the corresponding upstream and downstream initial flow rates.

Combining the three sub-cases, we have the following solution:

$$N(t, x) = \begin{cases} -k_2(x + wt) + w\kappa t, & x > v_s t; \\ -k_1(x - ut), & x < v_s t. \end{cases}$$

In this case, the discontinuity in the density travels along with $x = v_s t$. Therefore the solution is a shock wave, and v_s is the shock wave speed, which is consistent with the shock wave speed obtained for the LWR model in (5.27).

When $k_1 > \kappa_c > k_2$, there are also three sub-cases:

1. When $x \geq ut$, the initial traffic is uncongested inside $\partial \Omega(t, x)$. From Lemma 7.1.1 we have

$$N(t, x) = B(0, x - ut; t, x) = N_0(x - ut) = -k_2(x - ut).$$

2. When $x \leq -wt$, the initial traffic is congested inside $\partial \Omega(t, x)$. From Lemma 7.1.1 we have

$$N(t, x) = B(0, x + wt; t, x) = N_0(x + wt) + tC + wt\kappa_c$$
$$= -k_1(x + wt) + w\kappa t.$$

3. When $-wt < x < ut$, and the initial traffic is congested for $x - ut < y < 0$ and uncongested for $0 < y < x + wt$ inside $\partial \Omega(t, x)$. From Lemma 7.1.1 we have

$$N(t, x) = B(0, 0; t, x) = tC - x\kappa_c.$$

Combining the three sub-cases, we have the following solution:

$$N(t, x) = \begin{cases} -k_2(x - ut), & x \geq ut; \\ tC - x\kappa_c, & -wt < x < ut; \\ -k_1(x + wt) + w\kappa t, & x \leq -wt. \end{cases}$$

In this case, the middle part's density is neither k_1 nor k_2, but the critical density κ_c.

The four cases of Riemann solutions are shown in Fig. 7.3, where the solid arrows show the dependence relations between the initial and final states.

7.2 Newell's simplified kinematic wave model

Newell's simplified kinematic wave model determines traffic conditions inside a homogeneous road section with a triangular fundamental diagram from initial and boundary cumulative flows. That is, the Hamilton-Jacobi formulation of the LWR model, (7.1), is solved with a minimum principle inside a U-shaped spatial-temporal domain $\Omega = [0, L] \times [0, \infty)$ as shown in Fig. 7.4: where the initial conditions, $N_0(x) = N(0, x)$ ($x \in [0, L]$), and boundary conditions, $F(t) = N(0, t)$ and $G(t) = N(L, t)$ ($t \geq 0$), are given. Equivalently, the initial density $k(0, x)$, in-flux $f(t) = \dot{F}(t)$, and out-flux $g(t) = \dot{G}(t)$ are given.

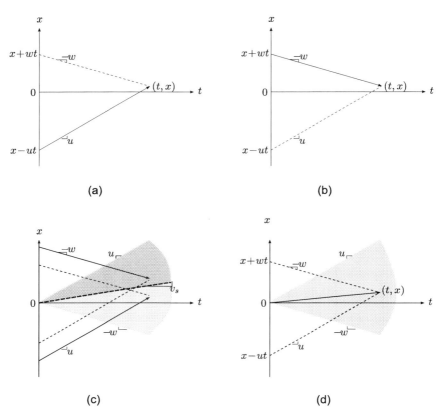

FIGURE 7.3 Four Riemann solutions for the Hamilton-Jacobi equation of the LWR model with the triangular fundamental diagram: (a) $k_1, k_2 \leq \kappa_c$; (b) $k_1, k_2 \geq \kappa_c$; (c) $k_1 < \kappa_c < k_2$; (d) $k_1 > \kappa_c > k_2$.

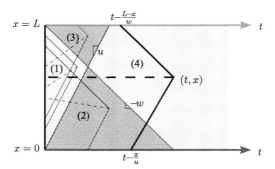

FIGURE 7.4 Newell's model for a U-shaped spatial-temporal domain with Dirichlet boundary conditions.

7.2.1 Derivation

Based on the Hopf-Lax formula, (7.13a), traffic conditions inside the U-shaped spatial-temporal domain can be determined for the four regions inside the domain, as shown in Fig. 7.4.

1. For any point (t, x) in region 1, we denote $x_1 = x - ut$ and $x_2 = x + wt$. Then (7.13a) is equivalent to

$$N(t, x) = \min_{y \in [x_1, x_2]} \{N_0(y) + Ct - (x - y)\kappa_c\}. \tag{7.20a}$$

2. For any point (t, x) in region 2, we denote $x_2 = x + wt$. From Lemma 7.1.3, (7.13a) is equivalent to

$$N(t, x) = \min_{y \in (0, x_2]} \{N_0(y) + Ct - (x - y)\kappa_c, F\left(t - \frac{x}{u}\right)\}. \tag{7.20b}$$

3. For any point (t, x) in region 3, we denote $x_1 = x - ut$. From Lemma 7.1.3, (7.13a) is equivalent to

$$N(t, x) = \min_{y \in [x_1, L)} \{N_0(y) + Ct - (x - y)\kappa_c,$$
$$G\left(t - \frac{L - x}{w}\right) + (L - x)\kappa\}. \tag{7.20c}$$

4. For any point (t, x) in region 4, from Lemma 7.1.3, (7.13a) is equivalent to

$$N(t, x) = \min_{y \in (0, L)} \{N_0(y) + Ct - (x - y)\kappa_c, F\left(t - \frac{x}{u}\right),$$
$$G\left(t - \frac{L - x}{w}\right) + (L - x)\kappa\}. \tag{7.20d}$$

The solutions of $N(t, x)$ in Regions 2, 3, and 4 imply that

Region 2: $\quad F(t) \leq N_0(wt) + \kappa wt,$ \hfill (7.21a)

Region 3: $\quad G(t) \leq N_0(L - ut),$ \hfill (7.21b)

Region 4: $\quad F(t) \leq G\left(t - \frac{L}{w}\right) + \kappa L, G(t) \leq F\left(t - \frac{L}{u}\right),$ \hfill (7.21c)

which are the necessary conditions for the initial-boundary problem to be well-posed. That is, if (7.21) is violated, then Newell's simplified model is not well defined.

In particular, when (7.16) is satisfied for the initial traffic density; i.e., when there is no transonic rarefaction wave initially, from Corollary 7.1.2 we have the following simplified version of (7.20):

Region 1: $N(t, x) = \min\{N_0(x - ut), N_0(x + wt) + \kappa wt\},$ \hfill (7.22a)

144　　　　　　　7. Newell's simplified kinematic wave model

$$\text{Region 2: } N(t,x) = \min\{F\left(t - \frac{x}{u}\right), N_0(x+wt) + \kappa wt\}, \quad (7.22\text{b})$$

$$\text{Region 3: } N(t,x) = \min\{N_0(x-ut),$$
$$G\left(t - \frac{L-x}{w}\right) + (L-x)\kappa\}, \quad (7.22\text{c})$$

$$\text{Region 4: } N(t,x) = \min\{F\left(t - \frac{x}{u}\right),$$
$$G\left(t - \frac{L-x}{w}\right) + (L-x)\kappa\}. \quad (7.22\text{d})$$

When the initial traffic density is constant at k_0, then $F(0) = G(0) + k_0 L$, and $N_0(x) = G(0) + k_0(L-x)$. Thus we have the following solutions:

$$\text{Region 1: } N(t,x) = F(0) - k_0 x + \min\{k_0 ut, (\kappa - k_0)wt\}, \quad (7.23\text{a})$$

$$\text{Region 2: } N(t,x) = \min\{F\left(t - \frac{x}{u}\right),$$
$$F(0) - k_0 x + (\kappa - k_0)wt\}, \quad (7.23\text{b})$$

$$\text{Region 3: } N(t,x) = \min\{F(0) + (ut-x)k_0,$$
$$G\left(t - \frac{L-x}{w}\right) + (L-x)\kappa\}, \quad (7.23\text{c})$$

$$\text{Region 4: } N(t,x) = \min\{F\left(t - \frac{x}{u}\right),$$
$$G\left(t - \frac{L-x}{w}\right) + (L-x)\kappa\}. \quad (7.23\text{d})$$

Furthermore, when the road is initially empty, then $N_0(x) = F(0) = G(0)$, and (7.22) is equivalent to

$$\text{Region 1: } N(t,x) = G(0), \quad (7.24\text{a})$$

$$\text{Region 2: } N(t,x) = F\left(t - \frac{x}{u}\right), \quad (7.24\text{b})$$

$$\text{Region 3: } N(t,x) = G(0), \quad (7.24\text{c})$$

$$\text{Region 4: } N(t,x) = \min\{F\left(t - \frac{x}{u}\right),$$
$$G\left(t - \frac{L-x}{w}\right) + (L-x)\kappa\}. \quad (7.24\text{d})$$

7.2.2 Properties

We focus on the solution of $N(t,x)$ inside region 4 when (7.16) is satisfied. Introducing two new variables, $N_1(t,x)$ and $N_2(t,x)$, which are defined by

$$N_1(t,x) = F\left(t - \frac{x}{u}\right), \quad (7.25)$$

7.2 Newell's simplified kinematic wave model

$$N_2(t, x) = G\left(t - \frac{L-x}{w}\right) + (L-x)\kappa. \quad (7.26)$$

Then inside region 4,

$$N(t, x) = \min\{N_1(t, x), N_2(t, x)\}. \quad (7.27)$$

Clearly both $N_1(t, x)$ and $N_2(t, x)$ are non-decreasing in t, as both $F(t)$ and $G(t)$ are non-decreasing. Without loss of generality, we assume that they are strictly increasing; i.e., the boundary flow-rates are always positive. We also assume that both $N_1(t, x)$ and $N_2(t, x)$ are differentiable with respect to x and t; i.e., $F(t)$ and $G(t)$ are differentiable. In the following lemma, we demonstrate that they are non-increasing in x.

Lemma 7.2.1. *At a time instant, both $N_1(t, x)$ and $N_2(t, x)$ are non-increasing in x, and their partial derivatives satisfy the following relation:*

$$-\kappa \leq \frac{\partial N_2(t, x)}{\partial x} \leq -\kappa_c \leq \frac{\partial N_1(t, x)}{\partial x} \leq 0. \quad (7.28)$$

This is equivalent to saying that the density is under-critical (between 0 and κ_c) along $N_1(t, x)$ and over-critical (between κ_c and κ) along $N_2(t, x)$.

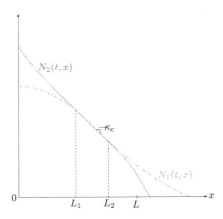

FIGURE 7.5 Three sub-segments on a road.

Lemma 7.2.2. *At any time instant t, the road segment $x \in [0, L]$ can be divided into three sub-segments, as shown in Fig. 7.5:*

1. *For $x \in [0, L_1)$, $N_1(t, x) < N_2(t, x)$, and $N(t, x) > N(t, L_1)$. In this sub-segment, traffic is strictly under-critical.*
2. *For $x \in [L_1, L_2]$, $N_1(t, x) = N_2(t, x)$, and $N(t, x) \in [N(t, L_2), N(t, L_1)]$. In this sub-segment, traffic is critical.*

3. For $x \in (L_2, L]$, $N_1(t, x) > N_2(t, x)$, and $N(t, x) < N(t, L_2)$. In this sub-segment, traffic is strictly over-critical.

Two special cases are when $L_1 = L_2 = 0$ when the whole road is congested or $L_1 = L_2 = L$ when the whole road is uncongested.

7.2.3 Newell's model in the trajectory coordinates

In the trajectory coordinates, the location and order of vehicle i are denoted by $X_i(t)$ and $\phi_i(t)$: $\phi_i(t) = N(t, X_i(t))$ (see (4.7) for the definition), respectively.

We denote $X_i^1(t)$ and $X_i^2(t)$ as the respective inverse functions of $N_1(t, x)$ and $N_2(t, x)$; i.e., $X_i^1(t)$ satisfies

$$N_1(t, X_i^1(t)) = \phi_i(t), \qquad (7.29)$$

and $X_i^2(t)$ satisfies

$$N_2(t, X_i^2(t)) = \phi_i(t). \qquad (7.30)$$

Without loss of generality, here we assume that $\frac{\partial N_1(t,x)}{\partial x} < 0$, which implies that $\frac{\partial N_2(t,x)}{\partial x} < 0$ from Lemma 7.2.1. Thus, both $N_1(t, x)$ and $N_2(t, x)$ are strictly decreasing, and $X_i^1(t)$ and $X_i^2(t)$ are well-defined and can be calculated from $\phi_i(t)$ as well as the boundary cumulative flows.

Then, we can state the following theorem.

Theorem 7.2.3. At t, the location of the ith vehicle on the road segment, $X_i(t)$, is given by

$$X_i(t) = \min\left\{X_i^1(t), X_i^2(t)\right\}. \qquad (7.31)$$

In particular, for FIFO traffic, $\phi_i(t) = i$, and we can label vehicles such that $i = n = N(t, X(t, n))$. That is, $X_i(t) = X(t, i)$, which is the inverse function of $N(t, x)$. In this case, Newell's simplified kinematic wave model in the trajectory coordinates becomes

$$X(t, n) = \min\{X_1(t, n), X_2(t, n)\}, \qquad (7.32)$$

where $X_1(t, n)$ and $X_2(t, n)$ are the inverse functions of $N_1(t, x)$ and $N_2(t, x)$, respectively: $N_1(t, X_1(t, n)) = n$, and $N_2(t, X_2(t, n)) = n$.

For non-FIFO but steady traffic, in which $k(t, x) = k$, $v(t, x) = v$, and $v_i(t) = v_i$ are all constant. Then from the definition of $\phi_i(t)$ we have

$$\phi_i'(t) = k(v - v_i),$$

which is also constant. Thus, we have

$$\phi_i(t) = k(v - v_i)t + b_i, \qquad (7.33)$$

where b_i is the initial order. In this case, the cumulative flows are

$$F(t) = kvt + kL,$$
$$G(t) = kvt,$$

which lead to

$$N_1(t, x) = kv(t - \frac{x}{u}) + kL = kvt + k(L - x\frac{v}{u}),$$
$$N_2(t, x) = kv(t - \frac{L-x}{w}) + (L-x)\kappa = kvt + (\kappa - k\frac{v}{w})(L - x).$$

It can be shown that

$$N(t, x) = \min\{N_1(t, x), N_2(t, x)\} = kvt + k(L - x), \tag{7.34}$$

since in the triangular fundamental diagram

$$k\frac{v}{u} \leq k \leq \kappa - k\frac{v}{w},$$

and at least one of the equal sign holds; in other words,

$$\min\{k - k\frac{v}{u}, \kappa - k\frac{v}{w} - k\} = 0. \tag{7.35}$$

Hence,

$$X_i^1(t) = \frac{u}{kv}(kv_i t - b_i) + \frac{u}{v}L,$$
$$X_i^2(t) = \frac{w}{\kappa w - kv}(kv_i t - b_i) + L.$$

It can also be shown that for $X_i(t) \in [0, L]$

$$X_i(t) = \min\{X_i^1(t), X_i^2(t)\} = v_i t + L - \frac{b_i}{k}. \tag{7.36}$$

Verification of these results is assigned in Problem 7.7.

7.3 Queueing dynamics on a road segment

According to Lemma 7.2.2, traffic conditions on a road segment at any time can be divided into three sub-segments (from upstream to downstream): strictly under-critical (SUC), critical (C), and strictly over-critical (SOC). Then the traffic conditions on a homogeneous road without internal bottlenecks can be illustrated by Fig. 7.6. In the figure, the downstream red (top shaded) region represents the SOC states, the middle yellow (middle shaded) region represents the C states, and the upstream blank region represents the SUC states. The duration of the red (top shaded) region is the peak period.

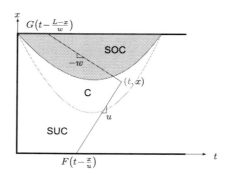

FIGURE 7.6 Traffic dynamics on a road segment.

Then the results in Section 5.3 can be extended here for a relatively large t. In the SUC and C states,

$$N(t, x) = N_0(x - ut) = F\left(t - \frac{x}{u}\right) = N_1(t, x).$$

In the SOC and C states,

$$N(t, x) = N_0(x + wt) + \frac{1}{\tau}t = G\left(t - \frac{L-x}{w}\right) + (L-x)\kappa = N_2(t, x).$$

Theorem 7.3.1. *For traffic dynamics illustrated in Fig. 7.6, we can demonstrate that (i) $N_1(t, x) < N_2(t, x)$ for SUC states; (ii) $N_1(t, x) = N_2(t, x)$ for C states; and (iii) $N_1(t, x) > N_2(t, x)$ for SOC states. Thus, $N(t, x) = \min\{N_1(t, x), N_2(t, x)\}$. This is another way to derive Newell's simplified kinematic wave model.*

If we define the queue length as the length of the strictly over-critical region and denote it by $B(t)$, then $N_1(t, x) > N_2(t, x)$ for $x \in (L - B(t), L]$.

Thus, given observed initial and boundary conditions, we can estimate how the queue grows and dissipates during a peak period.

Notes

Note 7.1. *Traditionally Hamilton-Jacobi equations usually arise from the classical mechanics problems (Goldstein et al., 2002) or the optimal control problems (Bardi and Capuzzo-Dolcetta, 2008). Refer to (Evans, 1998, Chapter 3) for the characteristic equations of a Hamilton-Jacobi equation.*

Note 7.2. *Refer to (Lanczos, 1986) for a basic introduction of the calculus of variations used in Section 7.1.2.*

Note 7.3. *Note that (7.10) is a more general variational principle than that in (Newell, 1993), where only characteristic paths are considered. Such a variational principle was derived in (Daganzo, 2005a,b), where numerical methods were also presented. The variational principle has been applied to study the macroscopic fundamental diagrams in a signalized network in (Daganzo and Geroliminis, 2008). The four Riemann solutions in Section 7.1.4 verify that Newell's minimization principle is equivalent to the Hopf-Lax formula.*

Note 7.4. *In Newell's simplified kinematic wave model, the initial and boundary cumulative flows are given; thus it can only handle boundary conditions of Dirichlet type. However, the Cauchy-Dirichlet problem may not be well-posed under general initial and boundary conditions for a Hamilton-Jacobi equation or a hyperbolic conservation law (Bardos et al., 1979). Here (7.21) is the necessary condition for Newell's model to be well-posed. In some studies, e.g., (Daganzo, 1997a, Section 4.4.3) and (Laval et al., 2012), (7.22d) in region 4 is also referred to as the three detector problem or method. Note that the solution of $N(t,x)$ in region 4 depends on the initial conditions when (7.16) is violated.*

Note 7.5. *Hopf-Lax formula for the Hamilton-Jacobi equation of the LWR model was also systematically discussed in (Claudel and Bayen, 2010). In particular, it was simplified for piecewise linear fundamental diagrams and piecewise linear initial cumulative flows. In (Laval and Leclercq, 2013) the Hopf-Lax formulas for the equivalent Hamilton-Jacobi equations in the three coordinates were derived from general, triangular, and piecewise linear fundamental diagrams.*

Note 7.6. *(7.31) is a new formulation of Newell's simplified kinematic wave model in the trajectory coordinates, since the independent variable is time t and vehicle ID i. Note that this formulation is different from Newell's simplified car-following model (G.F. Newell, 2002), which is also in the trajectory coordinates: (i) In the car-following model a vehicle's trajectory is determined by its leader's trajectory, but by the boundary cumulative flows in (7.31); (ii) more importantly the FIFO principle is always observed in the car-following model, but not necessarily in (7.31). These unique features make the new formulation, (7.31), a perfect model for estimating vehicles' trajectories from the boundary cumulative flows and vehicles' entry and exit times. The results in Sections 7.2.2 and 7.2.3 were from (Rey et al., 2019), where (7.31) was used to estimate vehicles' trajectories from the boundary cumulative flows and the vehicle orders.*

Problems

Problem 7.1. *Derive the Hopf-Lax formula of the Hamilton-Jacobi formulation of the LWR model with the Greenshields fundamental diagram: $Q_k = uk(1 - \frac{k}{\kappa})$.*

Problem 7.2. *Solve the Riemann problem of the Hamilton-Jacobi formulation of the LWR model with the Greenshields fundamental diagram.*

Problem 7.3. *Demonstrate that (7.22d) in region 4 may be wrong when (7.16) is violated. Hint: Consider a special initial-boundary value problem related to the following Riemann initial condition:*

$$N_0(x) = \begin{cases} -\kappa(x - \frac{L}{2}), & x < \frac{L}{2}; \\ 0, & x > \frac{L}{2}. \end{cases}$$

The corresponding boundary flows are

$$G(t) = \begin{cases} 0, & t \leq \frac{L}{2u}; \\ C(t - \frac{L}{2u}), & t > \frac{L}{2u}; \end{cases}$$

$$F(t) = \frac{\kappa L}{2} + \begin{cases} 0, & t \leq \frac{L}{2w}; \\ C(t - \frac{L}{2w}), & t > \frac{L}{2w}. \end{cases}$$

Problem 7.4. *Prove Lemma 7.2.1.*

Problem 7.5. *Prove Lemma 7.2.2.*

Problem 7.6. *Prove Theorem 7.2.3. Hint: Use Lemma 7.2.2.*

Problem 7.7. *For the triangular fundamental diagram, show that (7.35) is true. Verify that both (7.34) and (7.36) are correct.*

Problem 7.8. *Prove Theorem 7.3.1 with results in Section 5.3.*

CHAPTER 8

The Link Transmission Model (LTM)

This chapter introduces the Link Transmission Model of network traffic dynamics, in which each link is homogeneous with unifiable and FIFO traffic flow. In particular, with the triangular fundamental diagram, the Link Transmission Model complements Newell's simplified kinematic wave model. The Link Transmission Model tracks the evolution of the boundary cumulative flows of a link, given the initial cumulative flows and external demand and supply. Newell's simplified kinematic wave model then can be used to calculate traffic conditions inside each link. Hence, the Link Transmission Model is fundamentally different from the Cell Transmission Model, which tracks the evolution of the densities on a link, given the initial densities and external demand and supply.

This chapter is organized as follows. Section 8.1 defines the basic variables. Section 8.2 introduces link demand, supply, queue, and vacancy. Section 8.3 formulates the continuous version of the Link Transmission Model. Section 8.4 presents the discrete version of the Link Transmission Model. Section 8.5 applies the Link Transmission Model to describe traffic dynamics on a simple signalized road network. Section 8.6 defines the stationary states on a road segment and solves the simple boundary value problem with constant external demand and supply.

8.1 Basic variables

For a link $x \in [0, L]$, as illustrated in Fig. 8.1, the following variables are defined in the Link Transmission Model:

1. $N_0(x) = N(0, x)$ is the initial cumulative flow;
2. $d^-(t)$ is the external upstream demand, the maximum rate of flow that wishes to enter the link;
3. $s^+(t)$ is the external downstream supply, the maximum rate of flow the downstream link(s) can accept from the link;

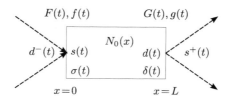

FIGURE 8.1 Variables in the Link Transmission Model.

4. $F(t) = N(t, 0)$ is the cumulative in-flow; $G(t) = N(t, L)$ the cumulative out-flow;
5. $f(t)$ and $g(t)$ are the in- and out-fluxes;
6. $s(t)$ and $d(t)$ are the link supply and demand, which define the maximum rate of flow the link can receive and send, respectively;
7. $\sigma(t)$ and $\delta(t)$ are the link vacancy and queue, which are the intermediate variables.

Here $N_0(x)$ defines the initial condition, $d^-(t)$ and $s^+(t)$ are the boundary conditions, and the other variables are unknown. Therefore, the Link Transmission Model describes how to solve the unknown variables from the initial and boundary conditions.

From the definitions and simple junction models for the upstream and downstream boundaries, we have the following four ordinary differential equations:

$$\frac{dF(t)}{dt} = f(t) = \min\{d^-(t), s(t)\}, \tag{8.1a}$$

$$\frac{dG(t)}{dt} = g(t) = \min\{d(t), s^+(t)\}, \tag{8.1b}$$

where both $d(t)$ and $s(t)$ will be defined by the initial and cumulative flows, $N_0(x)$, $F(t)$, and $G(t)$.

8.2 New link variables: link demand, supply, queue, and vacancy

Following the definitions of demand and supply of a cell in Section 6.2.1, we define the demand of a link between $x \in [0, L]$ at time t, $d(t)$, as the out-flux with an empty downstream link, and the supply, $s(t)$, as the in-flux with a jammed upstream link. Here we assume that $F(r)$ and $G(r)$ are known for $r \in [0, t]$, and $N_0(x)$ are known for $x \in [0, L]$.

1. To define the link demand, we extend the such that $x \in [0, \infty)$, but the downstream link is empty; i.e., $k(t, x) = 0$ for $x > L$. In this case, we first apply the Hopf-Lax formula to calculate the out-flow $\hat{G}(t + \Delta t)$ for

8.2 New link variables

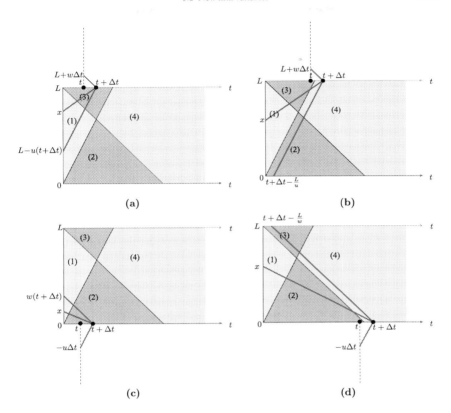

FIGURE 8.2 Definitions of link demands and supplies.

a small $\Delta t > 0$ with a pan-shaped spatial-temporal domain shown in Fig. 8.2(a) and (b), and then define the link demand $d(t)$ by

$$d(t) = \lim_{\Delta t \to 0^+} \frac{\hat{G}(t+\Delta t) - G(t)}{\Delta t}. \tag{8.2a}$$

From Lemma 7.1.3, we can obtain $\hat{G}(t+\Delta t)$ as follows:
(a) If $t + \Delta t \leq \frac{L}{u}$, as shown in Fig. 8.2(a),

$$\hat{G}(t+\Delta t) = \min_{x \in [L-(t+\Delta t)u, L)} \{B(0, x; t+\Delta t, L),$$
$$G(t) + C\Delta t\}. \tag{8.2b}$$

(b) If $t + \Delta t > \frac{L}{u}$, as shown in Fig. 8.2(b),

$$\hat{G}(t+\Delta t) = \min_{x \in (0, L)} \{F(t+\Delta t - \frac{L}{u}),$$
$$B(0, x; t+\Delta t, L), G(t) + C\Delta t\}. \tag{8.2c}$$

As expected, $\hat{G}(t + \Delta t)$ only depends on traffic conditions inside link a. Note that $\hat{G}(t + \Delta t)$ is the ideal value of $G(t + \Delta t)$ when the downstream is empty, but the two values may not be the same in reality when the downstream is not.

2. To define the link supply, we extend the link such that $x \in (-\infty, 0]$, but upstream part is jammed; i.e., $k(t, x) = \kappa$ for $x < 0$. In this case, we first apply the Hopf-Lax formula to calculate the in-flow $\hat{F}(t + \Delta t)$ for a small $\Delta t > 0$ with a pan-shaped spatial-temporal domain shown in Fig. 8.2(c) and (d), and then define the link supply $s(t)$ by

$$s(t) = \lim_{\Delta t \to 0^+} \frac{\hat{F}(t + \Delta t) - F(t)}{\Delta t}. \qquad (8.3a)$$

From Lemmas 7.1.1 and 7.1.3, we can obtain $\hat{F}(t + \Delta t)$ as follows:

(a) If $t + \Delta t \leq \frac{L}{w}$, as shown in Fig. 8.2(c),

$$\hat{F}(t + \Delta t) = \min_{x \in (0, (t+\Delta t)w]} \{B(0, x; t + \Delta t, 0), \\ F(t) + C\Delta t\}. \qquad (8.3b)$$

(b) If $t + \Delta t > \frac{L}{w}$, as shown in Fig. 8.2(d),

$$\hat{F}(t + \Delta t) = \min_{x \in (0, L)} \{G(t + \Delta t - \frac{L}{w}) + \kappa L, \\ B(0, x; t + \Delta t, 0), F(t) + C\Delta t\}. \qquad (8.3c)$$

Again, $\hat{F}(t + \Delta t)$ only depends on traffic conditions inside link a. Note that $\hat{F}(t + \Delta t)$ is the ideal value of $F(t + \Delta t)$ when the upstream is jammed, but the two values may not be the same in reality when the upstream is not jammed.

In the discussions hereafter, we assume that (7.16) is satisfied; i.e., there exists no initial transonic rarefaction wave on a link. Then from Corollary 7.1.2 $\hat{G}(t + \Delta t)$ and $\hat{F}(t + \Delta t)$ can be simplified as follows:

$$\hat{G}(t + \Delta t) = \begin{cases} \min\{N_0(L - u(t + \Delta t)), G(t) + C\Delta t\}, & t + \Delta t \leq \frac{L}{u}; \\ \min\{F(t + \Delta t - \frac{L}{u}), G(t) + C\Delta t\}, & t + \Delta t > \frac{L}{u}; \end{cases}$$

$$\hat{F}(t + \Delta t) = \begin{cases} \min\{N_0(w(t + \Delta t)) + (t + \Delta t)\kappa w, \\ \quad F(t) + C\Delta t\}, & t + \Delta t \leq \frac{L}{w}; \\ \min\{G(t + \Delta t - \frac{L}{w}) + \kappa L, \\ \quad F(t) + C\Delta t\}, & t + \Delta t > \frac{L}{w}. \end{cases}$$

8.2 New link variables

Then from (8.2a) and (8.3a), the link demand and supply can be re-written as:

$$d(t) = \begin{cases} \min\left\{k(0, L-ut)u + \frac{\delta(t)}{\epsilon}, C\right\}, & t \leq \frac{L}{u}; \\ \min\left\{f(t-\frac{L}{u}) + \frac{\delta(t)}{\epsilon}, C\right\}, & t > \frac{L}{u}; \end{cases} \quad (8.4a)$$

$$s(t) = \begin{cases} \min\left\{\kappa w - k(0, wt)w + \frac{\sigma(t)}{\epsilon}, C\right\}, & t \leq \frac{L}{w}; \\ \min\left\{g(t-\frac{L}{w}) + \frac{\sigma(t)}{\epsilon}, C\right\}, & t > \frac{L}{w}, \end{cases} \quad (8.4b)$$

where ϵ is a hyperreal infinitesimal number:

$$\epsilon = \lim_{\Delta t \to 0^+} \Delta t. \quad (8.5)$$

Two new variables, including the link queue size, $\delta(t)$, and the link vacancy size, $\sigma(t)$, are defined as follows:

$$\delta(t) = \begin{cases} N_0(L-ut) - G(t), & t \leq \frac{L}{u}; \\ F(t - \frac{L}{u}) - G(t), & t > \frac{L}{u}; \end{cases} \quad (8.6a)$$

$$\sigma(t) = \begin{cases} N_0(wt) + \kappa wt - F(t), & t \leq \frac{L}{w}; \\ G(t - \frac{L}{w}) + \kappa L - F(t), & t > \frac{L}{w}. \end{cases} \quad (8.6b)$$

From (8.6), we have $\delta(0) = \sigma(0) = 0$; from (7.21), we can see that both $\delta(t)$ and $\sigma(t)$ are non-negative. Note that the link queue size may not equal the number of vehicles on the road, which is $F(t) - G(t)$; rather, it equals the number of queued (delayed) vehicles, which would have left the link without congestion. For $t > \frac{L}{u}$, without congestion, the number of exiting vehicles at t is $F\left(t - \frac{L}{u}\right)$, but the actual number of exiting vehicles is $G(t)$.

For examples, we consider a steady state on the link with density k and flow-rate q. Then there are the following two cases.

1. For under-critical traffic, $k \leq \kappa_c$, and $q = uk$. If we denote $F(t) = qt$, then $G(t) = q(t - \frac{L}{u})$. In this case, for large t, the queue size $\delta(t) = 0$, and the vacancy size $\sigma(t) = \frac{u+w}{w}(\kappa_c - k)L$. Thus, the vacancy size linearly decreases with the density and reaches zero at the critical density. In addition, for an empty road, the vacancy size equals κL, which is the maximum number of vehicles on the road.

2. For over-critical traffic, $k \geq \kappa_c$, and $q = w(\kappa - k)$. If we denote $F(t) = qt$, then $G(t) = q(t - \frac{L}{v})$, where $v = w(\frac{\kappa}{k} - 1)$. In this case, for large t, $\sigma(t) = 0$, and the queue size is $\delta(t) = \frac{u+w}{u}(k - \kappa_c)L$. Thus, the queue size linearly increases with the density and reaches zero at the critical density. In addition, for a jammed road, the queue size equals κL, which is the maximum number of vehicles on the road.

In the following we consider two special cases of (7.16):

1. When the initial traffic density is constant on the link; i.e., when $k(0, x) = k$ for $x \in [0, L]$, we have

$$\delta(t) = \begin{cases} kut + G(0) - G(t), & t \leq \frac{L}{u}; \\ F(t - \frac{L}{u}) - G(t), & t > \frac{L}{u}; \end{cases} \quad (8.7a)$$

$$\sigma(t) = \begin{cases} (\kappa - k)wt + F(0) - F(t), & t \leq \frac{L}{w}; \\ G(t - \frac{L}{w}) + \kappa L - F(t), & t > \frac{L}{w}; \end{cases} \quad (8.7b)$$

$$d(t) = \begin{cases} \min\left\{ku + \frac{\delta(t)}{\epsilon}, C\right\}, & t \leq \frac{L}{u}; \\ \min\left\{f(t - \frac{L}{u}) + \frac{\delta(t)}{\epsilon}, C\right\}, & t > \frac{L}{u}; \end{cases} \quad (8.7c)$$

$$s(t) = \begin{cases} \min\left\{(\kappa - k)w + \frac{\sigma(t)}{\epsilon}, C\right\}, & t \leq \frac{L}{w}; \\ \min\left\{g(t - \frac{L}{w}) + \frac{\sigma(t)}{\epsilon}, C\right\}, & t > \frac{L}{w}. \end{cases} \quad (8.7d)$$

2. When the link is initially empty; i.e., when $k(0, x) = 0$ for $x \in [0, L]$, we have $\delta(t) = 0$ for $t \leq \frac{L}{u}$, and $d(t) = 0$ for $t \leq \frac{L}{u}$; $\sigma(t) \geq (\kappa w - C)t \geq 0$ for $t \leq \frac{L}{w}$, and $s(t) \geq \min\{\kappa w, C\} = C$ for $t \leq \frac{L}{w}$. In this case, from (8.6) and (8.4) we have the following demand and supply functions:

$$\delta(t) = \begin{cases} 0, & t \leq \frac{L}{u}; \\ F(t - \frac{L}{u}) - G(t), & t > \frac{L}{u}; \end{cases} \quad (8.8a)$$

$$\sigma(t) = \begin{cases} \kappa wt + F(0) - F(t), & t \leq \frac{L}{w}; \\ G(t - \frac{L}{w}) + \kappa L - F(t), & t > \frac{L}{w}; \end{cases} \quad (8.8b)$$

$$d(t) = \begin{cases} 0, & t \leq \frac{L}{u}; \\ f(t - \frac{L}{u}), & \text{if } F(t - \frac{L}{u}) = G(t), t > \frac{L}{u}; \\ C, & \text{if } F(t - \frac{L}{u}) > G(t), t > \frac{L}{u}; \end{cases} \quad (8.8c)$$

$$s(t) = \begin{cases} C, & t \leq \frac{L}{w}; \\ g(t - \frac{L}{w}), & \text{if } F(t) = G(t - \frac{L}{w}) + \kappa L, t > \frac{L}{w}; \\ C, & \text{if } F(t) < G(t - \frac{L}{w}) + \kappa L, t > \frac{L}{w}. \end{cases} \quad (8.8d)$$

8.3 Continuous Link Transmission Model

Thus, the Link Transmission Model is defined by (8.1), coupled with the link demand and supply. As the link demand and supply are computed from historical cumulative flows, the Link Transmission Model is a system of delay differential equation, which is also of an infinite number of dimensions, as the LWR model.

The unknown state variables in (8.1) are the boundary cumulative flows. The Link Transmission Model can also be formulated with the link vacancy and queue as state variables by differentiating (8.6):

$$\frac{d\delta(t)}{dt} = \begin{cases} k_0(L-ut)u - g(t), & t \leq \frac{L}{u}; \\ f(t-\frac{L}{u}) - g(t), & t > \frac{L}{u}; \end{cases} \quad (8.9a)$$

$$\frac{d\sigma(t)}{dt} = \begin{cases} -k_0(wt)w + \kappa w - f(t), & t \leq \frac{L}{w}; \\ g(t-\frac{L}{w}) - f(t), & t > \frac{L}{w}, \end{cases} \quad (8.9b)$$

where $f(t) = \min\{d^-(t), s(t)\}$, $g(t) = \min\{d(t), s^+(t)\}$, and $d(t)$ and $s(t)$ are defined by $\delta(t)$ and $\sigma(t)$ as in (8.4).

With the definitions of the link demand and supply functions, the Link Transmission Model can be readily extended for network traffic flow, by applying the junction models in the Cell Transmission Model, as discussed in Section 6.6. In the junction models, the upstream links' demands and the downstream links' supplies are used to determine the boundary fluxes. On link i, the commodity flow-rate proportions at $x_i = 0$ and $x_i = L_i$ are denoted by $\hat{\gamma}_{i \to j}(t)$ and $\gamma_{i \to j}(t)$, respectively. The travel time on link i for vehicles exiting the link at t is denoted by $\Upsilon_i(t)$; i.e.,

$$G_i(t) = F_i(t - \Upsilon_i(t)). \quad (8.10)$$

Then for FIFO traffic we have

$$\gamma_{i \to j}(t) = \hat{\gamma}_{i \to j}(t - \Upsilon_i(t)).$$

8.4 Discrete Link Transmission Model

Note that for a real number $y \geq 0$

$$\frac{y}{\epsilon} = \begin{cases} 0, & y = 0; \\ +\infty, & y > 0. \end{cases}$$

However, if we extend the domain of y to include hyperreal numbers, $\frac{y}{\epsilon}$ could be a real number even if $y > 0$. For example, if $y = \epsilon$, then $\frac{y}{\epsilon} = 1$. This can be illustrated in the discrete version, $\epsilon = \Delta t$, and $\frac{y}{\epsilon}$ could be finite when y is in the order of Δt.

The discrete link demand and supply can be calculated from the initial and boundary flows:

1. When the initial traffic density is constant on the link; i.e., when $k(0, x) = k$ for $x \in [0, L]$, we have

$$d(t)\Delta t = \hat{G}(t+\Delta t) - G(t)$$
$$\begin{cases} \min\{ku(t+\Delta t)+G(0)-G(t), C\Delta t\}, & t \leq \frac{L}{u}; \\ \min\{F(t+\Delta t-\frac{L}{u})-G(t), C\Delta t\}, & t > \frac{L}{u}; \end{cases}$$
$$s(t)\Delta t = \hat{F}(t+\Delta t) - F(t)$$
$$\begin{cases} \min\{(\kappa-k)w(t+\Delta t)+F(0)-F(t), C\Delta t\}, & t \leq \frac{L}{w}; \\ \min\{G(t+\Delta t-\frac{L}{w})-F(t), C\Delta t\}, & t > \frac{L}{w}. \end{cases}$$

2. When the link is initially empty; i.e., when $k(0,x)=0$ for $x \in [0,L]$, we have

$$d(t)\Delta t = \begin{cases} 0, & t \leq \frac{L}{u}; \\ \min\{F(t+\Delta t-\frac{L}{u})-G(t), C\Delta t\}, & t > \frac{L}{u}; \end{cases} \quad (8.11a)$$

$$s(t)\Delta t = \begin{cases} C\Delta t, & t \leq \frac{L}{w}; \\ \min\{G(t+\Delta t-\frac{L}{w})-F(t), C\Delta t\}, & t > \frac{L}{w}. \end{cases} \quad (8.11b)$$

(8.1) can be discretized by

$$F(t+\Delta t) = F(t) + \min\{d^-(t)\Delta t, s(t)\Delta t\},$$
$$G(t+\Delta t) = G(t) + \min\{d(t)\Delta t, s^+(t)\Delta t\},$$

which can be used to update the boundary cumulative flows.

The derivation of the discrete version with link queue and vacancy as state variables is assigned as Problem 8.1.

The computational cost of the Link Transmission Model is only proportional to the number of time-steps, as links are not divided into cells. Therefore, the Link Transmission Model is much more efficient than the Cell Transmission Model. However, the Link Transmission Model achieves the efficiency by omitting traffic conditions inside each road, which can be obtained through Newell's simplified kinematic wave model.

Compared with the Cell Transmission Model, however, the Link Transmission Model only applies for homogeneous links and multi-commodity traffic that is unifiable and FIFO.

The Link Transmission Model only works for two types of boundary conditions: Dirichlet and periodic. But it does not work for Neumann boundary conditions, since the internal supply at the downstream boundary and the internal demand at the upstream boundary inside a link are not available in the model.

But we can solve the Riemann problem with the Link Transmission Model under the following initial condition,

$$N_0(x) = \begin{cases} \frac{L}{2}k_2 + (\frac{L}{2}-x)k_1, & x \in [0, \frac{L}{2}); \\ (L-x)k_2, & x \in [\frac{L}{2}, L], \end{cases} \quad (8.12)$$

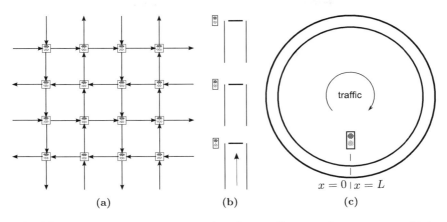

FIGURE 8.3 (a) A homogeneous network with insignificant turning movements; (b) An infinite street with identical roads; (c) A signalized ring road.

where k_1 is the upstream initial density, and k_2 the downstream initial density. The upstream external demand $d^-(t) = D(k_1)$, and the downstream external supply $s^+(t) = S(k_2)$. Then we can solve the Link Transmission Model to obtain the boundary cumulative flows $F(t)$ and $G(t)$, from which Newell's simplified kinematic wave model can be used to determine the cumulative flows inside the U-shaped domain. Note that, when $k_1 > \kappa_c > k_2$; i.e., when the Riemann problem is solved by a transonic rarefaction wave, the demand and supply functions need to include the initial state at $x = \frac{L}{2}$.

8.5 Homogeneous signalized road networks

In this section we apply the Link Transmission Model to describe traffic dynamics on a homogeneous signalized road networks, as shown in Fig. 8.3(a), in which all links are homogeneous and identical with the same length (L) and triangular fundamental diagram ($Q(k) = \min\{uk, w(\kappa - k)\}$). In addition, the signals have the same settings for the north-south or east-west streets, and the number of turning movements are insignificant and ignored. Then the north-south streets (similarly, the east-west streets) can be considered separately, as illustrated in Fig. 8.3(b). Furthermore, we assume that the in- and out-fluxes are almost the same at any time. Then the traffic dynamics on each link are equivalent to those on a signalized ring road in Fig. 8.3(c), for which the boundary conditions are periodic.

Assuming that the ring road's initial density is constant at k. Under the periodic boundary conditions, we also have

$$F(t) = G(t) + kL, \qquad (8.13)$$

8. The Link Transmission Model (LTM)

$$f(t) = g(t). \tag{8.14}$$

Let $G(0) = N_0(L) = 0$. Then $F(0) = N_0(0) = kL$. Thus, (8.7) can be simplified as follows:

$$\delta(t) = \begin{cases} kut - G(t), & t \leq \frac{L}{u}; \\ G(t - \frac{L}{u}) - G(t) + kL, & t > \frac{L}{u}; \end{cases} \tag{8.15a}$$

$$\sigma(t) = \begin{cases} (\kappa - k)wt - G(t), & t \leq \frac{L}{w}; \\ G(t - \frac{L}{w}) - G(t) + (\kappa - k)L, & t > \frac{L}{w}; \end{cases} \tag{8.15b}$$

$$d(t) = \begin{cases} \min\left\{ku + \frac{\delta(t)}{\epsilon}, C\right\}, & t \leq \frac{L}{u}; \\ \min\left\{g(t - \frac{L}{u}) + \frac{\delta(t)}{\epsilon}, C\right\}, & t > \frac{L}{u}; \end{cases} \tag{8.15c}$$

$$s(t) = \begin{cases} \min\left\{(\kappa - k)w + \frac{\sigma(t)}{\epsilon}, C\right\}, & t \leq \frac{L}{w}; \\ \min\left\{g(t - \frac{L}{w}) + \frac{\sigma(t)}{\epsilon}, C\right\}, & t > \frac{L}{w}. \end{cases} \tag{8.15d}$$

In addition, we have

$$\frac{d}{dt}G(t) = g(t). \tag{8.16}$$

At the intersection, the boundary flux is determined by the following model

$$g(t) = b(t) \cdot \min\{d(t), s(t)\}, \tag{8.17}$$

where $b(t)$ equals 1 in the effective green interval and 0 in the effective red interval. If we denote the cycle length by B and the effective green ratio by π, then we can define

$$b(t) = \begin{cases} 1, & \frac{t}{B} \in i + [0, \pi], i = 0, 1, 2, \cdots \\ 0, & \text{otherwise.} \end{cases} \tag{8.18}$$

That is, each cycle starts with an effective green interval with a length of πB and ends with an effective red interval with a length of $(1 - \pi)B$.

Clearly, (8.15)-(8.17) form the Link Transmission Model for the signalized ring road in Fig. 8.3(c). The model comprises six equations with six unknown variables, $G(t), g(t), \delta(t), \sigma(t), d(t),$ and $s(t)$. The initial condition is $G(0) = 0$.

8.6 Stationary states on a link

Stationary states on a link were defined with the Cell Transmission Model in Section 6.3; they can also be defined with the Link Transmission Model.

8.6.1 Definition

For a constant flow-rate q^*, the stationary cumulative flow on a road segment with $x \in [0, L]$ can be written as

$$N^*(t, x) = q^* t + N_0^*(x), \qquad (8.19)$$

where

$$N_0^*(x) = \begin{cases} N_0^*(0) - K\left(\frac{q^*}{C}\right) x, & x \in [0, yL]; \\ N_0^*(L) + (L - x) K\left(\frac{C}{q^*}\right), & x \in [yL, L], \end{cases} \qquad (8.20)$$

where $N_0^*(0) = N_0^*(L) + yLK\left(\frac{q^*}{C}\right) + (1 - y)LK\left(\frac{C}{q^*}\right)$. Clearly, when $y = 0$, the road segment is stationary at an over-critical state; when $y = 1$, the road segment is stationary at an under-critical state; when $y \in (0, 1)$, the road segment is stationary at a zero-speed shock wave.

Theorem 8.6.1. *On a stationary link, the in- and out-fluxes are equal and time-independent:*

$$f^*(t) = g^*(t) = q^*, \qquad (8.21)$$

and both queue and vacancy sizes are also time-independent

$$\delta^* = (1 - y)(1 - \frac{q^*}{C})\kappa L, \qquad (8.22a)$$

$$\sigma^* = y(1 - \frac{q^*}{C})\kappa L. \qquad (8.22b)$$

The link demand and supply are

$$d^* = \min\{q^* + \frac{\delta^*}{\epsilon}, C\}, \qquad (8.23a)$$

$$s^* = \min\{q^* + \frac{\sigma^*}{\epsilon}, C\}. \qquad (8.23b)$$

8.6.2 Simple boundary value problem for a road segment

For a road segment with $x \in [0, L]$, we consider the following simple boundary value problem where the external upstream demand and downstream supply are both constant at d^- and s^+, respectively, as illustrated in Fig. 8.1. Intuitively, the system reaches a stationary state after a long time.

In addition to the four equations in (8.22) and (8.23), we have

$$q^* = \min\{d^-, s^*\}, \qquad (8.24a)$$
$$q^* = \min\{d^*, s^+\}, \qquad (8.24b)$$

which are the stationary in- and out-fluxes at the upstream and downstream boundaries, respectively. Hence, we have six equations with six unknown variables: $q^*, \delta^*, \sigma^*, d^*, s^*$, and y, where ϵ, C, κ, and L are given.

Combining (8.23) and (8.24), we have

$$q^* = \min\{d^-, q^* + \frac{\sigma^*}{\epsilon}, C\}, \qquad (8.25a)$$
$$q^* = \min\{q^* + \frac{\delta^*}{\epsilon}, C, s^+\}. \qquad (8.25b)$$

We solve the problem in the following cases.

1. When $\min\{d^-, s^+\} \geq C$; i.e., when both the external demand and supply are not smaller than the road capacity, we have $q^* = s^* = d^*$, since $s^* \leq C$ and $d^* \leq C$ from their definitions in (8.23). Further from (8.23), we have $d^* = s^* = C$, since $\delta^* \geq 0$ and $\sigma^* \geq 0$ from (8.22). Then from (8.22) we have $\delta^* = \sigma^* = 0$, and y can take any value between 0 and 1, since $K\left(\frac{q^*}{C}\right) = K\left(\frac{C}{q^*}\right) = \kappa_C$. In this case, the road segment is stationary at the critical density.

2. When $d^- < \min\{s^+, C\}$, from (8.24) we have $q^* = d^* < s^+$, since $q^* \leq d^- < s^+$. From (8.23) we have $\delta^* = 0$, since $d^* < C$. Thus, from (8.22) we have $y = 1$ and $\sigma^* = (1 - \frac{q^*}{C})\kappa L \gg \epsilon$. Then from (8.23b) we have $s^* = C$, and from (8.24a) we have $q^* = d^-$. In this case, the road segment is stationary at a strictly under-critical state with a density of $K\left(\frac{d^-}{C}\right)$.

3. When $s^+ < \min\{d^-, C\}$, from (8.24) we have $q^* = s^* < d^-$, since $q^* \leq s^+ < d^-$. From (8.23) we have $\sigma^* = 0$, since $s^* < C$. Thus, from (8.22) we have $y = 0$ and $\delta^* = (1 - \frac{q^*}{C})\kappa L \gg \epsilon$. Then from (8.23a) we have $d^* = C$, and from (8.24b) we have $q^* = s^+$. In this case, the road segment is stationary at a strictly under-over state with a density of $K\left(\frac{C}{s^+}\right)$.

4. When $d^- = s^+ < C$, from (8.25) we have either $q^* = d^- = s^+$ or $q^* < d^- = s^+$. In the latter sub-case, either $\delta^* \gg \epsilon$ or $\sigma^* \gg \epsilon$, which implies that either $d^* = C$ or $s^* = C$ from (8.23), and either $q^* = d^-$ or $q^* = s^+$ from (8.24). Thus, the only possible solution is $q^* = d^- = s^+$. Furthermore, y can take any value between 0 and 1. When $y = 0$, the road segment is stationary at a strictly over-critical state; when $y = 1$, the road segment is stationary at a strictly under-critical state; when $y \in (0, 1)$, the road segment is stationary at a zero-speed shock wave.

Note that it is possible that the interface of the zero-speed shock wave is very close to the boundaries such that the distance is smaller than a cell size (which can be set at $u\epsilon$). That is, it is possible that y is a hyper-real number.

In all the above cases the stationary flow-rate is determined by

$$q^* = \min\{d^-, C, s^+\}, \qquad (8.26)$$

which can be directly proved without enumerating all the four cases. This is assigned as Problem 8.7.

Notes

Note 8.1. *The term of link transmission model was first introduced in (Yperman et al., 2006; Yperman, 2007), which presented the definition of the discrete demand and supply in (8.11). The most critical difference between the link transmission model and the cell transmission model is that the demand and supply are defined from cumulative flows, not the density. To the best of our knowledge, however, continuous link demand and supply defined from cumulative flows were first presented (Kuwahara and Akamatsu, 2001), where the definition is equivalent to (8.4), but the discrete version is different from (8.11).*

Note 8.2. *The link transmission model is closely related to Newell's simplified kinematic wave model, since both of them are based on the Hopf-Lax formula (or more generally the variational principle and Newell's minimization principle); but they are different, as the demand and supply were not defined in Newell's model explicitly. The link transmission model plus Newell's simplified kinematic wave is equivalent to the Cell Transmission Model, in the sense that they both seek to calculate the traffic conditions in a road network, given initial and boundary conditions.*

Note 8.3. *The link queue size was first defined in (Newell, 1993), which states that:*

> This is not the number of vehicles in the "physical queue", the number between the shock wave and the bottleneck; it is simply the difference between the number of vehicles which would like to pass x_i by t and the number which actually pass.

The link vacancy size was introduced in (Jin, 2015b), along with the continuous formulation of link demand and supply.

Problems

Problem 8.1. *Derive the discrete Link Transmission Model with the link vacancy and queue as unknown state variables, (8.9).*

Problem 8.2. Let the time-step size be Δt, write down the discrete Link Transmission Model for a signalized ring road. The continuous version is given in (8.15)-(8.17).

Problem 8.3. For a signalized ring road, let $L = 1200$ m, $u = 20$ m/s, $w = 5$ m/s, $\kappa = 1/7$ veh/m, $B = 60$ s, and $\pi = 0.5$. For $\Delta t = 1$ s and $k = \kappa_c = \frac{1}{5}\kappa$, numerically solve and plot the six variables in (8.15)-(8.17) until $E = 3600$ s. Also plot the moving average flow-rate $\phi(t) = \frac{G(t)}{t}$ for $t > 0$.

Problem 8.4. With the same set-up as in Problem 8.3 except that k varies from 0 to κ. For each k, the final moving average is denoted by $\Phi(k)$. Plot the diagram of k and $\Phi(k)$. This approximates the network fundamental diagram.

Problem 8.5. Prove Theorem 8.6.1.

Problem 8.6. (8.21) is a necessary condition for the traffic on a link to be stationary. Is it also sufficient? Why or why not?

Problem 8.7. Show that (8.26) is true directly from (8.22)-(8.25) without listing the four cases.

CHAPTER

9

Newell's simplified car-following model

Chapter 7 focuses on the equivalent Hamilton-Jacobi equation of the LWR model in the flow coordinates for a road segment without transonic rarefaction waves. With the triangular fundamental diagram, Newell's simplified kinematic wave model can predict traffic conditions inside the road segment from initial and boundary flows. An equivalent model in the trajectory coordinates was also derived. Such models make use of global information and are able to predict traffic conditions at a time and location without knowing the local information. Even though not applicable to transonic rarefaction waves, they are efficient for road and network level applications when integrated with the Link Transmission Model in Chapter 8.

However, such global models cannot be extended to incorporate more realistic, local interactions among vehicles, such as bounded acceleration and deceleration. This chapter discusses Newell's simplified car-following model, which is the local, approximate version of the LWR model in the trajectory coordinates. This model can be derived from the Hamilton-Jacobi equation as in Section 7.1 or the LWR model as in Section 5.3.

Section 9.1 derives Newell's simplified car-following model. Section 9.2 discusses the model's properties and presents its equivalent formulations. Section 9.3 applies the model to solve the simple acceleration and braking problems.

9.1 Derivation

In the trajectory coordinates, the Hamilton-Jacobi equation for the LWR model on a homogeneous road is given by (see Section 9.1)

$$X_t = W(-X_n), \qquad (9.1)$$

9. Newell's simplified car-following model

which is equivalent to the following hyperbolic conservation equation (with $z = -X_n$)

$$z_t + W(z)_n = 0. \tag{9.2}$$

(9.2) is the formulation of the LWR model in the flow-coordinates as shown in 5.1.

Note that $v = X_t$. The characteristic ordinary differential equations are

$$\dot{n} = W_z(z), \tag{9.3a}$$
$$\dot{z} = 0, \tag{9.3b}$$
$$\dot{X} = W(z) - zW_z(z), \tag{9.3c}$$
$$v = W(z). \tag{9.3d}$$

In (9.3), the first equation defines the characteristic curve $(t, n(t))$ in the time-vehicle plane, where $W_z(z)$ is the characteristic wave speed; the second equation is derived from the first equation and (9.2) and shows that the spacing z is constant along the characteristic curve; the third equation determines vehicle n's trajectory along the characteristic curve; and the fourth equation determines the speed.

For the triangular fundamental diagram,

$$W(z) = \min\{u, \frac{1}{\tau}(z - \zeta)\}, \tag{9.4}$$

the characteristic wave speed $\dot{n}$ is between 0 and $\frac{1}{\tau}$, and the Legendre transformation is

$$L(b) = \max_{z \in [\zeta, \infty)} \min\{u, \frac{1}{\tau}(z - \zeta)\} - bz = u - b\zeta_c, \tag{9.5}$$

where the critical spacing $\zeta_c = \zeta + u\tau$. The speed-spacing relation and its Legendre transformation are shown in Fig. 9.1. In Fig. 9.1(a), the thick curve illustrates the speed-spacing relation, and the dashed lines are for bz. From the figure we can see that the maximum value of $W(z) - bz$ occurs at $z = \zeta_c$; thus, $L(b) = u - b\zeta_c$. From Fig. 9.1(b), we can see that $L(0) = u$, $L\left(\frac{1}{\tau}\right) = -w = -\frac{\zeta}{\tau}$, and $L(C) = 0$, since $C = u\kappa_c = \frac{u}{\zeta_c}$.

The Hopf-Lax formula can be written as

$$X(t, n) = \min_{(r, y) \in \partial \Omega(t, n)} B(r, y; t, n), \tag{9.6}$$

where the relevant boundary values for (t, n) are on $\partial \Omega(t, n) = \{(r, y) | (r, y) \in \partial \Omega, b = \frac{n-y}{t-r} \in [0, \frac{1}{\tau}], t > r\}$, and

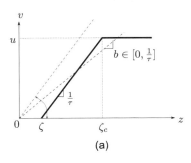 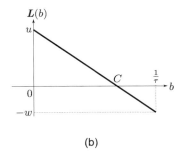

FIGURE 9.1 The speed-spacing relation and its Legendre transformation.

$$B(r, y; t, n) = X(r, y) + (t - r)L\left(\frac{n - y}{t - r}\right)$$
$$= X(r, y) + (t - r)u - (n - y)\zeta_c. \quad (9.7)$$

If we let $r = t - \Delta t$, then $y \in [n - \Delta n, n]$, where $\Delta n = \frac{1}{\tau}\Delta t$, and the Hopf-Lax formula can be written as

$$X(t, n) = \min_{y \in [n - \Delta n, n]} X(t - \Delta t, y) + u\Delta t - (n - y)(\zeta + u\tau).$$

If we assume that the spacing between vehicles $n - \Delta n$ and n is constant at $t - \Delta t$; i.e., if $z(t - \Delta t, y) = X(t - \Delta t, n - \Delta n) - X(t - \Delta t, n)$ for $y \in [n - \Delta n, n]$, then $X(t - \Delta t, y)$ is linear in y, and we have

$$X(t, n) = \min\{X(t - \Delta t, n) + u\Delta t, X(t - \Delta t, n - \Delta n) - \zeta \Delta n\}. \quad (9.8)$$

Further if we let $\Delta t = \tau$, then $\Delta n = 1$ and the above equation can be written as

$$X(t, n) = \min\{X(t - \tau, n) + u\tau, X(t - \tau, n - 1) - \zeta\}. \quad (9.9)$$

A heuristic derivation was given in Section 5.3.

(9.9) is Newell's simplified car-following model. In the model, vehicle n's location at t is determined by either its location at $t - \tau$ plus a free-flow travel distance, $u\tau$, or the location of its leader, vehicle $n - 1$, at $t - \tau$ minus the jam spacing ζ. The model is illustrated in Fig. 9.2 in both (t, n) and (t, x) coordinates. Fig. 9.2(a) shows that the location of vehicle n at t is determined by those of vehicles n and $n - 1$ at $t - \tau$, along the thick lines, which represent the characteristic curves in the (t, n) plane. Fig. 9.2(b) shows that $X(t, n)$ is determined by the smaller one of $X(t - \tau, n) + u\tau$ and $X(t - \tau, n - 1) - \zeta$.

With a small time-step size, Δt, (9.8) is the continuum version of Newell's simplified car-following model in the (t, n) plane. Fig. 9.2(a) il-

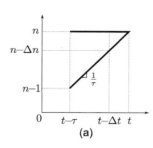 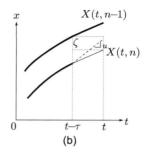

FIGURE 9.2 Illustration of Newell's simplified car-following model in (a) time-vehicle plane and (b) time-distance plane.

lustrates the model in the (t, n) plane. In this model, traffic flow is a continuum of sub-vehicles of Δn.

9.2 Properties

In Newell's car-following model, either the original version in (9.9) or the continuum version in (9.8), vehicle n's location at t depends on its leader's (vehicle $n - 1$ in (9.9) or $n - \Delta n$ in (9.8)) location at an earlier time not by its follower's (vehicle $n + 1$ or $n + \Delta n$). Thus, Newell's simplified car-following model satisfies the anisotropic property. This is different from isotropic systems in which molecules and particles can interact in different directions. Hence such models are also called follow-the-leader models.

In such anisotropic models, the spacing $z(t, n) = -\frac{\partial X(t,n)}{\partial n}$ is discretized implicitly:

$$z(t, n) = \frac{X(t, n - \Delta n) - X(t, n)}{\Delta n}, \tag{9.10}$$

which leads to $z(t, n) = X(t, n - 1) - X(t, n)$ for $\Delta n = 1$.

In this section we analyze the properties of (9.9).

9.2.1 First-order principles

When the forward-traveling principle is satisfied, vehicles do not travel backwards, and vehicle $n - 1$'s location at t is at least $X(t - \tau, n - 1)$, when it stops. Then we can show that Newell's simplified car-following model satisfies the collision-free condition, (3.21), in the following theorem. This is consistent with Tort law that the following vehicle needs to take "Duty of Care".

Theorem 9.2.1. *Newell's simplified car-following model satisfies the collision-free condition, (3.21), at t, if it is satisfied at $t - \tau$.*

Proof. If, at $t - \tau$, the collision-free condition is satisfied, then

$$z(t - \tau, n) = X(t - \tau, n - 1) - X(t - \tau, n) \geq \zeta.$$

Then as $X(t, n - 1) \geq X(t - \tau, n - 1)$, we have

$$z(t, n) = X(t, n - 1) - X(t, n) \geq X(t - \tau, n - 1) - X(t, n).$$

Since $X(t, n) \leq X(t - \tau, n - 1) - \zeta$ from (9.9), we have $z(t, n) \geq \zeta$. That is, the second term on the right-hand side of (9.9) leads to the collision-free principle. □

If we define the speed of vehicle n at t by

$$v(t, n) = \frac{X(t, n) - X(t - \tau, n)}{\tau}, \tag{9.11}$$

which is an implicit discretization of $v(t, n) = \frac{\partial X(t,n)}{\partial t}$, from (9.9) we then have

$$v(t, n) = \min\{u, \frac{z(t - \tau, n) - \zeta}{\tau}\}. \tag{9.12}$$

Hence the first term on the right-hand side of (9.9) leads to $v(t, n) \leq u$; that is, Newell's model satisfies the speed limit principle.

Furthermore, (9.12) shows that the speed is always maximized in Newell's model, subject to constraints by the speed limit and collision-free principles.

In steady states, $v(t, n) = v$ and $z(t, n) = z = \frac{1}{k}$ are both constant, and (9.12) leads to

$$v = \min\{u, \frac{z - \zeta}{\tau}\}, \tag{9.13}$$

which is the speed-spacing relation in the triangular fundamental diagram.

Thus, Newell's simplified car-following model is consistent with the collision-free, forward-traveling, speed limit, maximum speed, and fundamental diagram principles discussed in Chapter 3.

9.2.2 Equivalent formulations

In Newell's simplified car-following model, traffic states are always in equilibrium. When $v(t, n) = u$, it is in the under-critical regime; when

$v(t,n) = \frac{z(t-\tau,n)-\zeta}{\tau} < u$ in (9.12), it is in the strictly over-critical regime. Equivalently, in the latter case,

$$X(t,n) = X(t-\tau, n-1) - \zeta.$$

Taking the derivative with respect to t on both sides, we obtain the following equation:

$$v(t,n) = v(t-\tau, n-1). \tag{9.14}$$

That is, vehicle n's speed equals vehicle $n-1$'s speed at an earlier time. Furthermore, we have

$$a(t,n) = a(t-\tau, n-1). \tag{9.15}$$

Thus a small disturbance (acceleration or deceleration) in the speed of vehicle $n-1$ is propagated to vehicle n at a later time, without amplifying or reducing the oscillation magnitude. This suggests that Newell's car-following model is string stable, but not asymptotically stable, for a platoon of vehicles. In addition, if the leader's acceleration and deceleration rates are bounded, then the follower's too.

Newell's simplified car-following model, (9.9), can also be written as

$$X(t+\tau, n) = \min\{X(t,n) + u\tau, X(t, n-1) - \zeta\}, \tag{9.16}$$

which leads to (assuming constant speed between t and $t+\tau$)

$$v(t+\tau_1, n) \equiv \frac{X(t+\tau, n) - X(t,n)}{\tau}$$
$$= \min\{u, \frac{X(t, n-1) - X(t,n) - \zeta}{\tau}\}, \tag{9.17}$$

with $\tau_1 \in [0, \tau]$. (9.17) is a special case of the following car-following model with a general speed-spacing relation $v = W(z)$,

$$v(t+\tau_1, n) = W(X(t, n-1) - X(t,n)). \tag{9.18}$$

That is, (9.17) corresponds to (9.18) with the triangular fundamental diagram.

(9.17) can be discretized with a smaller time-step size $\Delta t \le \tau$ if we let $v(t+\tau_1, n) = \frac{X(t+\Delta t, n) - X(t,n)}{\Delta t}$ for $\tau_1 \in [0, \Delta t]$. That is, Newell's simplified car-following model can be approximated by

$$X(t+\Delta t, n) = X(t,n) + \Delta t \cdot \min\{u, \frac{X(t, n-1) - X(t,n) - \zeta}{\tau}\}, \tag{9.19}$$

which is equivalent to

$$X(t+\Delta t, n) = \min\{X(t,n) + u\Delta t,$$
$$(1 - \frac{\Delta t}{\tau})X(t,n) + \frac{\Delta t}{\tau}(X(t, n-1) - \zeta)\}. \quad (9.20)$$

In particular, when $\Delta t = \tau$, (9.19) is equivalent to (9.9). Even with a small Δt, (9.19) is different from (9.8), since the former still uses information of vehicle $n-1$ not $n - \Delta n$. In this sense, (9.19) is a (time-)continuous version of Newell's simplified car-following model.

It is straightforward to show that (9.19) or (9.20) satisfies all first-order principles defined in Chapter 3. This is assigned as Problem 9.1.

9.3 Applications

In this section we apply Newell's simplified car-following model to solve simple accelerating and braking problems at a signalized intersection, when the traffic signal turns green and red respectively. Both problems are the special cases of the simple lead vehicle problem discussed in Section 4.2.

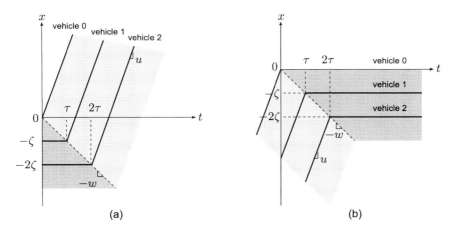

FIGURE 9.3 Illustration of the simple (a) acceleration and (b) deceleration problems.

9.3.1 Simple accelerating problem (queue discharge problem)

Consider the following simple accelerating problem. Vehicle n ($n = 0, 1, 2, \cdots$) stops at an intersection $X(0,n) = -n\zeta$ (this is the initial condition). Here the stop line is assumed to be at $x = 0$, and vehicles' front bumpers are used as the reference points. At $t = 0$, the signal turns green, and we assume that vehicles' response times are zero.

Then from (9.9), vehicle 0 immediately accelerates to the free-flow speed at τ, its trajectory is given by ($j = 0, 1, 2, \cdots$):

$$X(j\tau, 0) = ju\tau. \tag{9.21}$$

This is the boundary condition.

Vehicle 1's initial location is at $-\zeta$. At τ, from (9.9) we have $X(\tau, 1) = \min\{-\zeta + u\tau, X(0,0) - \zeta\} = -\zeta$. Thus, vehicle 1 stays at the same location during 0 and τ. But at 2τ,

$$X(2\tau, 1) = \min\{-\zeta + u\tau, X(\tau, 0) - \zeta\} = u\tau - \zeta.$$

That is, vehicle 1 accelerates to the free-flow speed at $t = \tau$. After that, it travels at the free-flow speed. Similarly, vehicle 2 accelerates to the free-flow speed at $t = 2\tau$. These vehicles' trajectories are illustrated in Fig. 9.3(a).

The results are consistent with the Riemann solutions with an upstream density of κ and a downstream density of 0 in Section 5.5.4, as this is a transonic rarefaction wave, and the intermediate density of κ_c is from vehicle 0's trajectory to the wave $x = -wt$.

From Fig. 9.3(a) we can also see that the acceleration rate is infinite in Newell's car-following model in this case. It is possible to incorporate the bounded acceleration principle to Newell's simplified car-following model and obtain more realistic solutions for the simple accelerating problem.

9.3.2 Simple braking problem

For a platoon of vehicles traveling at the free-flow speed and with a critical spacing ($\zeta_c = \zeta + u\tau$), if the traffic signal turns red at $t = 0$, and vehicle 0's front bumper stops at the stop line at $x = 0$. Then the initial condition is $X(0, n) = -n\zeta_c$, and the boundary condition is $X(j\tau, 0) = 0$ for $j = 0, 1, 2, \cdots$.

For vehicle 1, its location at $t = \tau$ is given by

$$X(\tau, 1) = \min\{-\zeta_c + u\tau, X(0, 0) - \zeta\} = -\zeta.$$

That is, it travels at the free-flow speed during 0 and τ. But at 2τ, we have

$$X(2\tau, 1) = \min\{-\zeta + u\tau, X(\tau, 0) - \zeta\} = -\zeta.$$

Thus, vehicle 1 stops at τ. Similarly, vehicle 2 stops at 2τ.

Vehicles' trajectories are illustrated in Fig. 9.3(b). The results are consistent with the Riemann solutions in Section 5.5.4. In this case, the upstream density is κ_c, and the downstream density κ; and the Riemann problem is solved by a shock wave with the speed of $-w$.

From Fig. 9.3(b) we can also see that the deceleration can be infinite in Newell's simplified car-following model.

Note that Newell's simplified car-following model is still an approximation of the LWR model and may cause numerical errors. See Problem 9.4 for an example.

Notes

Note 9.1. *Newell's simplified car-following model, (9.9), was first presented in (G.F. Newell, 2002; Daganzo, 2006).*

Note 9.2. *The derivation of Newell's simplified car-following in Section 9.1 was presented in (Laval and Leclercq, 2013).*

Note 9.3. *(9.14) was derived from the LWR model in (Del Castillo, 1996).*

Note 9.4. *String stability of car-following models for a platoon of vehicles was first defined and studied for the General Motors model in (Chandler et al., 1958).*

Note 9.5. *(9.18) was first presented in (Newell, 1961) and studied with an exponential fundamental diagram, where $v = u(1 - e^{-\frac{z-\zeta}{u\tau}})$.*

Note 9.6. *In (Jin and Laval, 2018), the extended version of Newell's simplified kinematic wave model with bounded acceleration was presented and solved for the simple accelerating problem. References on models with bounded acceleration were also provided in the article.*

Problems

Problem 9.1. Demonstrate that (9.19) or (9.20) satisfies all of the first-order principles defined in Chapter 3.

Problem 9.2. With a normalized triangular fundamental diagram, $v = \min\{1, \frac{1}{5}(z-1)\}$, solve Newell's simplified car-following model, (9.9), with the following initial and boundary conditions: initially, vehicle n's location is at $X(0, n) = -n$ for $n = 0, 1, 2, \cdots$; vehicle 0's trajectory is given by $X(t, 0) = t$ for $t \geq 0$. Compare the numerical results with the theoretical solutions with the LWR model.

Problem 9.3. With a normalized triangular fundamental diagram, $v = \min\{1, \frac{1}{5}(z-1)\}$, solve Newell's simplified car-following model, (9.9), with the following initial and boundary conditions: initially, vehicle n's location is at $X(0, n) = -6n$ for $n = 0, 1, 2, \cdots$; vehicle 0's trajectory is given by $X(t, 0) = 0$ for $t \geq 0$. Compare the numerical results with the theoretical solutions with the LWR model.

Problem 9.4. With a normalized triangular fundamental diagram, $v = \min\{1, \frac{1}{5}(z-1)\}$, solve Newell's simplified car-following model, (9.9), with the following initial and boundary conditions: initially, vehicle n's location is at $X(0,n) = -7n$ for $n = 0, 1, 2, \cdots$; vehicle 0's trajectory is given by $X(t,0) = 0$ for $t \geq 0$. Compare the numerical results with the theoretical solutions with the LWR model.

Problem 9.5. With a normalized triangular fundamental diagram, $v = \min\{1, \frac{1}{5}(z-1)\}$, solve the continuum version of Newell's simplified car-following model, (9.8), with $\Delta t = 1$ and the following initial and boundary conditions: initially, vehicle n's location is at $X(0,n) = -7n$ for $n = 0, 1, 2, \cdots$; vehicle 0's trajectory is given by $X(t,0) = 0$ for $t \geq 0$. Compare the numerical results with the theoretical solutions with the LWR model.

Problem 9.6. With a normalized triangular fundamental diagram, $v = \min\{1, \frac{1}{5}(z-1)\}$, solve the continuous version of Newell's simplified car-following model, (9.19), with $\Delta t = 1$ and the following initial and boundary conditions: initially, vehicle n's location is at $X(0,n) = -7n$ for $n = 0, 1, 2, \cdots$; vehicle 0's trajectory is given by $X(t,0) = 0$ for $t \geq 0$. Compare the numerical results with the theoretical solutions with the LWR model.

Problem 9.7. Calibrate the jam density and the shock wave speed in congested traffic from observed vehicle trajectories, for example, in the NGSim data sets.

PART III

Queueing models

All models are wrong, but some are useful. - George E. P. Box

CHAPTER 10

The link queue model

This chapter presents an approximation of the network kinematic wave model. At a time instant, we assume that traffic is steady on a link, and the density is constant at all locations. Then the link demand and supply can be defined from such a link density. With the junction models for the Cell Transmission Model, this leads to a new network traffic flow model. Numerically, such a model is as efficient as the Link Transmission Model, and, thus, more efficient than the Cell Transmission Model. Analytically, the model offers some advantages for solving complicated network traffic flow model, since it comprises ordinary differential equations.

We refer to this model as the link queue model, as vehicles on each link form a queue that is evenly distributed on the link. This is different from the Link Transmission Model (plus Newell's simplified kinematic wave model) or the Cell Transmission Model, as traffic conditions are undifferentiated at different locations, and there is a single queue on the link. It is also different from the point queue model, as the length of the queue equals the link's length. In addition, this is a deterministic queueing model, without considering the stochastic variations in traffic states.

In this model, the traffic conditions are uniform on a link; thus, there is no need to consider the space dimension inside a link. However, the topological characteristics of a network, including the origins, destinations, routes, and links, are still tracked. Thus, the space dimension is simplified in the link queue model.

Section 10.1 defines various variables for a link. Section 10.2 presents equivalent formulations of the link queue model. Section 10.3 discusses the collision-free condition for the link queue model to be well-defined. Section 10.4 solves the stationary states and dynamics for the simple boundary value problem. Section 10.5 presents applications and extensions of the link queue model.

10.1 Link density, demand, and supply

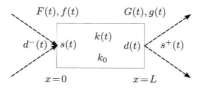

FIGURE 10.1 Variables for the link queue model.

As illustrated in Fig. 10.1, the variables for a link at time t include the cumulative in- and out-flows ($F(t)$ and $G(t)$, respectively), the in- and out fluxes ($f(t)$ and $g(t)$), the internal demand and supply ($d(t)$ and $s(t)$), and the average density $k(t)$. The initial density is k_0, and the boundary conditions include the external demand and supply ($d^-(t)$ and $s^+(t)$).

The link queue model is similar to the Link Transmission Model illustrated in Fig. 8.1, as both consider traffic dynamics on the whole road link with the help of internal and external demands and supplies. However, the link queue model tracks the dynamic changes in the average density, $k(t)$, or equivalently, the number of vehicles $Lk(t)$. More importantly, a link in the link queue model is considered a single unit, and traffic conditions at different locations $x \in [0, L]$ are undifferentiated. But in the Link Transmission Model, we can track traffic conditions at different locations with Newell's simplified kinematic wave model.

10.1.1 Basic relations

Among the seven variables, $F(t)$, $f(t)$, $G(t)$, $g(t)$, $s(t)$, $d(t)$, and $k(t)$, there are the following relationships from their definitions:

$$f(t) = \frac{d}{dt}F(t), \tag{10.1}$$

$$g(t) = \frac{d}{dt}G(t). \tag{10.2}$$

When there are no signals or other types of bottlenecks at the upstream and downstream boundaries, the in- and out-fluxes can be calculated as

$$f(t) = \min\{d^-(t), s(t)\}, \tag{10.3}$$

$$g(t) = \min\{d(t), s^+(t)\}. \tag{10.4}$$

In addition, from the conservation of the number of vehicles on the road we have

$$L\frac{d}{dt}k(t) = f(t) - g(t), \tag{10.5}$$

which is equivalent to

$$Lk(t) = F(t) - G(t). \tag{10.6}$$

Thus, from the initial condition we have $Lk_0 = F(0) - G(0)$.

Among the six equations above, five are independent. We need two more equations to complete the model.

10.1.2 Definitions of link demand and supply

We denote the link fundamental diagram by

$$q = Q(k), \tag{10.7}$$

which is the same as the fundamental diagram at each location for a homogeneous road. The jam density is denoted by κ, and the critical density by κ_c.

Extending the definitions of cell demand and supply in the Cell Transmission Model, we can define the link demand and supply as follows:

$$d(t) = D(k(t)) = Q(\min\{k(t), \kappa_c\}), \tag{10.8a}$$
$$s(t) = S(k(t)) = Q(\max\{k(t), \kappa_c\}). \tag{10.8b}$$

The demand- and supply-density relations are the same as those illustrated in Fig. 6.3(a) in Section 6.2.1.

In particular, demand increases in density and reaches the maximum value of C in over-critical traffic; supply decreases in density and reaches the maximum value of C in under-critical traffic.

In a sense, the link queue model is an approximation of the Cell Transmission Model by assuming all cells have the same density at a time instant. In other words, traffic on a link is always in steady states in the link queue model. This assumption makes the link queue model simpler than the Cell Transmission Model, but it also leads to certain limitations of the former.

10.2 Link queue model

With the definitions of and basic relations among the variables in the preceding section, the link queue model can be written as a system of ordinary differential equations or the corresponding discrete equations. There can be different formulations with respect to different unknown variables.

10.2.1 Continuous version

If we use the average link density $k(t)$ as the unknown variable, the link queue model can be written as the following single equation

$$L\frac{d}{dt}k(t) = \min\{d^-(t), Q(\max\{k(t), \kappa_c\})\} \\ - \min\{Q(\min\{k(t), \kappa_c\}), s^+(t)\}, \quad (10.9)$$

in which $d^-(t)$ and $s^+(t)$ are given as the boundary condition, and $k(0)$ is given as the initial condition.

In contrast, we can also use the cumulative flows, $F(t)$ and $G(t)$, as the unknown variables. In this case, the link queue model comprises of two ordinary differential equations:

$$\frac{d}{dt}F(t) = \min\{d^-(t), Q\left(\max\{\frac{F(t)-G(t)}{L}, \kappa_c\}\right)\}, \quad (10.10a)$$

$$\frac{d}{dt}G(t) = \min\{Q\left(\min\{\frac{F(t)-G(t)}{L}, \kappa_c\}\right), s^+(t)\}, \quad (10.10b)$$

in which $d^-(t)$ and $s^+(t)$ are given as the boundary condition, and $F(0)$ and $G(0)$ are given as the initial condition.

10.2.2 Discrete version

We use Euler's forward method to discretize the differential equations above to obtain the corresponding discrete versions of the link queue model.

With $k(t)$ as the unknown variable, we have the discrete version of (10.9) as

$$k(t+\Delta t) = k(t) + \frac{\Delta t}{L} \cdot [\min\{d^-(t), Q(\max\{k(t), \kappa_c\})\} \\ - \min\{Q(\min\{k(t), \kappa_c\}), s^+(t)\}]. \quad (10.11)$$

With $F(t)$ and $G(t)$ as the unknown variables, we have the discrete version of (10.10) as

$$F(t+\Delta t) = F(t) + \Delta t \cdot \\ \min\{d^-(t), Q\left(\max\{\frac{F(t)-G(t)}{L}, \kappa_c\}\right)\}, \quad (10.12a)$$

$$G(t+\Delta t) = G(t) + \Delta t \cdot \\ \min\{Q\left(\min\{\frac{F(t)-G(t)}{L}, \kappa_c\}\right), s^+(t)\}. \quad (10.12b)$$

10.3 Well-defined and collision-free conditions

In this section we examine under what conditions the link queue model is well-defined. We start with the following definitions.

Definition 10.3.1. *The link queue model is well-defined, if $f(t)$, $g(t)$, $s(t)$, and $d(t)$ are non-negative, and $k(t) \in [0, \kappa]$. Consequently, $F(t)$ and $G(t)$ are non-decreasing in time.*

These conditions are quite straightforward for the link queue model to be physically meaningful. In addition, the external demand and supply should be non-negative. It can be seen that $f(t)$, $g(t)$, $s(t)$, and $d(t)$ are non-negative if and only if $k(t) \in [0, \kappa]$. Therefore, we have the following lemma.

Lemma 10.3.2. *The link queue model is well-defined if and only if $k(t) \in [0, \kappa]$, which is the collision-free condition for the average density.*

Next we examine the collision-free condition for the discrete link queue model in (10.11).

Theorem 10.3.3. *The discrete link queue model, (10.11), is collision-free at $t + \Delta t$ if $k(t) \in [0, \kappa]$, and Δt satisfies the following condition:*

$$\frac{\Delta t}{L} \leq \min\{\min_{k \in [0, \kappa_c]} \frac{1}{V(k)}, \min_{k \in [\kappa_c, \kappa]} \frac{\kappa - k}{Q(k)}\}. \tag{10.13}$$

Proof. At t, $k(t) \in [0, \kappa]$ satisfies the collision-free condition. From (10.11), we have

$$k(t) - \frac{\Delta t}{L} Q(\min\{k(t), \kappa_c\}) \leq k(t + \Delta t) \leq k(t) + \frac{\Delta t}{L} Q(\max\{k(t), \kappa_c\}),$$

where the left equal sign occurs when the external demand $d^-(t) = 0$, but the external supply $s^+(t)$ is very large, and the right equal sign occurs when the external demand $d^-(t)$ is very large, but the external supply $s^+(t) = 0$.

Thus, $k(t + \Delta t) \in [0, \kappa]$ if and only if for any $k(t)$

$$\frac{\Delta t}{L} \leq \frac{k(t)}{Q(\min\{k(t), \kappa_c\})},$$

$$\frac{\Delta t}{L} \leq \frac{\kappa - k(t)}{Q(\max\{k(t), \kappa_c\})},$$

which lead to
$$\frac{\Delta t}{L} \le \min_{k\in[0,\kappa]}\{\frac{k}{Q(\min\{\kappa_c,k\})}, \frac{\kappa-k}{Q(\max\{\kappa_c,k\})}\},$$
or, equivalently (10.13). □

The collision-free condition for the discrete link queue model, (10.13), is similar to that for the Cell Transmission Model, (6.14). Similarly, Theorem 6.2.3 can be extended for the link queue model as follows.

Theorem 10.3.4. *The collision-free condition, (10.13), is equivalent to the CFL (Courant-Friedrichs-Lewy) condition,*
$$\frac{\Delta t}{L} \le \min_{k\in[0,\kappa]} \frac{1}{|Q'(k)|}, \quad (10.14)$$
when (i) the speed-density relation is non-increasing; and (ii) the flow-density relation is concave.

The proof of this theorem is the same as that of Theorem 6.2.3. Thus, it is omitted.

Clearly, for the triangular and Greenshields fundamental diagrams, Theorem 10.3.4 is valid.

10.4 Simple boundary value problem

In this section we consider the simple boundary value problem when the external demand and supply are constant: $d^-(t) = d^-$, and $s^+(t) = s^+$, respectively.

10.4.1 Stationary states

In the link queue model, the traffic system reaches a stationary state when the average density is constant: $k(t) = k^*$. In this case, the internal demand and supply are also constant: $d^* = Q(\min\{k^*, \kappa_c\})$ and $s^* = Q(\max\{k^*, \kappa_c\})$. In addition, the in- and out-fluxes are equal and constant:
$$f^* = g^* = \min\{d^-, s^*\} = \min\{d^*, s^+\}. \quad (10.15)$$

Thus in the stationary states, there are five unknown variables: k^*, d^*, s^*, f^*, and g^*; and there are five equations. In particular, if we can find k^*, all the other four variables can be directly solved.

There the following two types of solutions for k^*.

10.4 Simple boundary value problem

1. When $k^* \leq \kappa_c$; i.e., when the average traffic is under-critical, we have $d^* = Q(k^*)$ and $s^* = C$. In this case, (10.15) leads to

$$\min\{d^-, C\} = \min\{Q(k^*), s^+\},$$

   which is only possible when $s^+ \geq \min\{d^-, C\}$ and $Q(k^*) \geq \min\{d^-, C\}$. Furthermore, we have the following sub-cases:
   (a) When $s^+ > \min\{d^-, C\}$, then $Q(k^*) = \min\{d^-, C\}$, which leads to $k^* = K\left(\frac{\min\{d^-, C\}}{C}\right)$.
   (b) When $s^+ = \min\{d^-, C\}$, then any k^* that satisfies $Q(k^*) \geq s^+ = \min\{d^-, C\}$ is a solution. That is, $k^* \geq K\left(\frac{\min\{d^-, C\}}{C}\right)$ and $k^* \leq \kappa_c$.

2. When $k^* > \kappa_c$; i.e., when the average traffic is strictly over-critical, we have $d^* = C$ and $s^* = Q(k^*)$. In this case, (10.15) leads to

$$\min\{d^-, Q(k^*)\} = \min\{C, s^+\},$$

   which is only possible when $d^- \geq \min\{C, s^+\}$ and $Q(k^*) \geq \min\{C, s^+\}$. Furthermore, we have the following sub-cases:
   (a) When $d^- > \min\{C, s^+\}$, then $Q(k^*) = \min\{C, s^+\}$, which leads to $k^* = K\left(\frac{C}{\min\{C, s^+\}}\right)$.
   (b) When $d^- = \min\{C, s^+\}$, then any k^* that satisfies $Q(k^*) \geq \min\{C, s^+\}$ is a solution. That is, $k^* \leq K\left(\frac{C}{\min\{C, s^+\}}\right)$ and $k^* > \kappa_c$.

It can be verified that, in all cases, the stationary fluxes are

$$f^* = g^* = \min\{d^-, C, s^+\}. \tag{10.16}$$

In addition, we have the following four types of stationary states:

1. When $C \leq \min\{d^-, s^+\}$, the link becomes stationary at the critical density: $k^* = \kappa_c$. In this case, $d^* = s^* = f^* = g^* = C$.
2. When $d^- < \min\{C, s^+\}$, the link becomes stationary at a strictly under-critical state: $k^* = K\left(\frac{d^-}{C}\right)$. In this case, $d^* = f^* = g^* = d^-$, and $s^* = C$.
3. When $s^+ < \min\{d^-, C\}$, the link becomes stationary at a strictly over-critical state: $k^* = K\left(\frac{C}{s^+}\right)$. In this case, $s^* = f^* = g^* = s^+$, and $d^* = C$.
4. When $d^- = s^+ < C$, the link becomes stationary at an intermediate state: $k^* \geq K\left(\frac{d^-}{C}\right)$ and $k^* \leq K\left(\frac{C}{s^+}\right)$. In this case, $d^* \geq d^-$ and $s^* \geq s^+$, and $f^* = g^* = d^- = s^+$.

Compared with the stationary states for the simple boundary value problem in the Link Transmission Model in Section 8.6.2, the stationary states in the link queue model are the same in the boundary fluxes and the average density, but the internal demand and supply are the same except when $d^- = s^+ < C$.

10.4.2 Dynamic solution of a simple boundary value problem

In this subsection, we assume that $d^- = s^+ = C$. In addition, the road is initially empty: $k(0) = 0$. As $d(t) \leq C$ and $s(t) \leq C$, the link queue model, (10.9), can be simplified as (for $k(t) \leq \kappa_c$ and a triangular fundamental diagram)

$$L \frac{d}{dt} k(t) = C - uk(t) = u(\kappa_c - k(t)),$$

which is solved by

$$k(t) = \kappa_c (1 - e^{-\frac{u}{L} t}).$$

Thus,

$$f(t) = C,$$
$$g(t) = uk(t) = C(1 - e^{-\frac{u}{L} t}).$$

Therefore, the density converges to κ_c exponentially, and the out-flux increases to the capacity exponentially.

In contrast, in the LWR model, equivalently, the Cell Transmission and Link Transmission models, a forward-traveling rarefaction wave formed by an upstream density of κ_c and a downstream density of 0 forms on the link and travels at a speed of u. Once the wave reaches the downstream boundary at $\frac{L}{u}$, the whole link becomes stationary at the critical density. Thus, the density on the road is

$$k(t,x) = \begin{cases} 0, & t < \frac{x}{u}; \\ \kappa_c, & t \geq \frac{x}{u}, \end{cases}$$

and

$$f(t) = C,$$
$$g(t) = \begin{cases} 0, & t < \frac{L}{u}; \\ C, & t \geq \frac{L}{u}. \end{cases}$$

Thus, even though both the link queue model and the LWR model have the same stationary states, their dynamics are different. On one hand, the out-flux becomes positive immediately at $t > 0$ in the link queue model, but the first vehicle exits at $\frac{L}{u}$ in the LWR model. On the other hand, the out-flux reaches the capacity at $\frac{L}{u}$ in the LWR model, but it only converges to the capacity exponentially in the link queue model. Therefore, the speed limit principle is violated in the link queue model, and it is an approximation of the LWR model.

10.5 Applications and extensions

10.5.1 Network fundamental diagram on a signalized ring road

In this subsection, we assume that the link is a ring road and there is a signal at the boundary, such that the boundary flux is given by

$$f(t) = g(t) = b(t) \cdot \min\{d(t), s(t)\} = b(t) Q(k(t)), \qquad (10.17)$$

where $b(t)$ equals 1 in the effective green interval and 0 in the effective red interval. For a cycle length of B and an effective green ratio of π, $b(t)$ can be written as

$$b(t) = \begin{cases} 1, & \frac{t}{B} \in i + [0, \pi], i = 0, 1, 2, \cdots; \\ 0, & \text{otherwise.} \end{cases} \qquad (10.18)$$

In the link queue model, the average density is always constant, since (10.9) leads to

$$L \frac{d}{dt} k(t) = f(t) - g(t) = 0.$$

Therefore, given any initial density k, the boundary flux is a periodic function of time, as $b(t)$, and the average flux is

$$\bar{g}(k) = \frac{1}{B} \int_0^B g(t) dt = \pi Q(k). \qquad (10.19)$$

This is the network fundamental diagram for the average flow-density relation, which is illustrated in Fig. 10.2. In the figure, the dashed triangular fundamental diagram is for any point on the link, and the (red) solid triangular fundamental diagram is for the network, which has the same jam and critical densities but a smaller capacity, πC. But the network fundamental diagram with the LWR model can be a trapezoid in the shaded region.

10.5.2 Modified demand function and the queue discharge problem

Consider a link upstream to a signalized intersection, which is initially jammed with queued vehicles. That is, $k(0) = \kappa$. At $t = 0$, the signal turns green, and both external demand and supply are C. In this subsection, we solve the downstream discharge flow-rate, $g(t)$, for such a queue discharge problem, which is a special case of the simple boundary value problem.

With the triangular fundamental diagram, the internal demand and supply are given by

$$d(t) = D(k(t)) = u \min\{\kappa_c, k(t)\},$$

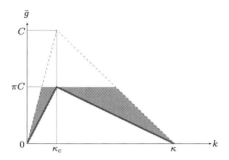

FIGURE 10.2 Network fundamental diagram for a signalized ring road.

$$s(t) = S(k(t)) = w(\kappa - \max\{\kappa_c, k(t)\}).$$

As $k(t) \geq \kappa_c$, we have $d(t) = u\kappa_c = C$, and $s(t) = w(\kappa - k(t))$. Hence, the link queue model, (10.9) can be simplified as

$$L\frac{d}{dt}k(t) = w(\kappa - k(t)) - C = w(\kappa_c - k(t)),$$

which is solved by

$$k(t) = \kappa_c + (\kappa - \kappa_c)e^{-\frac{w}{L}t}.$$

The discharge flow-rate is

$$g(t) = C.$$

That is, the density decreases from the jam density to the critical density exponentially, but the discharge flow-rate is always the capacity. That is, the headway is always the saturation headway. In reality, however, due to the reaction time of the first vehicle and the bounded deceleration, it has been observed that the headways of the first few vehicles are significantly higher than the saturation headway. Hence, the link queue model cannot capture such higher-order effects.

However, if we introduce a modified demand function as

$$\tilde{D}(k(t)) = \min\{uk(t), \tilde{w}(\tilde{\kappa} - k(t))\}, \tag{10.20}$$

which is a new triangular shape. In particular,

$$\tilde{w}(\tilde{\kappa} - \kappa_c) = w(\kappa - \kappa_c),$$

or equivalently,

$$\tilde{w}\tilde{\kappa} - w\kappa = (\tilde{w} - w)\kappa_c; \tag{10.21}$$

that is, the new triangular shape and the triangular fundamental diagram share the same critical density and capacity. Then the link queue model, (10.9) can be simplified as

$$L\frac{d}{dt}k(t) = w(\kappa - k(t)) - \tilde{w}(\tilde{\kappa} - k(t)) = (\tilde{w} - w)(k(t) - \kappa_c),$$

which is solved by

$$k(t) = \kappa_c + (\kappa - \kappa_c)e^{-\frac{w-\tilde{w}}{L}t}.$$

The corresponding discharge flow-rate is

$$g(t) = \tilde{D}(k(t)) = C - \tilde{w}(\kappa - \kappa_c)e^{-\frac{w-\tilde{w}}{L}t}. \quad (10.22)$$

The cumulative flow is

$$G(t) = \int_0^t g(y)dy = Ct - L\frac{\tilde{w}}{w-\tilde{w}}(\kappa - \kappa_c)(1 - e^{-\frac{w-\tilde{w}}{L}t}). \quad (10.23)$$

We denote the time for vehicle n passing the stop line by T_n for $n = 0, 1, 2, \cdots$. Then

$$G(T_n) = n, \quad (10.24)$$

and $T_0 = 0$. Hence we can calculate the headway of vehicle n ($n = 1, 2, \cdots$) as

$$h_n = T_n - T_{n-1}. \quad (10.25)$$

The modified demand function and the corresponding solutions of the queue discharge problem are shown in Fig. 10.3.

Notes

Note 10.1. *The link queue model was first introduced in (Jin, 2012a).*

Note 10.2. *The network fundamental diagram for a signalized ring road with the link queue model was presented in (Jin, 2012a). That with the LWR model was first solved with the variational principle in (Daganzo and Geroliminis, 2008).*

Note 10.3. *The modified demand function was first introduced in (Lebacque, 2002). It was applied to solve the queue discharge problem in (Srivastava et al., 2015), which also calibrated the modified demand function with observed headways at various locations.*

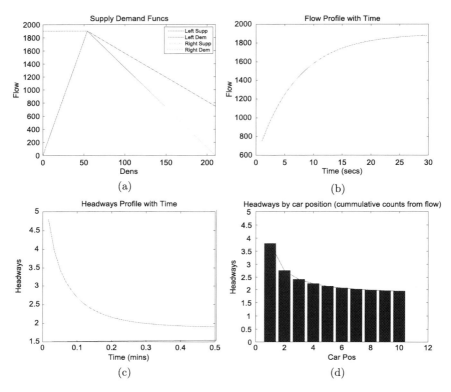

FIGURE 10.3 Queue discharge problem with a modified demand function: (a) modified demand function, (b) discharge flow-rate, (c) continuous headways as a function of time, and (d) the headways by queue positions.

Note 10.4. *The link queue model was applied to study the variable speed limit problem in (Jin and Jin, 2014, 2015). It was applied to study the network fundamental diagram in a signalized network with turning movements in (Gan et al., 2017). In (Gu et al., 2017), the link queue model was used to estimate traffic states in a large road network. In (Lopez et al., 2020), the model was used to analyze the security properties in a signalized road network.*

Problems

Problem 10.1. *Prove Theorem 10.3.4.*

Problem 10.2. *Solve the link queue model with $d^- = 0$, $s^+ = C$, and $k(0) = \kappa$. Compare the results with those of the LWR model under the same initial and boundary conditions. Here we assume the triangular fundamental diagram.*

Problem 10.3. *Observe vehicles' discharging headways at a signalized intersection when the signal turns green and calibrate the parameters in the modified demand function and the corresponding link queue model.*

CHAPTER 11
Point queue model

The link queue model in Chapter 10 approximates the LWR model by assuming the steady state on a link, in which traffic states are location-independent, and all vehicles are evenly distributed on the link. The link queue model violates the speed limit principle. This chapter introduces another approximation of the LWR model (the Link Transmission Model) by assuming that all vehicles are stacked at one point and form a point queue. Thus, in the point queue model the collision-free principle is violated, and the internal supply is infinite, but the internal demand is still well defined, depending on the queue size, and the boundary flow-rate is still bounded by the external supply. Such a point queue model can be extended for network traffic flow, and offers a simple approach to solve the boundary value problem for a point queue and evaluate the impacts of external demand and supply patterns at a single road bottleneck. Thus, the point queue model is very efficient for solving departure time choice and traffic control problems at single bottlenecks or road networks.

Similar to the link queue model, the point queue model also employs a simplified space dimension for a road network. In this model, only the topological characteristics are kept, and each link as a point queue is dimensionless.

Section 11.1 derives the point queue model from the Link Transmission Model. Section 11.2 presents equivalent continuous and discrete formulations of the point queue model. Section 11.3 discusses some properties of the point queue model. Section 11.4 applies the point queue model to study the departure time choice problem at a single bottleneck.

11.1 Derivation

11.1.1 Point queue as a limit of a road segment

For a road segment illustrated in Fig. 11.1, the number of lanes is l, and the length of the road segment is L. If the jam density per lane is κ, then the maximum number of vehicles the road segment can hold is

11. Point queue model

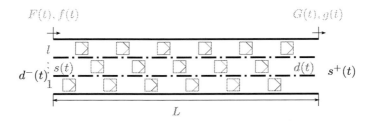

FIGURE 11.1 A road segment and the corresponding boundary value problem.

$\Lambda = lL\kappa$. Vehicles on the road segment form a horizontal queue: in the LWR model, the distribution of vehicles on the road segment may be location-dependent; but in the link queue model, the distribution is even and location-independent.

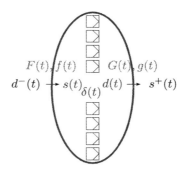

FIGURE 11.2 A point queue and the corresponding boundary value problem.

For a road segment illustrated in Fig. 11.1, the boundary value problem is to solve the boundary cumulative flows ($F(t)$ and $G(t)$), the boundary fluxes ($f(t)$ and $g(t)$), the internal demand and supply ($d(t)$ and $s(t)$), as well as the distribution of the number of vehicles, from the initial condition and the boundary condition in the external demand $d^-(t)$ and $s^+(t)$. Here, the distribution of vehicles inside the road segment depends on the traffic flow model. For example, in the LWR and Cell Transmission Model, the distribution is determined by the traffic densities at different locations or cells; in the Link Transmission Model, the distribution is determined by the queue and vacancy sizes; but in the link queue model, the distribution is simply determined by the number of vehicles inside the whole road segment.

For a fixed lane-miles of the road segment; i.e., for a fixed Λ, we let the length of the road segment L decrease to zero. Then the number of lanes l increases to infinite. Thus, the road segment is equivalent to a point facility, and vehicles form a vertical queue, whose spatial length is zero. We refer to such a traffic system as a point queue, as illustrated in Fig. 11.2.

Thus, in a point queue, all vehicles are at the same location, and the only other variable is the queue size, $\delta(t)$. Therefore, there are seven unknown variables in a point queue: $F(t)$, $f(t)$, $G(t)$, $g(t)$, $s(t)$, $d(t)$, and $\delta(t)$. Among these variables, we have the following standard equations: from the relationship between the cumulative flow and the flux, we have

$$f(t) = \frac{d}{dt}F(t), \tag{11.1a}$$

$$g(t) = \frac{d}{dt}G(t); \tag{11.1b}$$

from the junction model we have

$$f(t) = \min\{d^-(t), s(t)\}, \tag{11.2a}$$

$$g(t) = \min\{d(t), s^+(t)\}. \tag{11.2b}$$

Thus, we need three more equations to have a complete model. These equations are related to the definitions of the queue size as well as the internal demand and supply, as in the Link Transmission Model.

11.1.2 Definitions of queue and vacancy sizes and internal demand and supply

As a point queue can be considered a limit of a road segment, the queue size and the internal demand and supply of the point queue can be defined by taking the limits of the corresponding variables in the Link Transmission Model.

In the Link Transmission Model for the road segment shown in Fig. 11.1, the internal demand and supply are given by (8.4):

$$d(t) = \min\{f\left(t - \frac{L}{u}\right) + \frac{\delta(t)}{\epsilon}, lC\}, \quad t \geq \frac{L}{u}; \tag{11.3a}$$

$$s(t) = \min\{g\left(t - \frac{L}{w}\right) + \frac{\sigma(t)}{\epsilon}, lC\}, \quad t \geq \frac{L}{w}, \tag{11.3b}$$

where C is the per-lane capacity, lC is the capacity for the l-lane road segment, and the queue and vacancy sizes are

$$\delta(t) = F\left(t - \frac{L}{u}\right) - G(t), \quad t \geq \frac{L}{u}; \tag{11.3c}$$

$$\sigma(t) = G\left(t - \frac{L}{w}\right) + \Lambda - F(t), \quad t \geq \frac{L}{w}. \tag{11.3d}$$

11. Point queue model

When $L \to 0$ and $l \to \infty$, $\frac{L}{u} \to 0$, and $\frac{L}{w} \to 0$. At any $t \geq 0$, the queue and vacancy sizes for the point queue are given by

$$\delta(t) = F(t) - G(t), \tag{11.4a}$$
$$\sigma(t) = G(t) + \Lambda - F(t) = \Lambda - \delta(t). \tag{11.4b}$$

Thus, the queue size in the point queue equals the number of vehicles $F(t) - G(t)$. In addition, the internal demand and supply of the point queue are given by

$$d(t) = f(t) + \frac{\delta(t)}{\epsilon}, \tag{11.5a}$$
$$s(t) = g(t) + \frac{\sigma(t)}{\epsilon}. \tag{11.5b}$$

11.2 Equivalent formulations

This section discusses the equivalent formulations of the point queue model in both continuous and discrete forms, when the maximum queue size Λ is infinite. In this case, the vacancy size $\sigma(t) = \infty$.

11.2.1 Continuous versions

From (11.2) and (11.5), we have $s(t) = \infty$, and

$$f(t) = d^-(t), \tag{11.6a}$$
$$d(t) = d^-(t) + \frac{\delta(t)}{\epsilon}, \tag{11.6b}$$
$$g(t) = \min\{d(t), s^+(t)\}. \tag{11.6c}$$

If we use $\delta(t)$ as the unknown variable, then we have the following ordinary differential equation:

$$\frac{d}{dt}\delta(t) = d^-(t) - \min\{d^-(t) + \frac{\delta(t)}{\epsilon}, s^+(t)\}, \tag{11.7}$$

which is equivalent to

$$\frac{d}{dt}\delta(t) = \max\{-\frac{\delta(t)}{\epsilon}, d^-(t) - s^+(t)\}. \tag{11.8}$$

Here $s^+(t)$ can be understood as the handling capacity of the point queue, and $d^-(t)$ the demand. Thus, $s^+(t) - d^-(t)$ is the residue capacity of the point queue.

11.2 Equivalent formulations

Traditionally, (11.8) has been written as

$$\frac{d}{dt}\delta(t) = \begin{cases} \max\{0, d^-(t) - s^+(t)\}, & \delta(t) = 0; \\ d^-(t) - s^+(t), & \delta(t) > 0. \end{cases} \quad (11.9)$$

But this formulation could lead to negative queue sizes. See Problem 11.1.

If we use $F(t)$ and $G(t)$ as the unknown variables, we then have the following ordinary differential equations:

$$\frac{d}{dt} F(t) = d^-(t), \quad (11.10a)$$

$$\frac{d}{dt} G(t) = \min\{d^-(t) + \frac{F(t) - G(t)}{\epsilon}, s^+(t)\}. \quad (11.10b)$$

The cumulative flows and other variables are illustrated in Fig. 11.3. With respect to a point queue, $F(t)$ is called the arrival curve, and $G(t)$ the departure curve. On the other hand, $F(t)$ is the departure curve from the origin, and $G(t)$ the arrival curve to the destination. Correspondingly, $f(t)$ and $g(t)$ could be both the departure and arrival rates, depending on the reference points.

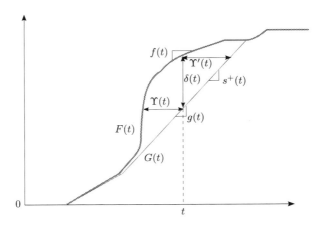

FIGURE 11.3 Cumulative flows and other variables in a point queue.

11.2.2 Discrete versions

We use Euler's forward method to discretize the point queue models. In addition we set $\epsilon = \Delta t$ in the discrete versions.

The discrete version of (11.8) is given by

$$\delta(t + \Delta t) = \max\{0, \delta(t) + (d^-(t) - s^+(t))\Delta t\}. \quad (11.11)$$

The point queue model is well-defined if the queue size is non-negative. From (11.11), we can see that the queue size is always non-negative at $t + \Delta t$. Thus, it is always well-defined.

The discrete version of (11.10) can be written as

$$F(t + \Delta t) = F(t) + d^-(t)\Delta t, \qquad (11.12a)$$
$$G(t + \Delta t) = \min\{F(t + \Delta t), G(t) + s^+(t)\Delta t\}. \qquad (11.12b)$$

In particular, (11.12b) shows that the cumulative out-flow at $t + \Delta t$, $G(t + \Delta t)$, is bounded by the cumulative in-flow at $t + \Delta t$, $F(t + \Delta t)$, and the cumulative out-flow at t, $G(t)$, plus the external supply between t and $t + \Delta t$, $s^+(t)\Delta t$.

If we divide a study period $[0, E]$ into I intervals with $\Delta t = \frac{E}{I}$. Then with (11.12) we can obtain $F(i\Delta t)$ and $G(i\Delta t)$ for $i = 0, \cdots, I$. For any $t \in [i\Delta t, (i+1)\Delta t]$, we can use the following linear interpolations of $F(t)$ and $G(t)$:

$$\tilde{F}(t) = (i + 1 - \frac{t}{\Delta t}) \cdot F(i\Delta t) + (\frac{t}{\Delta t} - i) \cdot F((i+1)\Delta t), \qquad (11.13a)$$
$$\tilde{G}(t) = (i + 1 - \frac{t}{\Delta t}) \cdot G(i\Delta t) + (\frac{t}{\Delta t} - i) \cdot G((i+1)\Delta t). \qquad (11.13b)$$

11.3 Properties

11.3.1 Queueing times

As shown in Fig. 11.3, the queueing time for a vehicle exiting the point queue at t is denoted by $\Upsilon(t)$, and that for a vehicle entering the point queue at t by $\Upsilon'(t)$. Then for a first-in-first-out facility, we have

$$F(t - \Upsilon(t)) = G(t), \qquad (11.14a)$$
$$F(t) = G(t + \Upsilon'(t)). \qquad (11.14b)$$

Numerically, we use the linear interpolations of $F(t)$ and $G(t)$ in (11.13) to calculate $\Upsilon(i\Delta t)$ and $\Upsilon'(i\Delta t)$ as follows:

$$\tilde{F}(i\Delta t - \Upsilon(i\Delta t)) = G(i\Delta t), \qquad (11.15a)$$
$$F(i\Delta t) = \tilde{G}(i\Delta t + \Upsilon'(i\Delta t)). \qquad (11.15b)$$

We can see that, given $F(i\Delta t)$, we can use (11.12b) to calculate $G(i\Delta t)$ and then use (11.15) to calculate the queueing times. Here $F(i\Delta t)$ corresponds to the travel demand at the origin, and it is the only boundary condition (other than s^+).

Inversely, given the arrival curve at the destination, $G(i\Delta t)$, there can be many possible departure curves at the origin, $F(i\Delta t)$. However, if we also

11.3 Properties

know $\Upsilon(i\Delta t)$, the queueing times for vehicles arriving at the destination at $i\Delta t$, it is possible to uniquely determine the departure curve as follows. First, from (11.15a) we can obtain $\tilde{F}(i\Delta t - \Upsilon(i\Delta t))$. Second, we construct the following linear interpolation of $F(t)$ for $t \in [t_i, t_{i+1}]$, where $t_i = i\Delta t - \Upsilon(i\Delta t)$ and $t_{i+1} = (i+1)dt - \Upsilon((i+1)\Delta t)$:

$$\bar{F}(t) = \frac{t_{i+1} - t}{t_{i+1} - t_i}\tilde{F}(t_i) + \frac{t - t_i}{t_{i+1} - t_i}\tilde{F}(t_{i+1}). \tag{11.16}$$

Here $\bar{F}(t)$ is well-defined if and only if $t_{i+1} > t_i$; i.e.,

$$\Upsilon((i+1)\Delta t) - \Upsilon(i\Delta t) < \Delta t, \tag{11.17}$$

whose continuous version is

$$\frac{d}{dt}\Upsilon(t) < 1. \tag{11.18}$$

Finally, we can let $F(i\Delta t) = \bar{F}(i\Delta t)$, which leads to another approximate linear interpolation of $F(t)$ in (11.13).

11.3.2 Integral version

Theorem 11.3.1. *When $\delta(0) = 0$, the point queue model, (11.10), or equivalently, (11.12), are solved by the following integral form:*

$$F(t) = \int_0^t d^-(y)dy, \tag{11.19a}$$

$$G(t) = \min_{0 \leq y \leq t}\{F(y) - \hat{G}(y)\} + \hat{G}(t), \tag{11.19b}$$

where

$$\hat{G}(t) = \int_0^t s^+(y)dy. \tag{11.19c}$$

The discrete versions of (11.19) are ($i = 0, 1, 2, \cdots$)

$$F((i+1)\Delta t) = F(i\Delta t) + d^-(i\Delta t)\Delta t, \tag{11.20a}$$
$$\hat{G}((i+1)\Delta t) = \hat{G}(i\Delta t) + s^+(i\Delta t)\Delta t, \tag{11.20b}$$

and

$$G(i\Delta t) = \min_{0 \leq j \leq i}\{F(j\Delta t) - \hat{G}(j\Delta t)\}$$
$$+ \hat{G}(i\Delta t), \tag{11.20c}$$

where $F(0) = G(0) = \hat{G}(0) = 0$. Correspondingly, the queue size is given by

$$\begin{aligned}\delta(t) &= F(t) - \hat{G}(t) - \min_{0 \leq y \leq t}\{F(y) - \hat{G}(y)\} \\ &= \max_{0 \leq y \leq t}\{F(t) - F(y) - (\hat{G}(t) - \hat{G}(y))\}. \end{aligned} \quad (11.21)$$

Proof. Since $\delta(0) = 0$, we have $F(0) = G(0) = 0$. (11.19a) directly follows from (11.10).

Next we prove the discrete version of (11.20c) by induction. When $i = 0$, (11.20c) is equivalent to

$$G(0) = F(0) - \hat{G}(0) + \hat{G}(0) = 0,$$

which is correct. Assume that (11.20c) is correct for i. Then from (11.12b) we have

$$\begin{aligned} G((i+1)\Delta t) &= \min\{F((i+1)\Delta t), G(i\Delta t) + s^+(i\Delta t)\Delta t\} \\ &= \min\{F((i+1)\Delta t), \\ &\quad \min_{0 \leq j \leq i}\{F(j\Delta t) - \hat{G}(j\Delta t)\} + \hat{G}(i\Delta t) + s^+(i\Delta t)\Delta t\} \\ &= \min\{F((i+1)\Delta t) - \hat{G}((i+1)\Delta t), \\ &\quad \min_{0 \leq j \leq i}\{F(j\Delta t) - \hat{G}(j\Delta t)\}\} + \hat{G}((i+1)\Delta t) \\ &= \min_{0 \leq j \leq i+1}\{F(j\Delta t) - \hat{G}(j\Delta t)\} + \hat{G}((i+1)\Delta t). \end{aligned}$$

Thus (11.20c) is also correct for $i+1$.

(11.21) directly follows from (11.19) and that $\delta(t) = F(t) - G(t)$. □

When the external supply $s^+(t) = s^+$ is constant, we have $\hat{G}(t) = s^+ t$, and the following corollary.

Corollary 11.3.2. *When the external supply $s^+(t) = s^+$ is constant, we have $\hat{G}(t) = s^+ t$,*

$$G(t) = \min_{0 \leq y \leq t}\{F(y) - s^+ y\} + s^+ t, \quad (11.22)$$

and

$$\begin{aligned}\delta(t) &= F(t) - s^+ t - \min_{0 \leq y \leq t}\{F(y) - s^+ y\} \\ &= \max_{0 \leq y \leq t}\{F(t) - F(y) - s^+ \cdot (t - y)\}. \end{aligned} \quad (11.23)$$

11.3.3 With a constant external supply

In this subsection, we further look at the case when the external supply $s^+(t) = s^+ > 0$ is constant. In this case, the out-flux is given by

$$g(t) = \min\{d^-(t) + \frac{\delta(t)}{\epsilon}, s^+\}. \tag{11.24}$$

(11.8) can be simplified as

$$\frac{d}{dt}\delta(t) = \max\{-\frac{\delta(t)}{\epsilon}, d^-(t) - s^+\}. \tag{11.25}$$

Theorem 11.3.3. *For a constant external supply s^+, we have*

$$F(t) = G\left(t + \frac{\delta(t)}{s^+}\right). \tag{11.26}$$

Thus the queueing time for vehicles entering the queue at t is

$$\Upsilon'(t) = \frac{\delta(t)}{s^+}. \tag{11.27}$$

Proof. (11.26) is correct when $\delta(t) = 0$, since $F(t) = G(t)$.

If $\delta(t) > 0$, for $y \in [0, \frac{\delta(t)}{s^+})$, we have from (11.24) that

$$G(t+y) = G(t) + \int_0^y g(x)dx \leq G(t) + s^+ y.$$

As $y < \frac{\delta(t)}{s^+}$, we have $\delta(t) > s^+ y$, and $F(t) - G(t) > s^+ y$. Thus, $G(t+y) < F(t) \leq F(t+y)$, as $d^-(t)$ is non-negative. Therefore, the queue length $\delta(t+y) > 0$ remains positive for $y \in [0, \frac{\delta(t)}{s^+})$. Then from (11.24) we have

$$g(t+y) = \min\{d^-(t+y) + \frac{\delta(t+y)}{\epsilon}, s^+\} = s^+.$$

Therefore,

$$G\left(t + \frac{\delta(t)}{s^+}\right) = G(t) + \delta(t) = F(t).$$

Thus (11.26) is correct. Then from the definition of $\Upsilon'(t)$ (11.27) is also correct. □

Further from (11.24) we have that $g(t) \leq s^+$, and the following theorem.

Theorem 11.3.4. *For a constant external supply s^+ we have*

$$(s^+ - g(t)) \cdot \delta(t) = 0, \tag{11.28a}$$

or equivalently

$$(s^+ - g(t)) \cdot \Upsilon'(t) = 0. \tag{11.28b}$$

Proof. From (11.24) we can see that if $\delta(t) = 0$, then $g(t) \leq s^+$. But if $\delta(t) > 0$, then $g(t) = s^+$. Thus, (11.28a) is correct. Then from (11.27) we have (11.28b). □

Then we have following theorem regarding the rate of change in the queue length, $\frac{d}{dt}\delta(t)$.

Theorem 11.3.5. *The rate of change in the queue length is bounded during a study period $t \in [0, E]$ as follows:*

$$\frac{d}{dt}\delta(t) \geq -s^+, \tag{11.29a}$$

$$\frac{d}{dt}\delta(t) \leq \max\{0, \max_{t \in [0,E]} d^-(t) - s^+\}. \tag{11.29b}$$

Then we have the following corollary regarding the rate of change in the queueing time.

Corollary 11.3.6. *The rate of change in the queueing time is bounded during a study period $t \in [0, E]$ as follows:*

$$\frac{d}{dt}\Upsilon'(t) \geq -1, \tag{11.30}$$

$$\frac{d}{dt}\Upsilon'(t) \leq \max\{0, \max_{t \in [0,E]} \frac{d^-(t)}{s^+} - 1\}. \tag{11.31}$$

11.4 Departure time choice at a single bottleneck

This section applies the point queue model for the departure time choice at a single bottleneck, whose service rate (capacity) is constant at s^+.

11.4.1 Costs

Fig. 11.4(a) shows a pair of arrival and departure curves on a day. Fig. 11.4(b) shows the in-flux $f(t)$ and the corresponding costs. Here, a passenger arrives at the destination before or after his/her desired arrival time, t^*, would face an early/late penalty:

$$\phi_2(t) = \mu \cdot \max\{t^* - t, 0\} + \nu \cdot \max\{t - t^*, 0\}, \tag{11.32}$$

where μ and ν are the values of time. Some example values are $\mu = \$3.9/\text{hr}$, and $\nu = \$15.2/\text{hr}$. $\phi_2(t)$ is referred to as the scheduling cost, which

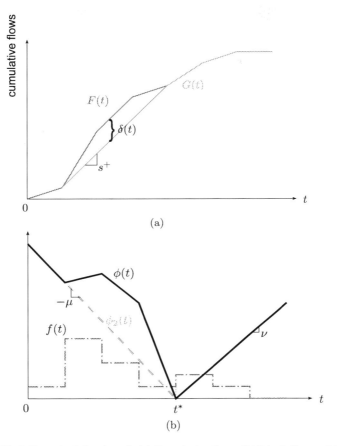

FIGURE 11.4 For a single bottleneck, (a) Cumulative flows; (b) Scheduling and total costs.

is a V-shaped curve as illustrated in Fig. 11.4(b). In addition to the scheduling cost, there is also a queueing cost, which is proportional to the queueing time. Thus, the total cost for a vehicle departing the origin at t is given by

$$\phi(t) = \alpha \cdot \Upsilon'(t) + \phi_2(t + \Upsilon'(t)), \qquad (11.33)$$

which is also illustrated in Fig. 11.4(b). Here

$$\alpha > \mu. \qquad (11.34)$$

An example value of α is \$6.4/hr.

Then the rate of change in the total cost is

$$\frac{d}{dt}\phi(t) = (\alpha + \frac{\partial}{\partial t}\phi_2(t + \Upsilon'(t))) \cdot \frac{d}{dt}\Upsilon'(t) + \frac{\partial}{\partial t}\phi_2(t + \Upsilon'(t)), \quad (11.35)$$

which is also bounded as shown in the following theorem.

Theorem 11.4.1. *The rate of change of the total cost is bounded as follows:*

$$\frac{d}{dt}\phi(t) \geq -\alpha, \quad (11.36a)$$

where the equal sign holds when the queue discharges with $d^-(t) = 0$ and $\delta(t) > 0$; and

$$\frac{d}{dt}\phi(t) \leq (\alpha + \nu) \cdot \max\{0, \max_{t \in [0,E]} \frac{d^-(t)}{s^+} - 1\} + \nu. \quad (11.36b)$$

Proof. Since $\frac{\partial}{\partial t}\phi_2(t + \Upsilon'(t)) = -\mu$ for early arrivals ($t + \Upsilon'(t) < t^*$) and $\frac{\partial}{\partial t}\phi_2(t + \Upsilon'(t)) = \nu$ for late arrivals ($t + \Upsilon'(t) > t^*$), then $\alpha + \frac{\partial}{\partial t}\phi_2(t + \Upsilon'(t)) = \alpha - \mu$ or $\alpha + \nu$. In both cases, $\alpha + \frac{\partial}{\partial t}\phi_2(t + \Upsilon'(t)) > 0$. Thus, $\frac{d}{dt}\phi(t)$ increases in $\frac{d}{dt}\Upsilon'(t)$.

From Corollary 11.3.6, we have $\frac{d}{dt}\phi(t) \geq -\alpha$ when $\frac{d}{dt}\Upsilon'(t) \geq -1$. The equal sign holds when $\frac{d}{dt}\Upsilon'(t) = -1$; i.e., when $d^-(t) = 0$ and $\delta(t) > 0$. The equal sign can occur for both early and late arrivals.

Also from Corollary 11.3.6, we have $\frac{d}{dt}\Upsilon'(t) \leq \max\{0, \max_{t \in [0,E]} \frac{d^-(t)}{s^+} - 1\}$. In addition, $\frac{\partial}{\partial t}\phi_2(t + \Upsilon'(t)) \leq \nu$. Thus, (11.36b) is true. The equal sign only occurs for late arrivals. □

11.4.2 User equilibrium

Clearly, the departure pattern, $F(t)$, in Fig. 11.4(a) is not in equilibrium, as the costs for vehicles arriving at different times are different. Intuitively, in the user equilibrium, vehicles departing and arriving at different times should have the same total cost, and no vehicles can improve their total costs by unilaterally change their departure and arrival times. The equilibrium cumulative flows and costs are illustrated in Fig. 11.5.

From Fig. 11.5(a), we can see that Λ vehicles take $\frac{\Lambda}{s^+}$ to complete their trips. Here $\frac{\Lambda}{s^+}$ is the length of the peak period, which depends on the number of travelers and the service rate of the bottleneck. Among the travelers, $\frac{\nu}{\mu+\nu}\Lambda$ arrive early, and $\frac{\mu}{\mu+\nu}\Lambda$ arrive late. The corresponding departure flow-rate for the early arrivals is $\frac{\alpha}{\alpha-\mu}s^+$, and that for the late arrivals is $\frac{\alpha}{\alpha+\nu}s^+$.

11.4 Departure time choice at a single bottleneck

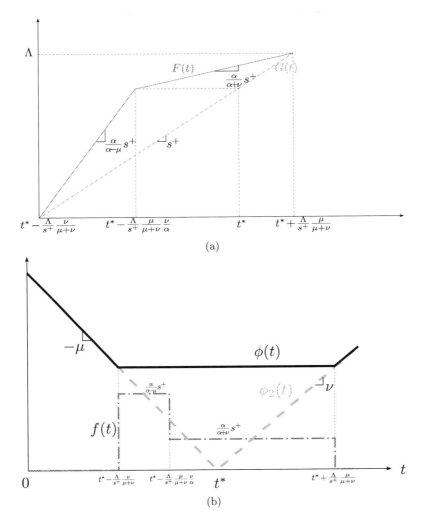

FIGURE 11.5 In the departure time user equilibrium, (a) Cumulative flows; (b) Scheduling and total costs.

The departure flow-rate $f(t)$ is also illustrated in Fig. 11.5(b), from which we can see that all vehicles have the same total cost, $\phi^* = \frac{\Lambda}{s^+}\frac{\mu\nu}{\mu+\nu}$. If any vehicle switches to an arrival time outside the peak period, s/he will experience a larger scheduling cost, even s/he does not have any queueing cost.

From the figure, we can see that the maximum queueing time and cost are experienced by the vehicle arriving at the desired arrival time: $\frac{\Lambda}{s^+}\frac{\mu}{\mu+\nu}\frac{\nu}{\alpha}$. The average queueing time for all vehicles is half of this: $B\frac{\Lambda}{s^+}$, where $B =$

$\frac{1}{2\alpha}\frac{\mu\nu}{\mu+\nu} \approx 0.24$ for the typical values. If the constant travel time from the origin to the destination without congestion is denoted by Υ_0, then the average travel time for all travelers during the peak period is

$$\bar{\Upsilon}(\Lambda) = \Upsilon_0 + B\frac{\Lambda}{s^+}, \qquad (11.37)$$

which resembles the BPR (Bureau of Public Roads) link performance function. But (11.37) is fundamentally different from the BPR link performance function, in which the explanatory variable is volume, whose unit is the same as that of capacity. In addition, a typical BPR link performance function is

$$\Upsilon = \Upsilon_0[1 + 0.15\left(\frac{\text{volume}}{\text{capacity}}\right)^4]. \qquad (11.38)$$

But such a link performance function conflicts with the fundamental diagram, and volume should not be larger than capacity, if volume is interpreted as the flow-rate on a road.

In contrast, (11.37) is coherent with the fundamental diagram, and Λ can be larger than the capacity. However, the point queue model does not capture the hypercongestion phenomenon, and the average travel time only increases in the demand linearly.

Notes

Note 11.1. *The point queue model is a fluid queue model (Kulkarni, 1997), in which the dynamics of a queueing system are described by changes in cumulative flows of queueing contents. Such models were first proposed for dam processes in 1950's (Moran, 1956, 1959). Since then, both discrete and continuous versions of fluid queue models have been extensively discussed with random arrival and service patterns.*

Note 11.2. *In the transportation literature, the point queue model was first applied to study the congestion effect of a bottleneck with deterministic, dynamic arrival patterns in (Vickrey, 1969). (Newell, 1982) systematically discussed the application of point queue models in transportation.*

Note 11.3. *Continuous formulations of the point queue model in Section 11.2 were systematically discussed in (Jin, 2015c), where other equivalent formulations were also presented.*

Note 11.4. *(11.23) was proved as Lemma 1.2.2 in (Le Boudec and Thiran, 2001), where the point queue model was applied to analyze deterministic queueing systems for the Internet.*

Note 11.5. *(11.26) was from (Li et al., 2000). (11.28b) was from (Iryo and Yoshii, 2007).*

Note 11.6. *The service rate s^+ was assumed to depend on the queue length in (Yang and Huang, 1997). Such a modification can capture the hypercongestion phenomenon as discussed in (Small and Chu, 2003).*

Note 11.7. *The example values of α, μ, and ν in Section 11.4 are from (Arnott et al., 1990). The departure time choice problem at a single bottleneck was first studied by (Vickrey, 1969).*

Note 11.8. *The BPR link performance function was introduced on V-20 of (BPR, 1964). Refer to (Small and Chu, 2003) for more detailed discussions on the relationship between the BPR link performance function and the fundamental diagram.*

Note 11.9. *Point queue models have been applied to study dynamic traffic assignment problems (Drissi-Kaïtouni and Hameda-Benchekroun, 1992; Kuwahara and Akamatsu, 1997; Li et al., 2000; Cominetti et al., 2015). It was also used to analyze signalized road networks in (Muralidharan et al., 2015). In (Yin and Lou, 2009; Wang et al., 2020; Jin et al., 2020), the point queue model was applied to study the dynamic pricing control of high-occupancy-toll lanes.*

Problems

Problem 11.1. *Show that (11.9) could lead to negative queue sizes. (Hint: Use the discrete version of (11.9) with $d^-(t) = 0$, and a small $\delta(t)$.)*

Problem 11.2. *Show that (11.18) is the sufficient and necessary condition for $\Upsilon(t)$ to be well-defined. (Hint: Use (11.14a).)*

Problem 11.3. *Prove Theorem 11.3.5.*

Problem 11.4. *Critically review Small, Kenneth A. "The bottleneck model: An assessment and interpretation." Economics of Transportation 4.1-2 (2015): 110-117.*

# CHAPTER 12

The bathtub model

A transportation system is to accommodate various trips, including vehicular trips, passenger trips, or freight trips. Among them, passenger trips and freight trips could be served by vehicles and coincide with vehicular trips. Here vehicular trips could correspond to different modes, such as privately operated vehicles, for-hire vehicles, or public transit vehicles. In addition, a surface transportation system is usually enabled by a network of roads.

Compared with the network kinematic wave model, the link queue and point queue models substantially simplified traffic dynamics on a road or point queue. However, the junctions, origins, destinations, and routes still need to be defined for a road network. Thus, when simulating traffic dynamics or estimating traffic conditions in a road network, we need to prepare such network topology data, collect origin-destination demand data, and consider the route choice behaviors. In addition, models are still needed to describe merging and diverging behaviors at various junctions. Therefore, such models are still too complicated for studies on drivers' departure time, destination, and mode choice behaviors or on the control, planning, and design problems for network-wide, multi-modal transportation systems.

This chapter introduces the bathtub model of network trip flow, for vehicular, passenger, or freight trips. In this model, trips of different origins, destinations, and routes adopt a unified relative space dimension, which is the remaining distances to their respective destinations. Such a space dimension is independent of network topology and helps to simplify and generalize the model. Then all trips' trajectories can be represented by curves in the same space-time plane, in which the travel demand can be represented by a joint distribution of trips' entering times and distances. Then based on the conservation law and the assumptions of undifferentiated traffic conditions on different roads and a network-level vehicular speed-density relation, the evolution of the distribution of trips in the space-time domain is described by the bathtub model, which is a partial differential equation, or an ordinary differential equation, depending on the distribution pattern of trip distances.

The bathtub model can be considered the counterpart of the LWR model for network traffic dynamics. But it is fundamentally different, since the interactions among trips are non-local, and all trips in the whole network can impact each other. As shock or rarefaction waves are caused by local interactions (particularly, the car-following rule), they cannot arise in the bathtub model. In addition, the characteristic curves in the bathtub model always overlap with the trip trajectories, and there exists a single characteristic travel distance for the whole traffic system. Furthermore, each trip has an individual characteristic trip distance, and trips' exiting times can be sorted according to their characteristic trip distances.

In addition, the traffic system in a road network forms a network queue, whose dynamics are described by the queue size of trips with different remaining trip distances. In this sense, the bathtub model can be considered a network queue model, which has a space dimension relative to the remaining trip distance but independent of network topology. This is different from the link and point queue models, for which the space dimension is irrelevant for a link or point queue, but the network topology is still relevant.

The bathtub model naturally describes the hypercongestion phenomenon, since the service rate of trips, i.e., the completion rate of trips, depends on the queue of active trips in a network. Also due to its simplicity, the bathtub model has been or can potentially be used for studying passengers' network-wide choice behaviors in departure times and modes (but not routes) as well as formulating and solving network-level traffic control and design problems.

Different from vehicles' trajectories described by the LWR model or Newell's simplified car-following model in the absolute space, trajectories described by the bathtub model do not reveal the exact locations of the origins, destinations, and routes; thus, travelers' privacy is totally preserved in the new space dimension. In addition, the space dimension can lead to a new paradigm for research, education, and practice in transportation, as the traditional topics on the travel demand analysis and estimation, traffic flow modeling, traffic management, and transportation network design and planning for a large-scale road network can all be simplified in the new space dimension.

Section 12.1 introduces the remaining distance as a unified space dimension for all trips in a road network. Section 12.2 defines variables for the demand, evolution, and completion of trips. Section 12.3 presents three conservation laws. Section 12.4 presents three simplification assumptions. Section 12.5 derives the bathtub models based on the three assumptions. Section 12.6 presents two numerical methods and one example for solving the bathtub model.

12.1 A unified space dimension

We can use two types of space coordinates to locate trips and describe their dynamics in a road network. Traditionally, we have to track individual vehicles' movements or the evolution of traffic states on all roads and routes; in this case, the coordinates are absolute with respect to the network topology. A relatively new paradigm is to track vehicles' movements with respect to their distances to the destinations; in this case, the space dimension is relative to different trips, and the absolute location inside the network is implicit. That is, the new space dimension is independent of network topology.

12.1.1 Traditional transportation system analysis

In the traditional transportation system analysis, a road network is divided into a number of traffic analysis zones (TAZs), which are the origins and destinations of various trips. In addition, the network topology is represented by junctions, links, and routes.

In the traditional four-step method, the trip generation step estimates the total number of trips originated from each zone; the trip distribution step calculates the travel demands among different origins and destinations; the mode choice step allocates these trips to different modes; and the route choice step solves the traffic assignment problem and determines the flows on different links and routes. In the route choice step, the link performance function is used to estimate the average travel time on each link. As discussed in Section 11.4, the link performance function implicitly captures the departure time choice behaviors during the peak period.

The network kinematic wave models as well as the link queue and point queue models can be incorporated into the analysis framework to study the traffic dynamics in a road network. These models can capture the time-dependent congestion patterns and travel times, which are essential for explicitly modeling the departure time choice behaviors.

However, in a dynamic road network, vehicles belong to different origins, destinations, routes, and roads. Thus, to track the traffic dynamics in a road network, we have to introduce different coordinates for different road topology and describe vehicles' movements or the evolution of aggregate traffic variables in such coordinates. The resulted model would be a system of networked ordinary differential equations (with the point queue and link queue models) or partial differential equations (with the Cell Transmission Model) or delay-differential equations (with Link Transmission Model). Such models are still too complicated to obtain useful analytical insights into understanding drivers' behaviors, evaluating the system performance, and designing control and management schemes.

12.1.2 A new paradigm

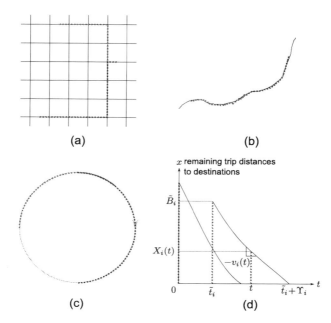

FIGURE 12.1 Trips in various road networks and trajectories in the relative space-time plane.

For a grid network in Fig. 12.1(a), a freeway or arterial corridor in Fig. 12.1(b), or a ring road in Fig. 12.1(c), vehicles may differ in their origins, destinations, routes, and links. For a vehicle, to indicate its location in the absolute space at a time, we need to specify the road and the location on the road. Thus, their trajectories, as illustrated by the red (mid gray in print version) and blue (dark gray in print version) dotted curves, belong to different coordinates and spaces.

However, we can unify the space dimension of different vehicles of different origins, destinations, routes, and roads by considering their (remaining) distances to their respective destinations. Such a space dimension is relative to each vehicle's route. In other words, the route as well as the origin, destination, and road for a vehicle is not explicitly tracked in such a space coordinate, and the space dimension is independent of network topology.

With such a unified space dimension, we can describe different vehicles' trajectories in the same space-time domain, as illustrated in Fig. 12.1(d), where the horizontal axis is for the time t, and the vertical axis for the remaining distance x. The blue and red trips have different entering times and (initial) trip distances. Their trajectories are represented by the solid curves: as time goes, the vehicles get closer and closer to their respective destinations, and the remaining trip distances decrease to zero, until they reach their destinations. Therefore, all vehicles' trajectories can be shown in the same space-time plane.

For a trip or vehicle i, the time for it to enter the network is denoted by $\tilde{t}_i$, and its total travel distance is $\tilde{B}_i$. At t, its remaining distance is denoted by $X_i(t)$, and the travel speed is $v_i(t)$. Then

$$\tilde{B}_i = X_i(\tilde{t}_i), \qquad (12.1a)$$

and

$$v_i(t) = -\frac{d}{dt} X_i(t); \qquad (12.1b)$$

i.e., the remaining trip distance is reduced at the rate of $v_i(t)$.

Here $v_i(t)$ could depend on the local traffic conditions surrounding vehicle i at time t. For example, it could be determined by car-following and lane-changing behaviors of other vehicles at the location. But such detailed driving behaviors can only be tracked in the absolute space coordinates, and the resulted model would be as in the preceding chapters. We will introduce simplification assumptions such that the local dependence can be ignored, and trips can be studied at the whole network level.

If the trip travel time is denoted by Υ_i, then we have

$$X_i(\tilde{t}_i + \Upsilon_i) = 0. \qquad (12.2)$$

Equivalently, we have

$$\int_{\tilde{t}_i}^{\tilde{t}_i + \Upsilon_i} v_i(t) dt = \tilde{B}_i. \qquad (12.3)$$

12.2 Definitions of network-wide trip variables

Ignoring individual trips' local dependence and interactions, we aim to describe trips at the network level. In this section we define some variables to dynamically track all trips in the network. In particular, we define variables to describe the demand or generation of trips, the evolution of trips, and the completion of trips.

12.2.1 Travel demand

In Fig. 12.2, each cross represents a trip demand in the space-time plane. The horizontal and vertical coordinates of the cross represent, respectively, the trip's entering time and distance.

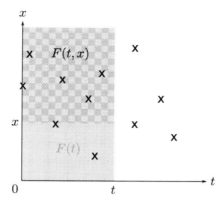

FIGURE 12.2 Aggregate travel demand.

Total in-flow and in-flux

The number of trips entering the network before t is denoted by $F(t)$. It is illustrated by the red (light gray in print version) shaded region in Fig. 12.2. The derivative of $F(t)$ is denoted by $f(t)$, which is the entering rate of trips:

$$f(t) = \frac{d}{dt}F(t). \qquad (12.4)$$

Thus, $F(t)$ and $f(t)$ are respectively the in-flow and in-flux to the road network. The units of $F(t)$ and $f(t)$ are the number of vehicles (trips) and vehicles (trips) per hour, respectively.

For a study period $[0, E]$, the total number of entering trips is

$$\Lambda = F(E) = \int_0^E f(t)dt. \qquad (12.5)$$

In a sense, $\frac{f(t)}{\Lambda}$ is a distribution function of the number of trips in time. It is a valid distribution function, since

$$\frac{f(t)}{\Lambda} \geq 0, \qquad (12.6a)$$

$$\int_0^E \frac{f(t)}{\Lambda}dt = 1. \qquad (12.6b)$$

Relative in-flows and in-fluxes

Different trips have different distances, and their contributions to the congestion patterns are different. Thus, the travel demand also depends on the trip distances. We denote $F(t, x)$ as the number of trips entering the network before t with a trip distance of at least x. It is illustrated by the checkerboard region in Fig. 12.2.

We denote the rate of entering trips with a distance not smaller than x by $f(t, x)$. Then

$$f(t, x) = \frac{\partial}{\partial t} F(t, x). \qquad (12.7)$$

From the definitions we can see that both $F(t, x)$ and $f(t, x)$ are non-negative and decrease in x. In particular, we have

$$\frac{\partial}{\partial x} F(t, x) \leq 0, \qquad (12.8a)$$
$$F(t, x) \geq 0, \qquad (12.8b)$$
$$F(t) = F(t, 0), \qquad (12.8c)$$
$$F(t, \infty) = 0, \qquad (12.8d)$$

and

$$\frac{\partial}{\partial x} f(t, x) \leq 0, \qquad (12.9a)$$
$$f(t, x) \geq 0, \qquad (12.9b)$$
$$f(t) = f(t, 0), \qquad (12.9c)$$
$$f(t, \infty) = 0. \qquad (12.9d)$$

The units of $F(t, x)$ and $f(t, x)$ are also the number of trips and the number of trips per hour, respectively.

$F(t, x)$ and $f(t, x)$ are relative in-flow and in-flux, respectively, as they are relative to the trip distance x.

Proportion and proportion density of entering trips

We denote the proportion of the entering trips with distances not smaller than x by $\tilde{\Phi}(t, x)$. Thus,

$$\tilde{\Phi}(t, x) = \frac{f(t, x)}{f(t)}, \qquad (12.10)$$

which is non-negative and decreases from 1 to 0; i.e.,

$$\frac{\partial}{\partial x} \tilde{\Phi}(t, x) \leq 0, \qquad (12.11a)$$
$$\tilde{\Phi}(t, x) \geq 0, \qquad (12.11b)$$
$$\tilde{\Phi}(t, 0) = 1, \qquad (12.11c)$$
$$\tilde{\Phi}(t, \infty) = 0. \qquad (12.11d)$$

$\tilde{\Phi}(t, x)$ is unit-less.

In addition, we denote the proportion density of entering trips per unit distance at a trip distance of x by $\tilde{\varphi}(t, x)$. Then

$$\tilde{\varphi}(t, x) = -\frac{\partial}{\partial x}\tilde{\Phi}(t, x), \tag{12.12}$$

which is non-negative and integrates to 1; i.e.

$$\tilde{\varphi}(t, x) \geq 0, \tag{12.13a}$$

$$\int_0^\infty \tilde{\varphi}(t, x)dx = 1, \tag{12.13b}$$

$$\tilde{\varphi}(t, \infty) = 0. \tag{12.13c}$$

The unit of $\tilde{\varphi}(t, x)$ is mile^{-1}.

If we define a joint distribution of the trips in the (t, x)-plane illustrated in Fig. 12.2 by $\tilde{\phi}(t, x)$, then

$$\tilde{\phi}(t, x) = \frac{f(t)}{\Lambda}\tilde{\varphi}(t, x), \tag{12.14}$$

which is a valid joint distribution for $t \in [0, E]$ and $x \in [0, \infty)$, since

$$\tilde{\phi}(t, x) \geq 0, \tag{12.15a}$$

$$\int_0^E \int_0^\infty \tilde{\phi}(t, x)dxdt = 1. \tag{12.15b}$$

In this sense, $\frac{f(t)}{\Lambda}$ is the marginal distribution of $\tilde{\phi}(t, x)$ in time, and $\tilde{\varphi}(t, x)$ is the conditional distribution:

$$\frac{f(t)}{\Lambda} = \int_0^\infty \tilde{\phi}(t, x)dx, \tag{12.16a}$$

$$\tilde{\varphi}(t, x) = \frac{\tilde{\phi}(t, x)}{f(t)/\Lambda}. \tag{12.16b}$$

Average trip distance and trip-miles-traveled

The average distance of trips entering at t is denoted by $\tilde{B}(t)$. Thus we have

$$\tilde{B}(t) = \int_0^\infty x\tilde{\varphi}(t, x)dx. \tag{12.17}$$

Lemma 12.2.1. *The average distance of trips entering at t is also given by*

$$\tilde{B}(t) = \int_0^\infty \tilde{\Phi}(t, x)dx. \tag{12.18}$$

The proof of Lemma 12.2.1 is assigned in Problem 12.1.

The total demand for a road network in terms of trip-miles traveled (TMT) during a period of $[0, t]$ is thus

$$\tilde{Y}(t) = \int_0^t \int_0^\infty f(b, x) \, dx \, db, \qquad (12.19)$$

which is the total TMT of entering trips during $[0, t]$.

Theorem 12.2.2. *The total TMT of entering trips during a period of $[0, t]$ can also be written as*

$$\tilde{Y}(t) = \int_0^t f(b) \tilde{B}(b) \, db, \qquad (12.20)$$

or

$$\tilde{Y}(t) = \int_0^\infty F(t, x) \, dx. \qquad (12.21)$$

The proof is assigned as Problem 12.2.

In contrast, the total number of trips during the period $[0, t]$ is

$$F(t) = \int_0^t f(b) \, db. \qquad (12.22)$$

In a sense, $f(t)$ is the generation rate in the number of trips, and $f(t)\tilde{B}(t)$ is the generation rate in the TMT. In a network, the latter better represents the travel demand.

12.2.2 Active trips

A trip is considered active in a road network after it enters and before it exits. That is, for trip i illustrated in Fig. 12.1(d), it is active when $\tilde{t}_i \leq t \leq \tilde{t}_i + \Upsilon_i$.

Total number of active trips

At time t, the total number of active trips is denoted by $\delta(t)$, which can be considered the queue size in the road network.

Relative number of active trips and relative trip density

In addition, the number of active trips with a remaining distance not smaller than x is denoted by $\delta(t, x)$. From the definition, $\delta(t, x)$ is nonnegative and decreases in x from $\delta(t)$ to 0, and

$$\frac{\partial}{\partial x} \delta(t, x) \leq 0, \qquad (12.23a)$$

$$\delta(t, x) \geq 0, \quad (12.23b)$$
$$\delta(t) = \delta(t, 0), \quad (12.23c)$$
$$\delta(t, \infty) = 0. \quad (12.23d)$$

The units of $\delta(t)$ and $\delta(t, x)$ are the same: the number of trips or vehicles.

The density of active trips, i.e., the number of active trips per unit distance, with a remaining distance of x, is denoted by $k(t, x)$. Then it is non-negative and related to $\delta(t, x)$ as follows:

$$k(t, x) = -\frac{\partial}{\partial x}\delta(t, x). \quad (12.24)$$

In other words,

$$\delta(t, x) = \int_x^\infty k(t, y)dy. \quad (12.25)$$

Note that $k(t, x)$ is the relative density of trips, with respect to the relative space dimension, i.e., the remaining trip distance.

Proportion and proportion density in the relative space

We denote the proportion of active trips with a remaining distance not smaller than x by $\Phi(t, x)$. Then

$$\Phi(t, x) = \frac{\delta(t, x)}{\delta(t)}, \quad (12.26)$$

which is non-negative and decreases from 1 to 0; i.e.,

$$\frac{\partial}{\partial x}\Phi(t, x) \leq 0, \quad (12.27a)$$
$$\Phi(t, x) \geq 0, \quad (12.27b)$$
$$\Phi(t, 0) = 1, \quad (12.27c)$$
$$\Phi(t, \infty) = 0. \quad (12.27d)$$

$\Phi(t, x)$ is unit-less.

In addition, we denote the proportion density of active trips per unit distance with a remaining distance of x by $\varphi(t, x)$. Then

$$\varphi(t, x) = -\frac{\partial}{\partial x}\Phi(t, x), \quad (12.28)$$

which is non-negative and integrates to 1; i.e.

$$\varphi(t, x) \geq 0, \quad (12.29a)$$
$$\int_0^\infty \varphi(t, x)dx = 1, \quad (12.29b)$$

12.2 Definitions of network-wide trip variables

$$\varphi(t, \infty) = 0. \tag{12.29c}$$

The unit of $\varphi(t, x)$ is mile^{-1}.

Lemma 12.2.3. *The density of active trips is related to the proportion density as follows:*

$$k(t, x) = \delta(t)\varphi(t, x). \tag{12.30}$$

The proof is assigned as Problem 12.3.

Average remaining trip distance and total remaining TMT

The average remaining distance of active trips at t is denoted by $B(t)$. Thus we have

$$B(t) = \int_0^\infty x\varphi(t, x)dx. \tag{12.31}$$

Lemma 12.2.4. *The average remaining distance of active trips at t is also given by*

$$B(t) = \int_0^\infty \Phi(t, x)dx. \tag{12.32}$$

The proof of Lemma 12.2.4 is assigned in Problem 12.4.
The total remaining TMT of active trips at t is denoted by $Y(t)$. Then

$$Y(t) = \delta(t)B(t). \tag{12.33}$$

We have the following theorem.

Theorem 12.2.5. *The total remaining TMT of active trips at t can also be written as*

$$Y(t) = \int_0^\infty \delta(t, x)dx, \tag{12.34}$$

or

$$Y(t) = \int_0^\infty xk(t, x)dx. \tag{12.35}$$

The proof of the theorem is assigned as Problem 12.5.

Initial condition

Initially at $t = 0$, there can be some active trips inside the road network. Thus, the initial condition can be given by (for $x \in [0, \infty)$): $\delta(0)$, $\delta(0, x)$, $k(0, x)$, $\Phi(0, x)$, $\varphi(0, x)$, $B(0)$, and $Y(0)$.

These variables are all related. In particular, $\delta(0, x)$ and $k(0, x)$ one-to-one related; and $\Phi(0, x)$ and $\varphi(0, x)$ are one-to-one related. But $\delta(0, x)$ is equivalent to $\delta(0)$ and $\Phi(0, x)$, which imply $B(0)$ and $Y(0)$.

Thus, if we know $\delta(0, x)$ or $k(0, x)$, the other values can be calculated. Alternatively, if we know $\delta(0)$, and $\Phi(0, x)$, or $\varphi(0, x)$, the other values can also be calculated. But $B(0)$ and $Y(0)$ only contain the aggregate information, not the detailed information with respect to the remaining trip distance.

12.2.3 Averages speed and completion rates

At t, there are $\delta(t)$ active trips or running vehicles. For vehicle $i = 1, 2, \cdots, \delta(t)$, its speed is denoted by $v_i(t)$, as illustrated in Fig. 12.1(d). If different vehicles have different speeds at the same time, we can define the distributions of active trips with respect to the speed.

Distributions with respect to the speed

For a remaining distance of x, the density of active trips is $k(t, x)$. Equivalently, the number of active trips with a remaining distance between x and $x + \Delta x$ is $k(t, x)\Delta x$. Then we denote the distribution of the speeds among these vehicles at t by $\mu(t; x, v)$. Thus, $\mu(t; x, v)$ is a valid distribution function in v, if

$$\mu(t; x, v) \geq 0, \tag{12.36a}$$

$$\int_0^u \mu(t; x, v)dv = 1, \tag{12.36b}$$

where we assume that the speed is always non-negative and smaller than the speed limit u.

In contrast, we denote the distribution of the speeds among all active trips at t by $\mu(t; v)$. Thus, $\mu(t; v)$ is a weighted average of $\mu(t; x, v)$:

$$\mu(t; v) = \frac{1}{\delta(t)} \int_0^\infty \mu(t; x, v) k(t, x) dx, \tag{12.37}$$

which is equivalent to

$$\mu(t; v) = \int_0^\infty \mu(t; x, v) \varphi(t, x) dx. \tag{12.38}$$

In addition, $\mu(t; v)$ is a valid distribution function in v, if

$$\mu(t; v) \geq 0, \tag{12.39a}$$

$$\int_0^u \mu(t; v)dv = 1. \tag{12.39b}$$

12.2 Definitions of network-wide trip variables

If we denote the joint distribution function of active trips in the (x, v)-plane at t by $\phi(t; x, v)$, then

$$\phi(t; x, v) = \mu(t; x, v)\varphi(t, x), \quad (12.40)$$

which is a valid joint distribution function for $v \in [0, u]$ and $x \in [0, \infty)$, since

$$\phi(t; x, v) \geq 0, \quad (12.41a)$$

$$\int_0^\infty \int_0^u \phi(t; x, v)\,dv\,dx = 1. \quad (12.41b)$$

In this sense, $\varphi(t, x)$ is the marginal distribution function of $\phi(t; x, v)$ in the remaining trip distance:

$$\varphi(t, x) = \int_0^u \phi(t; x, v)\,dv, \quad (12.42)$$

and $\mu(t; v)$ is the marginal distribution function $\phi(t; x, v)$ in the speed:

$$\mu(t; v) = \int_0^\infty \phi(t; x, v)\,dx. \quad (12.43)$$

Average speeds

The average speed for all vehicles in the road network at t is denoted by $v(t)$ and can be written as

$$v(t) = \int_0^u v\mu(t; v)\,dv. \quad (12.44)$$

In contrast, the average speed for vehicles with a remaining distance x at t is denoted by $v(t, x)$:

$$v(t, x) = \int_0^u v\mu(t; x, v)\,dv. \quad (12.45)$$

The relationship between the two average speeds is given in the following lemma.

Lemma 12.2.6. *The average speed for all vehicles, $v(t)$, is the weighted average of the average speed for vehicles with a remaining distance x:*

$$v(t) = \int_0^\infty \varphi(t, x)v(t, x)\,dx. \quad (12.46)$$

The proof of the lemma is assigned in Problem 12.6

Completion rate in TMT

For vehicles whose remaining trip distance is between x and $x + \Delta x$, the reduction in the TMT between t and $t + \Delta t$ is $k(t, x)\Delta x v(t, x)\Delta t$.

Between t and $t + \Delta t$, the total vehicle-miles-traveled of $\delta(t)$ vehicles is reduced by $\delta(t)v(t)\Delta t$. That is, $\delta(t)v(t)$ is the reduction or completion rate of TMT.

Lemma 12.2.7. *We have*

$$\delta(t)v(t) = \int_0^\infty k(t, x)v(t, x)dx. \tag{12.47}$$

The proof of the lemma is assigned in Problem 12.7.

Furthermore, during $[0, t]$ the total trip-miles-traveled is reduced by

$$\Delta Y(t) = \int_0^t \delta(b)v(b)db, \tag{12.48}$$

which is the total TMT served during $[0, t]$.

Completion rate in total number of trips

The number of trips exiting the network before t is denoted by $G(t)$, which is the total number of served trips between 0 and t. The exiting rate of trips is $g(t)$. Then

$$g(t) = \frac{d}{dt}G(t). \tag{12.49}$$

Thus, $G(t)$ and $g(t)$ are respectively the out-flow and out-flux of the network. $g(t)$ is also the completion or service rate of trips. The units of $G(t)$ and $g(t)$ are the number of trips and trips per hour, respectively.

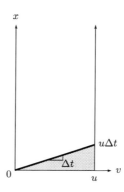

FIGURE 12.3 Illustration of the completion rate of trips in the (x, v)-plane.

In the (x,v)-plane as illustrated in Fig. 12.3, the shaded region is defined by $\{(x,v)|0 \le x \le v\Delta t\}$. Thus, the trips inside the shaded region all exit during t and $t+\Delta t$, since their remaining distances at $t+\Delta t$ is $x - v\Delta t \le 0$. For a small Δt, the number of trips inside the shaded region are

$$\delta(t)\int_0^u \int_0^{v\Delta t} \phi(t;x,v)dxdv = \delta(t)\int_0^u \phi(t;0,v)v\Delta t dv$$
$$= \delta(t)\int_0^u \varphi(t,0)\mu(t;0,v)v\Delta t dv.$$

From (12.45), the number of trips in the shaded region is $\delta(t)\varphi(t,0)v(t,0)\Delta t$. Thus, the completion rate $g(t)$ is given by

$$g(t) = \varphi(t,0)\delta(t)v(t,0). \qquad (12.50)$$

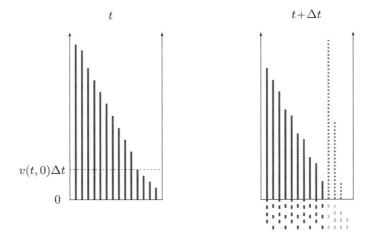

FIGURE 12.4 Illustration of the completion rate of trips in a road network.

On the left-hand side of Fig. 12.4 we show the active trips at t with blue (dark gray in print version) bars in a bin, whose lengths represent the remaining trip distances. On the right-hand side of the figure, we demonstrate the active trips at $t+\Delta t$ with blue (dark gray in print version) and red (mid gray in print version) bars in the bin, among which the blue trips are those active at t, and the red trips enter the network between t and $t+\Delta t$. During the time interval, the remaining distances of all trips active at t are reduced, and the reduced portions are illustrated by the dotted bars under the bin on the right-hand side. Note that, if these trips (vehicles) travel at different speeds, their reduced distances may be different.

In particular, the trips whose remaining distances are between 0 and $v(t,0)\Delta t$ exit the network before $t+\Delta t$. These trips are under the line of $v(t,0)\Delta t$ on the left-hand side, and the green (light gray in print version) dotted bars below the bin on the right-hand side. The number of exiting trips is $g(t)\Delta t$, which also equals $\int_0^{v(t,0)\Delta t} k(t,x)dx$. Letting $\Delta t \to 0$, we have

$$g(t) = k(t,0)v(t,0), \qquad (12.51)$$

which is equivalent to (12.50).

12.2.4 A network queue

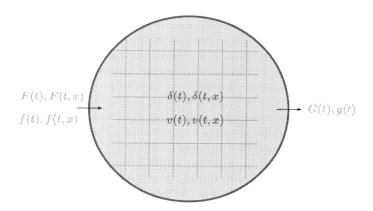

FIGURE 12.5 The queue representation of a network trip flow system.

In this sense, a network trip flow system can be considered a network queue as illustrated in Fig. 12.5. In the queue, the in-flow is given by $F(t,x)$, which represents the demand pattern and determines $F(t)$, $f(t)$, and $f(t,x)$; the out-flow is $G(t)$, which determines $g(t)$; and the aggregate state is determined by $\delta(t,x)$ and $v(t,x)$, which determine $\delta(t)$ and $v(t)$.

Among these ten variables, $F(t,x)$, $F(t)$, $f(t)$, and $f(t,x)$ are given; and $\delta(t,x)$, $\delta(t)$, $v(t,x)$, $v(t)$, $G(t)$, and $g(t)$ are unknown. In addition, with (12.23c) and (12.49), the network queue model is complete if $\delta(t,x)$ and $v(t,x)$ are determined. Here, $\delta(0,x)$ gives the complete initial condition.

From the perspective of a network queue, $F(t)$ and $G(t)$ are also the arrival and departure curves.

However, different from a link queue in Chapter 10 and a point queue in Chapter 11, which have no explicit space, a network queue has an explicit space dimension. Therefore, the demand for a network queue has to include both the rate of trips ($f(t)$) and the distribution of their distances ($\tilde{\varphi}(t,x)$), and the state of the network queue also needs to be characterized by its size, $\delta(t)$, and the distribution of the active trips' remaining distances, $\varphi(t, x)$. That is, the total demand for a network queue depends on the TMT defined in (12.19), not just the total number of trips in (12.22). In addition, with the space dimension, the travel speeds $v(t, x)$ and $v(t)$ need to be explicitly tracked in the network queue.

12.3 Three conservation equations

This section presents three conservation equations with respect to the total number of trips, the total vehicle-miles-traveled, and the relative number of trips with a remaining distance. These conservation equations apply to the general road networks, which may not satisfy the assumptions in the following sections.

12.3.1 Conservation in total number of trips

From the definitions of the total number of active trips, $\delta(t)$, the total number of entering flows, $F(t)$, and the total number of exiting flows, $G(t)$, we have the following relation:

$$\delta(t) = \delta(0) + F(t) - G(t), \tag{12.52}$$

where $\delta(0)$ is the initial number of active trips.

Clearly, (12.52) is a conservation equation for the whole road network: during $[0, t]$, the total number of trips at t equals the initial number of trips, plus the in-flow, minus the out-flow.

Its derivative form can be written as

$$\frac{d}{dt}\delta(t) = f(t) - g(t). \tag{12.53}$$

That is, the rate of change in the total number of trips equals the in-flux minus the out-flux.

Further from (12.50) we have

$$\frac{d}{dt}\delta(t) = f(t) - \varphi(t, 0)\delta(t)v(t, 0). \tag{12.54}$$

This is the conservation law in the total number of trips.

12.3.2 Conservation in the trip-miles-traveled

As explained in Section 12.2, the initial TMT $Y(0) = \delta(0)B(0)$, the remaining TMT for active trips at t is $Y(t) = \delta(t)B(t)$, the generated TMT during $[0, t]$ is $\tilde{Y}(t) = \int_0^t f(b)\tilde{B}(b)dt$, and the total TMT served during $[0, t]$

is $\Delta Y(t) = \int_0^t \delta(b) v(b) db$. Thus, from the conservation in the TMT, we have

$$\delta(t)B(t) = \delta(0)B(0) + \int_0^t f(b)\tilde{B}(b)dt - \int_0^t \delta(b)v(b)db, \quad (12.55)$$

whose derivative version is

$$\frac{d}{dt}\delta(t)B(t) = f(t)\tilde{B}(t) - \delta(t)v(t). \quad (12.56)$$

12.3.3 Conservation in the relative number of trips

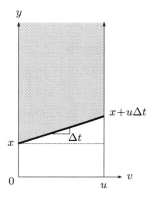

FIGURE 12.6 Illustration of conservation in the relative number of trips in the (x, v)-plane.

In the (y, v)-plane illustrated in Fig. 12.6, the shaded region is defined by $y \geq x + v\Delta t$ for $v \in [0, u]$ and $x \geq 0$. Thus, the trips inside the shaded region will have remaining distances not smaller than x at $t + \Delta t$, since their remaining distances at $t + \Delta t$ are $y - v\Delta t \geq x$. The number of trips inside the shaded region is

$$\delta(t) \int_0^u \int_{x+v\Delta t}^\infty \phi(t; y, v) dy dv = \delta(t) \int_0^u \int_{x+v\Delta t}^\infty \varphi(t, y) \mu(t; y, v) dy dv,$$

which for a small Δt equals

$$\delta(t) \int_0^u \int_{x+v\Delta t}^\infty \varphi(t, y) \mu(t; y, v) dy dv = \delta(t) \int_0^u \int_x^\infty \varphi(t, y) \mu(t; y, v) dy dv$$

$$- \delta(t) \int_0^u \varphi(t, x) \mu(t; x, v) v \Delta t dy dv.$$

$$(12.57)$$

12.3 Three conservation equations

The first term of the right-hand side of the above equation, (12.57), can be simplified as

$$\delta(t) \int_0^u \int_x^\infty \varphi(t, y)\mu(t; y, v)\,dy\,dv = \delta(t) \int_x^\infty \varphi(t, y) \int_0^u \mu(t; y, v)\,dv\,dy$$

$$= \delta(t) \int_x^\infty \varphi(t, y)\,dy = \delta(t, x).$$

From (12.45), the second term of the right-hand side of the above equation, (12.57), can be simplified as

$$\delta(t) \int_0^u \varphi(t, x)\mu(t; x, v)v\Delta t\,dy\,dv = \delta(t)\varphi(t, x)v(t, x)\Delta t.$$

Thus, at $t + \Delta t$, the number of trips that are active at t and have a remaining trip distance not smaller than x is given by $\delta(t, x) - \delta(t)\varphi(t, x)v(t, x)\Delta t$, which equals for a small Δt

$$\delta(t, x + v(t, x)\Delta t) = \delta(t, x) - \delta(t)\varphi(t, x)v(t, x)\Delta t. \quad (12.58)$$

In addition, during t and $t + \Delta t$, the number of entering trips with a distance not smaller than x is

$$F(t + \Delta t, x) - F(t, x) = f(t, x)\Delta t \quad (12.59)$$

Thus, the total number of active trips at $t + \Delta t$ with a remaining distance not smaller than x is

$$\delta(t + \Delta t, x) = \delta(t, x + v(t, x)\Delta t) + f(t, x)\Delta t, \quad (12.60)$$

which leads to for $\Delta t \to 0$

$$\frac{\partial}{\partial t}\delta(t, x) - v(t, x)\frac{\partial}{\partial x}\delta(t, x) = f(t, x). \quad (12.61)$$

This is the conservation law in the relative number of trips, $\delta(t, x)$. It is a partial differential equation.

Fig. 12.7 presents another illustration of (12.60). The number of trips with a remaining distance not smaller than x at $t + \Delta t$ in the right figure, $\delta(t + \Delta t, x)$, equals the number of the (blue (dark gray in print version)) trips with a remaining distance not smaller than $x + v(t, x)\Delta t$ at t in the left figure, $\delta(t, x + v(t, x)\Delta t)$, plus the number of the (red (light gray in print version)) entering trips between t and $t + \Delta t$ with a distance not smaller than x, $f(t, x)\Delta t$.

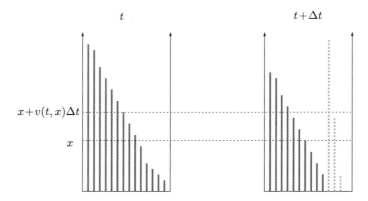

FIGURE 12.7 Illustration of conservation in the relative number of trips.

12.3.4 Relationship among the three conservation laws

In the following theorem, we show that the conservation equation in the relative number of trips, (12.61), is the most general form of the conservation law, since the other two conservation equations are its special cases and can be derived from it. Therefore, in the ensuing discussions, we focus on the conservation equation (12.61).

Theorem 12.3.1. *Both the conservation equations in the total number of trips, (12.54), and in the TMT, (12.56), are special cases of and can be derived from the conservation equation in the relative number of trips, (12.61). In particular, (12.61) with $x = 0$ leads to (12.54), and the integral version of (12.61) for x from 0 to ∞ leads to (12.56).*

Proof. If we let $x = 0$ in (12.61), then $\delta(t, 0) = \delta(t)$, $f(t, 0) = f(t)$, and $\frac{\partial}{\partial x}\delta(t, x) = -\delta(t)\varphi(t, 0)$. Thus (12.61) leads to the conservation equation in the total number of trips, (12.54).

We integrate both sides of (12.61) for x from 0 to ∞. Then from (12.18) we have

$$\int_0^\infty f(t, x)dx = f(t)\int_0^\infty \tilde{\Phi}(t, x)dx = f(t)\tilde{B}(t).$$

From (12.32) we have

$$\int_0^\infty \frac{\partial}{\partial t}\delta(t, x)\Delta x = \frac{d}{dt}\delta(t)\int_0^\infty \Phi(t, x)dx = \frac{d}{dt}\delta(t)B(t).$$

From (12.46) we have

$$\int_0^\infty v(t, x)\frac{\partial}{\partial x}\delta(t, x)dx = -\delta(t)\int_0^\infty v(t, x)\varphi(t, x)dx = -\delta(t)v(t).$$

12.4 Three simplification assumptions

In the general conservation equation in (12.61), $\delta(t,x)$ is the unknown state variable, $f(t,x)$ is the demand function and should be given exogenously, and $v(t,x)$ is also unknown. Once $\delta(t,x)$ and $v(t,x)$ are known, from (12.50) we can calculate $g(t)$. Thus, the variables in the network queue illustrated in Fig. 12.5 are well-defined if $v(t,x)$ can be calculated.

In practice, $v(t,x)$ could be inferred from observed data. In theory, $v(t,x)$ could depend on the traffic state, $\delta(t,x)$, road geometry, driving behaviors, traffic control policies, and other environmental factors. This section introduces three simplification assumptions that lead to simple models of $v(t,x)$ and $\delta(t,x)$.

12.4.1 The bathtub assumption

Undifferentiated roads

First, we assume that all active trips at different locations have the same speed at the same time. Thus, at t, the speeds of vehicles with any remaining distance x are the same at $v(t)$. In other words, $\mu(t;x,v)$ is a Delta function centered around $v = v(t)$. Then from (12.45) we have

$$v(t,x) = v(t). \qquad (12.62)$$

With this assumption, the absolute location of a trip is no longer relevant, and the only relevant space dimension is the relative remaining trip distance. That is, we only need to track each trip's relative location with the distance to its destination and can ignore the exact location it is in the road network.

With this assumption, the conservation law in (12.61) can be simplified as

$$\frac{\partial}{\partial t}\delta(t,x) - v(t)\frac{\partial}{\partial x}\delta(t,x) = f(t,x), \qquad (12.63)$$

whose discrete version can be derived from (12.60) as

$$\delta(t+\Delta t, x) = \delta(t, x + v(t)\Delta t) + f(t,x)\Delta t. \qquad (12.64)$$

The conservation equation in the total number of active trips, (12.54), is simplified as

$$\frac{d}{dt}\delta(t) = f(t) - \varphi(t,0)\delta(t)v(t). \tag{12.65}$$

But the conservation equation in TMT, (12.56), still the same.

With this assumption, all streets are effectively undifferentiated, and the road network can be considered a single unit. The traffic system is similar to a bathtub, in which the rise and fall of traffic in the morning rush hour resemble the filling and emptying process of a bathtub. Thus, we refer to this as the "bathtub" assumption.

Characteristic travel distance and characteristic trip distance

As all vehicles have the same speed, $v(t)$ characterizes the traffic conditions in the whole network. We denote the characteristic travel distance of the network by $z(t)$:

$$z(t) = \int_0^t v(b)db, \tag{12.66}$$

which is equivalent to $z(0) = 0$ and

$$v(t) = \frac{d}{dt}z(t). \tag{12.67}$$

When $v(t) > 0$, $z(t)$ strictly increases in t, and its inverse function is denoted by $\theta(z)$; i.e.,

$$\theta(z(t)) = t. \tag{12.68}$$

Thus, $\theta(z)$ is the time for a vehicle to travel a distance of z from $t = 0$.

For trip i in Fig. 12.1(d), its speed is

$$v_i(t) = v(t). \tag{12.69}$$

Thus, all trips' trajectories are parallel at t, since their slopes are the same as $v(t)$. In particular, trip i's trajectory can be represented by the characteristic travel distance:

$$X_i(t) = \tilde{B}_i - z(t) + z(\tilde{t}_i), \tag{12.70}$$

which satisfies (12.1). In addition, (12.2) can be written as

$$\tilde{B}_i - z(\tilde{t}_i + \Upsilon_i) + z(\tilde{t}_i) = 0, \tag{12.71}$$

and (12.3) can be simplified as

$$z(\tilde{t}_i + \Upsilon_i) - z(\tilde{t}_i) = \tilde{B}_i. \tag{12.72}$$

Clearly, (12.71) and (12.72) are equivalent and lead to

$$\Upsilon_i = \theta(\tilde{B}_i + z(\tilde{t}_i)) - \tilde{t}_i. \tag{12.73}$$

If we denote the exiting time of trip i by $\hat{t}_i$, then

$$\hat{t}_i = \tilde{t}_i + \Upsilon_i. \tag{12.74}$$

From (12.73), we have

$$\hat{t}_i = \theta(\tilde{B}_i + z(\tilde{t}_i)). \tag{12.75}$$

As $\theta(z)$ is an increasing function in z, the exiting time increases in $\tilde{B}_i + z(\tilde{t}_i)$, which can be considered a characteristic of trip i. Thus, we refer to this the characteristic distance of trip i and denote it by:

$$\hat{B}_i = \tilde{B}_i + z(\tilde{t}_i). \tag{12.76}$$

Furthermore, (12.75) can be written as

$$\hat{t}_i = \theta(\hat{B}_i), \tag{12.77}$$

or equivalently,

$$\hat{B}_i = z(\hat{t}_i). \tag{12.78}$$

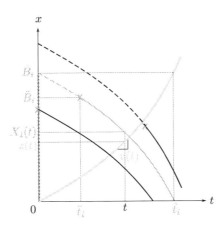

FIGURE 12.8 Illustration of characteristic travel distance and characteristic trip distance.

Fig. 12.8 illustrates the characteristic travel distance curve $z(t)$, which increase in t, as well as three trip trajectories. For trip i, the figure also illustrates its characteristic trip distance, $\hat{B}_i$, its exiting time $\hat{t}_i$, its trip distance, $\tilde{B}_i$, and its entering time $\tilde{t}_i$. From the figure, we can also see that the characteristic distance of trip i, $\hat{B}_i$, also equals the characteristic travel distance in the network when trip i exits the network at $\hat{t}_i$; this is consistent with (12.78). In addition, trip i's trajectory overlaps with that of a trip entering the network at $t=0$ with a distance of $\hat{B}_i$.

By comparing the three trips' trajectories, we can see that trips entering the network earlier may not exit the network earlier. That is, the first-in-first-out principle is violated. But the trip with the smaller characteristic distance exits the network earlier. We refer to this as the shorter-(characteristic) distance-first-out principle.

As trips with the same distance and entering the network at the same time share exactly the same trajectory, we can define the characteristic trip distance of a vehicle entering at t with a trip distance of x by $\hat{B}(t,x)$, which equals

$$\hat{B}(t,x) = z(t) + x. \tag{12.79}$$

The exit time for such a trip is denoted by $\hat{t}(t,x)$, which equals

$$\hat{t}(t,x) = \theta(\hat{B}(t,x)). \tag{12.80}$$

Equivalently,

$$\hat{B}(t,x) = z(\hat{t}(t,x)). \tag{12.81}$$

If we denote the trip travel time by $\Upsilon(t,x)$, then

$$\Upsilon(t,x) = \hat{t}(t,x) - t. \tag{12.82}$$

We denote the average travel time for trips entering at t by $\bar{\Upsilon}(t)$, which equals

$$\bar{\Upsilon}(t) = \int_0^\infty \Upsilon(t,x)\tilde{\varphi}(t,x)dx. \tag{12.83}$$

Lemma 12.4.1. *The average travel time in (12.83) can also be written as*

$$\bar{\Upsilon}(t) = \int_0^\infty \tilde{\Phi}(t,x)\frac{1}{v(\theta(z(t)+x))}dx. \tag{12.84}$$

The proof is assigned as Problem 12.8.

In (12.84), the speed varies with x, since $v(\theta(z(t)+x))$ is the speed when a trip entering at t with a distance x exits the network. There are two ways to approximate $\bar{\Upsilon}(t)$, if we approximate the speed by that when all trips enter the network, $v(t)$, or by that when the trip with an average distance exits the network, $v(\theta(z(t) + \tilde{B}(t)))$. That is, we have the following two approximations:

$$\tilde{\Upsilon}(t) \approx \tilde{\Upsilon}_1(t) \equiv \frac{\tilde{B}(t)}{v(t)}, \qquad (12.85a)$$

$$\tilde{\Upsilon}(t) \approx \tilde{\Upsilon}_2(t) \equiv \frac{\tilde{B}(t)}{v(\theta(z(t) + \tilde{B}(t)))}. \qquad (12.85b)$$

Characteristic curves and integral conservation equations

In the (t, x) plane, we define the characteristic curve emanated from $(0, x_0)$ as

$$x(t) = x_0 - z(t). \qquad (12.86)$$

Thus, along the characteristic curve we have

$$\dot{x}(t) = -v(t). \qquad (12.87)$$

Comparing (12.70) and (12.86), we can see that the characteristic curve coincides with the trajectory of the trip entering the network at 0 with a distance of x_0.

Along the characteristic curve, we have the total derivative of $\delta(t, x_0 - z(t))$ as follows:

$$\frac{d}{dt}\delta(t, x_0 - z(t)) = \frac{\partial}{\partial t}\delta(t, x_0 - z(t)) - v(t)\frac{\partial}{\partial x}\delta(t, x_0 - z(t)).$$

Thus, from (12.63) we have

$$\frac{d}{dt}\delta(t, x_0 - z(t)) = f(t, x_0 - z(t)),$$

whose integral version is

$$\delta(t, x_0 - z(t)) = \delta(0, x_0) + \int_0^t f(b, x_0 - z(b))db.$$

Let $x = x_0 - z(t)$, the characteristic curve passes (t, x), and the above equation is equivalent to

$$\delta(t, x) = \delta(0, x + z(t)) + \int_0^t f(b, x + z(t) - z(b))db. \qquad (12.88)$$

This is the integral version of (12.63). As a special case, when $x = 0$, we have the queue size at t as follows

$$\delta(t) = \delta(0, z(t)) + \int_0^t f(b, z(t) - z(b))db. \qquad (12.89)$$

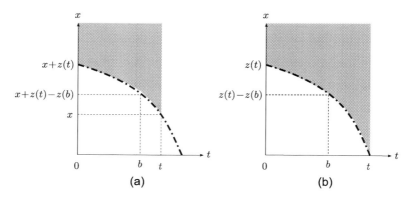

FIGURE 12.9 Illustration of the integral conservation equations.

Fig. 12.9(a) illustrates the integral conservation equation in (12.88) graphically. The dash-dotted curve represents a characteristic curve passing (t, x). Since $\delta(t, x)$ represents the number of trips with a distance not shorter than x at t, it includes the initial trips that are not shorter than $x + z(t)$, whose number is $\delta(0, x + z(t))$, and all trips that enter the network at $b \leq t$ with a distance not shorter than $x + z(t) - z(b)$, whose number is $\int_0^t f(b, x + z(t) - z(b))ds$; and all such trips are in the shaded region in the figure.

Similarly, Fig. 12.9(b) illustrates the integral conservation equation in (12.89).

12.4.2 Network fundamental diagram

If $v(t)$ is given, the conservation equation with the bathtub assumption, (12.63), is a complete model.

Note that $v(t)$ is the speed of running vehicles and also the speed of active trips. It could depend both the vehicle density and the trip density.

If the number of lane-miles of the network is denoted by L, then the density of running vehicles per lane-mile, denoted by $\rho(t)$. Thus, the total number of vehicles (or the fleet size) at t is $L\rho(t)$.

In the preceding sections, we have defined various trip densities. Here we first discuss the relationship between vehicle density and trip density. Then we introduce the second assumption of the network fundamental diagram.

Relationship between the vehicle density and trip density

If all passenger trips are served by privately operated vehicles (POVs), and the occupancy of each vehicle is 1, or if we are interested in vehicular trips, then the number of running vehicles in the road network equals the number of active trips. That is, $\rho(t)$ is given by

$$\rho(t) = \frac{\delta(t)}{L}. \tag{12.90}$$

Further, the relationship between the relative trip density $k(t,x)$ and the vehicle density $\rho(t)$ in (12.90) is as follows:

$$\rho(t) = \frac{\int_0^\infty k(t,x)dx}{L}. \tag{12.91}$$

In contrast, if trips are served by for-hire vehicles (FHVs), buses, metro, or other shared mobility systems, then $\rho(t)$ is determined by the corresponding fleet-size management schemes. In the traditional shared mobility system, the fleet size depends on the planning, operation, and control processes; but with FHVs, the fleet size could be adjusted in real time to reduce the wait time of passengers.

For a mixed mobility system, the relationship between the vehicle density and trip density can be more complicated.

Network fundamental diagram of vehicular traffic

For a road network, we assume that there exists a speed-density relation for all vehicles in the network. That is,

$$v(t) = V(\rho(t)), \tag{12.92}$$

which leads to the following flow-density relation:

$$q(t) = \rho(t)v(t) = Q(\rho(t)). \tag{12.93}$$

Here the unit of $q(t)$ is vehicle (or trip) per hour per lane. These relations constitute the network fundamental diagram for vehicular traffic.

In particular, for freeway networks, we can still use the triangular fundamental diagram:

$$V(\rho) = \min\{u, w(\frac{K}{\rho} - 1)\}. \tag{12.94}$$

For signalized road networks, we can use the following trapezoidal fundamental diagram:

$$V(\rho) = \min\{u, \frac{C}{\rho}, w(\frac{K}{\rho} - 1)\}, \tag{12.95}$$

where C is the average capacity determined by signal settings.

In addition, in shared mobility systems, the average running speeds of vehicles could also depend on the boarding and alighting times of passengers.

12.4.3 Time-independent negative exponential distribution of trip distances

In this subsection, we consider the special case when the distributions of the entering trips' distances and the remaining distances of active trips are the same and time-independent; i.e.,

$$\Phi(t,x) = \tilde{\Phi}(t,x) = \Phi(x); \tag{12.96}$$

equivalently,

$$\varphi(t,x) = \tilde{\varphi}(t,x) = \varphi(x). \tag{12.97}$$

The following Theorem 12.4.2 establishes that such a time-independent distribution has to be negative exponential; i.e.,

$$\Phi(x) = e^{-\frac{x}{B}}, \tag{12.98a}$$

$$\varphi(x) = \frac{1}{B}e^{-\frac{x}{B}}, \tag{12.98b}$$

where B is the average trip distance.

In this case, (12.63) can be simplified as

$$\frac{d}{dt}\delta(t) + \frac{1}{B}v(t)\delta(t) = f(t), \tag{12.99}$$

whose integral form can be simplified from (12.89) as

$$\delta(t) = \delta(0)e^{-\frac{z(t)}{B}} + \int_0^t f(b)e^{-\frac{z(t)-z(b)}{B}}db. \tag{12.100}$$

(12.99) can also be derived from the other two conservation equations: (12.54) and (12.56).

Theorem 12.4.2. *For the conservation equation in (12.63) with $v(t) > 0$, the following six statements are equivalent:*

(i) $\Phi(t,x) = \tilde{\Phi}(t,x) = e^{-\frac{x}{B}}$; i.e., the entering trips' distances and the remaining distances of active trips follow the same time-independent negative exponential distribution.
(ii) The remaining distances of active trips follow a time-independent negative exponential distribution: $\Phi(t,x) = e^{-\frac{x}{B}}$;
(iii) The distributions of the initial trips' remaining distances and the entering trips' total distances follow the same, time-independent negative exponential distribution: $\Phi(0,x) = \tilde{\Phi}(t,x) = e^{-\frac{x}{B}}$;
(iv) $\Phi(t,x) = \tilde{\Phi}(t,x) = \Phi(x)$; i.e., the entering trips' distances and the remaining distances of active trips follow the same time-independent distribution;

12.4 Three simplification assumptions

(v) *The entering trips' average distance and the active trips' average distance are equal and time-independent:*

$$B(t) = \tilde{B}(t) = B. \tag{12.101}$$

(vi) $\varphi(t, 0)$ *is time-independent:*

$$\varphi(t, 0) = \varphi(0) = \frac{1}{B}, \tag{12.102a}$$

$$g(t) = \frac{1}{B}\delta(t)v(t). \tag{12.102b}$$

Proof. From the definitions of the variables, (i) $\Rightarrow$ (ii), (iii), (iv), (v), and (vi); and (iv) $\Rightarrow$ (v).

If (ii) is correct, then substituting $\Phi(t, x) = e^{-\frac{x}{B}}$ into (12.63) we obtain

$$\frac{\partial}{\partial t}\delta(t)e^{-\frac{x}{B}} + \frac{1}{B}v(t)\delta(t)e^{-\frac{x}{B}} = f(t)\Phi(t, x),$$

which with $x = 0$ leads to

$$\frac{\partial}{\partial t}\delta(t) + \frac{1}{B}v(t)\delta(t) = f(t).$$

The above two equations lead to $\tilde{\Phi}(t, x) = e^{-\frac{x}{B}}$. Thus (ii) $\Rightarrow$ (i); and (ii) $\Rightarrow$ (iii).

We prove that (iii) $\Rightarrow$ (ii) by induction with the discrete equation in (12.64) as follows. First, $\Phi(0, x) = e^{-\frac{x}{B}}$ is given. Second, we assume that $\Phi(t, x) = e^{-\frac{x}{B}}$ at t. Third, we prove that $\Phi(t + \Delta t, x) = e^{-\frac{x}{B}}$ for an arbitrarily small Δt. From (12.64) we have

$$\delta(t + \Delta t)\Phi(t + \Delta t, x) = \delta(t)e^{-\frac{v(t)\Delta t}{B}}e^{-\frac{x}{B}} + f(t)\Delta t e^{-\frac{x}{B}},$$

which with $x = 0$ leads to

$$\delta(t + \Delta t) = \delta(t)e^{-\frac{v(t)\Delta t}{B}} + f(t)\Delta t.$$

Comparing the above two equations we have $\Phi(t + \Delta t, x) = e^{-\frac{x}{B}}$. By induction we have $\Phi(t, x) = e^{-\frac{x}{B}}$ at any $t \geq 0$. Thus, (iii) $\Rightarrow$ (ii). Therefore, (i), (ii), and (iii) are equivalent statements and imply (iv), (v), and (vi).

Next we prove (iv) $\Rightarrow$ (ii). In (12.64) we let $\Phi(t + \Delta t, x) = \Phi(t, x) = \tilde{\Phi}(t, x) = \Phi(x)$ according to (iv):

$$\delta(t + \Delta t)\Phi(x) = \delta(t)\Phi(x + v\Delta t) + f(t)\Delta t\Phi(x),$$

which with $x = 0$ leads to

$$\delta(t + \Delta t) = \delta(t)\Phi(v\Delta t) + f(t)\Delta t.$$

Comparing the above two equations we have

$$\Phi(x+v\Delta t) = \Phi(x)\Phi(v\Delta t).$$

Assuming that $\Phi(1) = e^{-\frac{1}{B}}$, we have from the above equation

$$\Phi(1) = \Phi(v\Delta t)^{\frac{1}{v\Delta t}},$$

which leads to $\Phi(v\Delta t) = e^{-\frac{v\Delta t}{B}}$ or $\Phi(x) = e^{-\frac{x}{B}}$. Thus, (iv) $\Rightarrow$ (ii), and the first four statements are equivalent.

If $B(t) = \tilde{B}(t) = B$, then (12.56) leads to

$$\frac{d}{dt}\delta(t) = f(t) - \frac{1}{B}\delta(t)v(t).$$

Comparing this equation with (12.65) we have $\varphi(t,0) = \frac{1}{B}$. Thus, (v) $\Rightarrow$ (vi).

When $\varphi(t,0) = \frac{1}{B}$, (12.65) leads to (12.99), whose integral version is (12.100). Comparing (12.100) and (12.88), we can conclude that $\Phi(0,x) = \tilde{\Phi}(t,x) = e^{-\frac{x}{B}}$. Thus (vi) $\Rightarrow$ (iii).

Therefore, all the six statements are equivalent. □

12.5 Bathtub models

In this section we derive bathtub models for vehicular trips or passenger trips served by privately operated vehicles with a unit occupancy. In these cases, the vehicle and trip densities are related by (12.90).

In addition, we adopt the bathtub and network fundamental diagram assumptions.

12.5.1 Derivation

For vehicular trips, we have the following speed-queue relation:

$$v(t) = V\left(\frac{\delta(t)}{L}\right). \qquad (12.103)$$

Combined with (12.63), this leads to the following bathtub model:

$$\frac{\partial}{\partial t}\delta(t,x) - V\left(\frac{\delta(t)}{L}\right)\frac{\partial}{\partial x}\delta(t,x) = f(t,x). \qquad (12.104)$$

In this model, the only unknown variable is $\delta(t,x)$ with $\delta(t) = \delta(t,0)$, $f(t,x)$ is the boundary condition and represents the demand pattern, and the initial condition is given by $\delta(0,x)$ for $x \in [0,\infty)$.

12.5 Bathtub models

If we use $k(t, x)$ as the unknown variable, (12.104) is equivalent to

$$\frac{\partial}{\partial t}k(t, x) - V\left(\frac{\int_0^\infty k(t, y)dy}{L}\right)\frac{\partial}{\partial x}k(t, x) = f(t)\tilde{\varphi}(t, x), \quad (12.105)$$

for which $f(t)$ and $\tilde{\varphi}(t, x)$ represent the demand pattern and boundary condition, and $k(0, x)$ is the initial condition.

Both (12.104) and (12.105) are partial differential equations. In particular, (12.105) resembles the LWR model discussed in Chapter 5. But (12.105) has a source term on the right-hand side, and the characteristic wave speed $-V\left(\frac{\int_0^\infty k(t,y)dy}{L}\right)$ is a function of the integral of the unknown variable $k(t, x)$; thus, (12.105) is a non-local model.

After solving $\delta(t, x)$ in (12.104) or $k(t, x)$ in (12.105), we can obtain $\varphi(t, x)$, $\Phi(t, x)$, $v(t)$, $z(t)$, and other variables.

The integral version of the bathtub model, (12.104), is given by the integral version of the conservation equation in (12.88), or (12.89), plus the following differential equation

$$\dot{z}(t) = V\left(\frac{\delta(t)}{L}\right), \quad (12.106)$$

which is derived from (12.103) and (12.67). In particular, (12.89) and (12.106) form a complete model, in which $\delta(t)$ is the unknown variable, and $\delta(t, x)$ does not need to be explicitly tracked.

For shared or mixed mobility systems, we can also derive the corresponding bathtub model, given the corresponding speed-queue relation.

12.5.2 Vickrey's bathtub model

When the trip distances follow a time-independent negative exponential distribution, the bathtub model, (12.104), can be simplified as

$$\frac{d}{dt}\delta(t) = f(t) - \frac{1}{B}\delta(t)V\left(\frac{\delta(t)}{L}\right), \quad (12.107)$$

which can be derived from (12.99) and (12.103). Its integral version is given by (12.100) and (12.106).

(12.107) is a special bathtub model, as it is an ordinary differential equation, compared with a partial differential equation in (12.104). We can see that this model is derived based on the three assumptions discussed in Section 12.4: (i) the bathtub assumption; (ii) the network fundamental diagram, and (iii) the time-independent negative exponential distribution of trip distances. This model is referred to as Vickrey's bathtub model, since Vickrey was the first one to derive the model from the three assumptions.

12.6 Numerical methods

12.6.1 A numerical method for solving the integral form

To solve the integral form of the bathtub model numerically, a difference-integration method can be developed to solve $\delta(t)$ and $z(t)$ from (12.89) and (12.106), and then $\delta(t, x)$ from (12.88) as follows.

We divide the range of trip distances $[0, X]$ into I intervals with $\Delta x = \frac{X}{I}$, where X is the maximum trip distance. We discretize the study period $[0, T]$ to J time steps with $\Delta t = \frac{T}{J}$. At $j\Delta t$ ($j = 0, 1, \cdots, J$), the number of active trips in the network is δ^j, the travel speed by v^j, and the characteristic travel distance by z^j.

$$v^j = V\left(\frac{\delta^j}{L}\right), \qquad (12.108a)$$

$$z^{j+1} = z^j + v^j \Delta t, \qquad (12.108b)$$

$$\delta^{j+1} = \delta(0, z^{j+1}) + \sum_{m=0}^{j} f(m\Delta t)\tilde{\Phi}(m\Delta t, z^{j+1} - z^m)\Delta t. \qquad (12.108c)$$

Then for $j = 0, \cdots, J-1$ and $i = 0, \cdots, I$

$$\delta((j+1)\Delta t, i\Delta x) = \delta(0, i\Delta x + z^{j+1})$$
$$+ \sum_{m=0}^{j} f(m\Delta t)\tilde{\Phi}(m\Delta t, i\Delta x + z^{j+1} - z^m)\Delta t.$$

12.6.2 A numerical method for solving the differential form

The differential form of the bathtub model, (12.104), can be numerically solved to obtain $\delta(t, x)$ as follows.

At jth time step, the time is denoted by t_j ($j = 0, 1, \cdots$), where $t_0 = 0$. At t_j, $\delta(t_j, i\Delta x)$ is denoted by δ_i^j ($i = 0, \cdots, I$), and the number of active trips in the network is $\delta^j = \delta_0^j$. Further the corresponding speed is denoted by $v^j = V(\frac{\delta^j}{L})$. If we denote the step-size $\Delta t^j = \frac{\Delta x}{v^j}$, which may be different at different time steps, then $t_{j+1} = t_j + \Delta t^j$, and $z(t_j) = j\Delta x$.

From (12.64) we can update δ_i^{j+1} ($i = 0, \cdots, I-1$) as follows:

$$\delta_i^{j+1} = \delta_{i+1}^j + \tilde{\delta}_i^j, \qquad (12.109)$$

where $\tilde{\delta}_i^j = f(t_j)\tilde{\Phi}(t_j, i\Delta x)\Delta t^j$.

The algorithm stops when the network is gridlocked with $v^j = 0$ or when t_{j+1} is beyond the study period T.

12.6.3 A numerical example

As an example of the second numerical method in Section 12.6.2, we consider a network with $L = 10$ lane-miles, the speed-density relation is

$$V(\rho) = \min\{30, \frac{750}{\rho}, 10(\frac{200}{\rho} - 1)\}.$$

Initially the network is empty, the in-flux during a peak period is given by the following trapezoidal function:

$$f(t) = \max\{0, \min\{10000t, 4000, 10000(1-t)\}\},$$

and the trip distance follows a uniform distribution:

$$\tilde{\Phi}(t, x) = \max\{0, 1 - \frac{x}{2\tilde{B}(t)}\},$$

where $\tilde{B}(t)$ is the time-dependent average trip distance at t:

$$\tilde{B}(t) = 2 + \max\{0, \min\{7.5t, 3, 7.5(1-t)\}\}.$$

Here the maximum remaining trip distance is $X = 5$ miles, and both the in-flux and the average trip distance are symmetric and reach their respective maximum values between 0.4 and 0.6 hr. The initial condition is given by $\delta_i^0 = 0$. We simulate the system until the characteristic travel distance reaches 30 miles.

We first let $\Delta x = 2^{-6}$ mile and $I = 320$. The evolution of $K(t, x)$ is illustrated in Fig. 12.10(a), which shows that the number of active trips reaches the maximum value between 0.75 and 1 hr. Thus the network is most congested between 0.75 and 1 hr, even though the demand pattern peaks between 0.4 and 0.6 hr.

In Fig. 12.10(b) we present the solutions of $z(t)$ for different Δx's. From this figure we can see that the solutions converge with diminishing Δx; it suggests that the numerical solution converges to the theoretical one when Δx diminishes. By comparing the times for the characteristic travel distance to reach 30 miles, we obtain an approximate convergence rate of 1.

Notes

Note 12.1. *Please refer to (McNally, 2007) for a review of the four-step method.*

Note 12.2. *The remaining trip distance was used as the new space dimension in (Vickrey, 1991, 2020).*

Note 12.3. *The main state variable in the bathtub model is $\delta(t, x)$, see e.g. the general conservation equation in (12.61), which is the number of active trips with*

240   12. The bathtub model

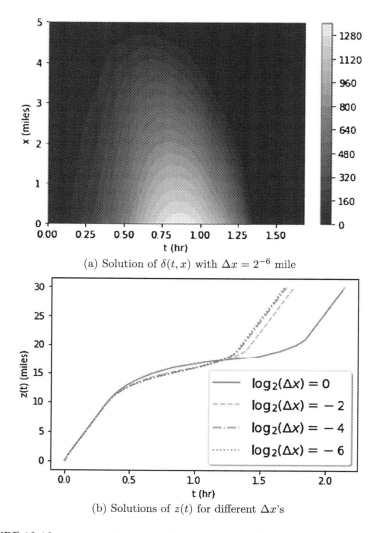

(a) Solution of $\delta(t,x)$ with $\Delta x = 2^{-6}$ mile

(b) Solutions of $z(t)$ for different Δx's

FIGURE 12.10 A numerical example of the bathtub model.

a remaining distance not smaller than x. This variable was first introduced in (Vickrey, 1991, 2020) as "the number of vehicles having a remaining trip distance greater than x".

Note 12.4. *The "bathtub" assumption in Section 12.4 was introduced by Vickrey around 1990. In (Vickrey, 1994, 2019), he started the discussions on bathtub models by "a maze of congested streets is treated as an undifferentiated movement area in which movement takes place at a speed". In (Vickrey, 2020), co-editor Arnott commented that "Vickrey coined the term 'bathtub model' not only because the* filling and emptying of a bathtub provides an intuitively appealing analogy to the rise and fall of traffic density in the morning rush hour but also because Manhattan is shaped like a bathtub and in the early morning rush hour its bridges and tunnels act like taps, providing the entry flow."

Note 12.5. *Refer to (Ibarra-Rojas et al., 2015) for a comprehensive literature review on the planning, operation, and control process of bus transport systems. Refer to (Schaller, 2018; Castiglione et al., 2018) for empirical studies on transportation network companies and for-hire vehicles.*

Note 12.6. *The network fundamental diagram for signalized road network was first observed in (Godfrey, 1969). In (Vickrey, 1991, 1994, 2019, 2020), it was assumed that "speed is a function of the density of cars in the area" to derive the bathtub model, without knowing Godfrey's work. In (Vickrey, 1991), it was mentioned that "Actual data are available for a period in 1983 (for the city of New York), and are indeed somewhat sketchy". In (Vickrey, 1994), it was mentioned that "The dry run in Hong Kong should have yielded data of this kind but as far as I know the data was not processed for this purpose." More recently, (Falcocchio and Afshar, 2005) calibrated the network fundamental diagram for a lower Manhattan road network with observed and simulated data; (Geroliminis and Daganzo, 2008) calibrated the network fundamental diagram for a signalized road network in Yokohama, Japan; in (Cassidy et al., 2011), the network fundamental diagram was calibrated for a freeway network.*

Note 12.7. *The bathtub model (12.104) was presented in (Jin, 2020), and it was referred to as the generalized bathtub model.*

Note 12.8. *Vickrey's bathtub model (12.107) was also independently derived in (Small and Chu, 2003; Daganzo, 2007). But both of the articles did not include the third assumption of the time-independent negative exponential distribution of trip distances. Many follow-up studies of (Daganzo, 2007) applied the model to constant trip distances, which would lead to physically unreasonable results (Mariotte et al., 2017).*

Note 12.9. *When all entering trips have the same constant distances, the bathtub model, (12.104), becomes the basic bathtub model, which has been studied in (Arnott et al., 2016; Arnott and Buli, 2018; Jin, 2020). In (Fosgerau, 2015), a bathtub model was developed for deterministic distributions of trip distances, and trips are "regularly sorted" such that shorter trips enter the network later but exit earlier than longer ones (last-in-first-out).*

Note 12.10. *Vickrey's bathtub model has been applied to study congestion pricing problem in (Vickrey, 1991, 2020), the departure time choice user equilibrium problem in (Small and Chu, 2003), and perimeter travel demand control problem in (Daganzo, 2007). The basic bathtub model was applied to solve the departure time user equilibrium problem in (Arnott et al., 2016; Arnott and Buli, 2018). Another bathtub model was used to solve the departure time user equilibrium problem in (Fosgerau, 2015).*

Problems

Problem 12.1. *Prove Lemma 12.2.1.*

Problem 12.2. *Prove Theorem 12.2.2.*

Problem 12.3. *Prove Lemma 12.2.3.*

Problem 12.4. *Prove Lemma 12.2.4.*

Problem 12.5. *Prove Theorem 12.2.5.*

Problem 12.6. *Prove Lemma 12.2.6.*

Problem 12.7. *Prove Lemma 12.2.7.*

Problem 12.8. *Prove Lemma 12.4.1*

Problem 12.9. *Critically review (Vickrey, 2020).*

Problem 12.10. *Critically review (Small and Chu, 2003).*

Problem 12.11. *Critically review (Daganzo, 2007).*

Problem 12.12. *Numerically solve the example in Section 12.6.3 with the method in Section 12.6.1.*

Bibliography

Agogino, A., Goebel, K., Alag, S., 1995. Intelligent sensor validation and sensor fusion for reliability and safety enhancement in vehicle control. Technical report. California Partners for Advanced Transit and Highways (PATH).

Akiva, M.E.B., Lerman, S.R., 1985. Discrete Choice Analysis: Theory and Application to Predict Travel Demand, vol. 9. The MIT Press.

Allen, R.W., Harwood, D., Chrstos, J., Glauz, W., 2000. The capability and enhancement of VDANL and TWOPAS for analyzing vehicle performance on upgrades and downgrades within IHSDM. Technical report. Federal Highway Administration. 00-078.

Ambühl, L., Loder, A., Menendez, M., Axhausen, K.W., 2017. Empirical macroscopic fundamental diagrams: new insights from loop detector and floating car data. In: Transportation Research Board 96th Annual Meeting. Number 17-03331.

Ansorge, R., 1990. What does the entropy condition mean in traffic flow theory? Transportation Research Part B 24 (2), 133–143.

Arnott, A., et al., 1990. Departure time and route choice for the morning commute. Transportation Research Part B 24 (3), 209–228.

Arnott, R., Buli, J., 2018. Solving for equilibrium in the basic bathtub model. Transportation Research Part B 109, 150–175.

Arnott, R., Kokoza, A., Naji, M., 2016. Equilibrium traffic dynamics in a bathtub model: a special case. Economics of Transportation 7, 38–52.

Asano, M., Sumalee, A., Kuwahara, M., Tanaka, S., 2007. Dynamic cell transmission–based pedestrian model with multidirectional flows and strategic route choices. Transportation Research Record 2039 (1), 42–49.

Baker, R., Christenson, C., Orde, H., 2004. Bernhard Riemann Collected Papers. Kendrick Press.

Banks, J., 1990. Flow processes at a freeway bottleneck. Transportation Research Record (1287), 20–28.

Banks, J.H., 1991a. Two-capacity phenomenon at freeway bottlenecks: a basis for ramp metering? Transportation Research Record: Journal of the Transportation Research Board 1320, 91–98.

Banks, J.H., 1991b. The two-capacity phenomenon: some theoretical issues. Transportation Research Record: Journal of the Transportation Research Board 1320, 234–241.

Bar-Gera, H., Ahn, S., 2010. Empirical macroscopic evaluation of freeway merge-ratios. Transportation Research Part C (ISSN 0968-090X) 18 (4), 457–470.

Bardi, M., Capuzzo-Dolcetta, I., 2008. Optimal Control and Viscosity Solutions of Hamilton-Jacobi-Bellman Equations. Springer Science & Business Media.

Bardos, C., Leroux, A., Nedelec, J., 1979. First order quasilinear equations with boundary conditions. Communications in Partial Differential Equations (ISSN 0360-5302) 4 (9), 1017–1034.

Barth, M., Malcolm, C., Younglove, T., Hill, N., 2001. Recent validation efforts for a comprehensive modal emissions model. Transportation Research Record: Journal of the Transportation Research Board (1750), 13–23.

Benzoni-Gavage, S., Colombo, R., 2003. An n-populations model for traffic flow. European Journal of Applied Mathematics 14 (05), 587–612.

Bliemer, M., 2007. Dynamic queuing and spillback in analytical multiclass dynamic network loading model. Transportation Research Record: Journal of the Transportation Research Board 2029, 14–21.

BPR, 1964. Traffic Assignment Manual for Application with a Large, High Speed Computer, vol. 2. United States Bureau of Public Roads.

Bui, D., Nelson, P., Narasimhan, S., Institute, T.T., T.D. of Transportation, 1992. Computational realizations of the entropy condition in modeling congested traffic flow. Technical report.

Buisson, C., Ladier, C., 2009. Exploring the impact of homogeneity of traffic measurements on the existence of macroscopic fundamental diagrams. Transportation Research Record: Journal of the Transportation Research Board 2124, 127–136.

Burd, M., Archer, D., Aranwela, N., Stradling, D., 2002. Traffic dynamics of the leaf-cutting ant, Atta cephalotes. American Naturalist 159 (3), 283–293.

Burger, R., Kozakevicius, A., 2007. Adaptive multiresolution weno schemes for multi-species kinematic flow models. Journal of Computational Physics 224 (2), 1190–1222.

Bürger, R., García, A., Karlsen, K., Towers, J., 2008. A family of numerical schemes for kinematic flows with discontinuous flux. Journal of Engineering Mathematics 60 (3), 387–425.

Burgers, J., 1948. A mathematical model illustrating the theory of turbulence. Advances in Applied Mechanics 1 (171–199), 677.

Burgers, J.M., 1940. Application of a model system to illustrate some points of the statistical theory of free turbulence. In: Proc. Acad. Sci. Amsterdam, vol. 43.

Carlson, R.C., Papamichail, I., Papageorgiou, M., 2011. Local feedback-based mainstream traffic flow control on motorways using variable speed limits. IEEE Transactions on Intelligent Transportation Systems 12 (4), 1261–1276.

Carlson, R.C., Papamichail, I., Papageorgiou, M., 2013. Comparison of local feedback controllers for the mainstream traffic flow on freeways using variable speed limits. Journal of Intelligent Transportation Systems 17 (4), 268–281.

Cascetta, E., 2009. Transportation Systems Analysis: Models and Applications, vol. 29. Springer Science & Business Media.

Cassidy, M., 1998. Bivariate relations in nearly stationary highway traffic. Transportation Research Part B 32 (1), 49–59.

Cassidy, M., Jang, K., Daganzo, C.F., 2011. Macroscopic fundamental diagrams for freeway networks. Transportation Research Record: Journal of the Transportation Research Board 2260, 8–15.

Cassidy, M.J., Bertini, R.L., 1999. Some traffic features at freeway bottlenecks. Transportation Research Part B 33 (1), 25–42.

Castiglione, J., Cooper, D., Sana, B., Tischler, D., Chang, T., Erhardt, G.D., Roy, S., Chen, M., Mucci, A., 2018. TNCs & Congestion. Technical report. SF County Transportation Authority.

Chandler, R., Herman, R., Montroll, E., 1958. Traffic dynamics: studies in car following. Operations Research 6 (2), 165–184.

Chanut, S., Buisson, C., 2003. Macroscopic model and its numerical solution for two-flow mixed traffic with different speeds and lengths. Transportation Research Record: Journal of the Transportation Research Board 1852, 209–219.

Chung, K., Rudjanakanoknad, J., Cassidy, M., 2007. Relation between traffic density and capacity drop at three freeway bottlenecks. Transportation Research Part B 41 (1), 82–95.

Claudel, C.G., Bayen, A.M., 2010. Lax–Hopf based incorporation of internal boundary conditions into Hamilton-Jacobi equation. Part II: Computational methods. IEEE Transactions on Automatic Control 55 (5), 1158–1174.

Coclite, G., Garavello, M., Piccoli, B., 2005. Traffic flow on a road network. SIAM Journal on Mathematical Analysis 36 (6), 1862–1886.

Cominetti, R., Correa, J., Larré, O., 2015. Dynamic equilibria in fluid queueing networks. Operations Research 63 (1), 21–34.

Courant, R., Friedrichs, K., Lewy, H., 1928. Über die partiellen Differenzengleichungen der mathematischen Physik. Mathematische Annalen 100 (1), 32–74.

Daganzo, C.F., 1994. The cell transmission model: a dynamic representation of highway traffic consistent with hydrodynamic theory. Transportation Research Part B 28 (4), 269–287.

Daganzo, C.F., 1995a. The cell transmission model II: network traffic. Transportation Research Part B 29 (2), 79–93.

Daganzo, C.F., 1995b. A finite difference approximation of the kinematic wave model of traffic flow. Transportation Research Part B 29 (4), 261–276.

Daganzo, C.F., 1996. The nature of freeway gridlock and how to prevent it. In: Proceedings of the 13th International Symposium on Transportation and Traffic Theory, pp. 629–646.

Daganzo, C.F., 1997a. Fundamentals of Transportation and Traffic Operations. Pergamon-Elsevier, Oxford, U.K.

Daganzo, C.F., 1997b. A continuum theory of traffic dynamics for freeways with special lanes. Transportation Research Part B 31 (2), 83–102.

Daganzo, C.F., 2005a. A variational formulation of kinematic waves: basic theory and complex boundary conditions. Transportation Research Part B 39 (2), 187–196.

Daganzo, C.F., 2005b. A variational formulation of kinematic waves: solution methods. Transportation Research Part B 39 (10), 934–950.

Daganzo, C.F., 2006. In traffic flow, cellular automata = kinematic waves. Transportation Research Part B 40 (5), 396–403.

Daganzo, C.F., 2007. Urban gridlock: macroscopic modeling and mitigation approaches. Transportation Research Part B 41 (1), 49–62.

Daganzo, C.F., Geroliminis, N., 2008. An analytical approximation for the macroscopic fundamental diagram of urban traffic. Transportation Research Part B 42 (9), 771–781.

Daganzo, C.F., Lin, W.-H., Del Castillo, J.M., 1997. A simple physical principle for the simulation of freeways with special lanes and priority vehicles. Transportation Research Part B 31 (2), 103–125.

Del Castillo, J., 1996. A car following model based on the Lighthill-Whitham theory. In: Proceedings of the 13th International Symposium on Transportation and Traffic Theory, pp. 517–538.

Del Castillo, J., Pintado, P., Benitez, F., 1994. The reaction time of drivers and the stability of traffic flow. Transportation Research Part B 28 (1), 35–60.

Del Castillo, J.M., Benitez, F.G., 1995. On the functional form of the speed-density relationship - II: empirical investigation. Transportation Research Part B 29 (5), 391–406.

Dixon, K.K., Hummer, J.E., Lorscheider, A.R., 1996. Capacity for North Carolina freeway work zones. Transportation Research Record: Journal of the Transportation Research Board 1529, 27–34.

Downs, A., 2004. Still Stuck in Traffic: Coping with Peak-Hour Traffic Congestion. Brookings Institution Press.

Drake, J.S., Schofer, J.L., May, A.D., 1967. A statistical analysis of speed-density hypotheses. Highway Research Record 156, 53–87.

Drissi-Kaïtouni, O., Hameda-Benchekroun, A., 1992. A dynamic traffic assignment model and a solution algorithm. Transportation Science 26 (2), 119–128.

Edie, L., 1961. Car following and steady-state theory for non-congested traffic. Operations Research 9 (1), 66–76.

Engquist, B., Osher, S., 1980a. Stable and entropy satisfying approximations for transonic flow calculations. Mathematics of Computation 34 (149), 45–75.

Engquist, B., Osher, S., 1980b. One-sided difference schemes and transonic flow. Proceedings of the National Academy of Sciences 77 (6), 3071–3074.

Evans, L., 1998. Partial Differential Equations. American Mathematical Society.

Falcocchio, J.C., Afshar, A., 2005. Traffic Mobility and Real-Time Congestion Management for Lower Manhattan: a Case Study. Technical report. URBAN ITS CENTER, Polytechnic University.

Federal Highway Administration, 2004. Traffic Flow Theory: A State of the Art Report. Transportation Research Board.

Flötteröd, G., Rohde, J., 2011. Operational macroscopic modeling of complex urban road intersections. Transportation Research Part B 45 (6), 903–922.

Fosgerau, M., 2015. Congestion in the bathtub. Economics of Transportation 4 (4), 241–255.
Gan, Q.-J., Jin, W.-L., 2013. Validation of a macroscopic lane-changing model. Transportation Research Record: Journal of the Transportation Research Board 2391, 113–123.
Gan, Q.-J., Jin, W.-L., Gayah, V.V., 2017. Analysis of traffic statics and dynamics in signalized networks: a Poincaré map approach. Transportation Science 51 (3), 1009–1029.
Gartner, N.H., Wagner, P., 2004. Analysis of traffic flow characteristics on signalized arterials. Transportation Research Record: Journal of the Transportation Research Board 1883, 94–100.
Geroliminis, N., Daganzo, C.F., 2008. Existence of urban-scale macroscopic fundamental diagrams: some experimental findings. Transportation Research Part B 42 (9), 759–770.
Gipps, P., 1981. Behavioral car-following model for computer simulation. Transportation Research Part B 15 (2), 105–111.
Godfrey, J., 1969. The mechanism of a road network. Traffic Engineering and Control 8 (8), 323–327.
Godunov, S.K., 1959. A difference method for numerical calculations of discontinuous solutions of the equations of hydrodynamics. Matematicheskii Sbornik 47 (3), 271–306. In Russian.
Goldstein, H., Poole, C., Safko, J., 2002. Classical Mechanics. American Association of Physics Teachers.
Greenberg, H., 1959. An analysis of traffic flow. Operations Research 7 (1), 79–85.
Greenberg, H., Daou, A., 1960. The control of traffic flow to increase the flow. Operations Research 8 (4), 524–532.
Greenshields, B.D., 1935. A study of traffic capacity. Highway Research Board Proceedings 14, 448–477.
Gu, Y., Qian, Z., Zhang, G., 2017. Traffic state estimation for urban road networks using a link queue model. Transportation Research Record 2623 (1), 29–39.
Haberman, R., 1977. Mathematical Models. Prentice Hall, Englewood Cliffs, NJ.
Haight, F.A., 1963. Mathematical Theories of Traffic Flow. Academic Press, New York.
Hall, F., Hurdle, V., Banks, J., 1992. Synthesis of recent work on the nature of speed-flow and flow-occupancy (or density) relationships on freeways. Transportation Research Record 1365, 12–18.
Hall, F.L., Agyemang-Duah, K., 1991. Freeway capacity drop and the definition of capacity. Transportation Research Record: Journal of the Transportation Research Board 1320, 91–98.
Hankin, B., Wright, R., 1958. Passenger flow in subways. Operations Research 9 (2), 81–88.
Hegyi, A., De Schutter, B., Hellendoorn, H., 2005. Model predictive control for optimal coordination of ramp metering and variable speed limits. Transportation Research Part C (ISSN 0968-090X) 13 (3), 185–209.
Hiraoka, T., Kunimatsu, T., Nishihara, O., Kumamoto, H., 2005. Modeling of driver following behavior based on minimum-jerk theory. In: Proc. 12th World Congress ITS.
Holden, H., Risebro, N.H., 1995. A mathematical model of traffic flow on a network of unidirectional roads. SIAM Journal on Mathematical Analysis 26 (4), 999–1017.
Hopf, E., 1950. The partial differential equation $u_t + uu_x = \mu u_{xx}$. Communications on Pure and Applied Mathematics (ISSN 1097-0312) 3 (3), 201–230.
Ibarra-Rojas, O.J., Delgado, F., Giesen, R., Muñoz, J.C., 2015. Planning, operation, and control of bus transport systems: a literature review. Transportation Research Part B: Methodological 77, 38–75.
Iryo, T., Yoshii, T., 2007. Equivalent optimization problem for finding equilibrium in the bottleneck model with departure time choices. In: Mathematics in Transport: Selected Proceedings of the 4th IMA International Conference on Mathematics in Transport: in Honour of Richard Allsop. Emerald Group Pub Ltd, p. 231.
Isaacson, E.I., Temple, J.B., 1992. Nonlinear resonance in systems of conservation laws. SIAM Journal on Applied Mathematics 52 (5), 1260–1278.

Jabari, S.E., 2016. Node modeling for congested urban road networks. Transportation Research Part B: Methodological 91, 229–249.

Jiang, Y., 1999. Traffic capacity, speed, and queue-discharge rate of Indiana's four-lane freeway work zones. Transportation Research Record: Journal of the Transportation Research Board 1657, 10–17.

Jin, H.-Y., Jin, W.-L., 2015. Control of a lane-drop bottleneck through variable speed limits. Transportation Research Part C 58, 568–582.

Jin, W.-L., 2003. Kinematic Wave Models of Network Vehicular Traffic. PhD thesis. University of California, Davis. http://arxiv.org/abs/math.DS/0309060.

Jin, W.-L., 2009. Asymptotic traffic dynamics arising in diverge-merge networks with two intermediate links. Transportation Research Part B 43 (5), 575–595.

Jin, W.-L., 2010a. A kinematic wave theory of lane-changing traffic flow. Transportation Research Part B 44 (8–9), 1001–1021.

Jin, W.-L., 2010b. Macroscopic characteristics of lane-changing traffic. Transportation Research Record: Journal of the Transportation Research Board 2188, 55–63.

Jin, W.-L., 2010c. Continuous kinematic wave models of merging traffic flow. Transportation Research Part B 44 (8–9), 1084–1103.

Jin, W.-L., 2012a. A link queue model of network traffic flow. arXiv preprint. arXiv:1209.2361.

Jin, W.-L., 2012b. A kinematic wave theory of multi-commodity network traffic flow. Transportation Research Part B 46 (8), 1000–1022.

Jin, W.-L., 2012c. The traffic statics problem in a road network. Transportation Research Part B 46 (10), 1360–1373.

Jin, W.-L., 2013. A multi-commodity Lighthill–Whitham–Richards model of lane-changing traffic flow. Transportation Research Part B 57, 361–377.

Jin, W.-L., 2015a. On the existence of stationary states in general road networks. Transportation Research Part B 81, 917–929.

Jin, W.-L., 2015b. Continuous formulations and analytical properties of the link transmission model. Transportation Research Part B 74, 88–103.

Jin, W.-L., 2015c. Point queue models: a unified approach. Transportation Research Part B 77, 1–16.

Jin, W.-L., 2016. On the equivalence between continuum and car-following models of traffic flow. Transportation Research Part B 93, 543–559.

Jin, W.-L., 2017a. A first-order behavioral model of capacity drop. Transportation Research Part B 105, 438–457.

Jin, W.-L., 2017b. Kinematic wave models of lane-drop bottlenecks. Transportation Research Part B 105, 507–522.

Jin, W.-L., 2017c. A Riemann solver for a system of hyperbolic conservation laws at a general road junction. Transportation Research Part B 98, 21–41.

Jin, W.-L., 2017d. On the stability of stationary states in general road networks. Transportation Research Part B: Methodological 98, 42–61.

Jin, W.-L., 2017e. Unifiable multi-commodity kinematic wave model. In: Transportation Research Procedia: Proceedings of the 22nd International Symposium on Transportation and Traffic Theory, vol. 23, pp. 137–156.

Jin, W.-L., 2018. Kinematic wave models of sag and tunnel bottlenecks. Transportation Research Part B 107, 41–56.

Jin, W.-L., 2020. Generalized bathtub model of network trip flows. Transportation Research Part B 136, 138–157.

Jin, W.-L., Jin, H.-Y., 2014. Analysis and design of a variable speed limit control system at a freeway lane-drop bottleneck: a switched systems approach. In: Proceedings of the 53rd IEEE Conference on Decision and Control.

Jin, W.-L., Laval, J., 2018. Bounded acceleration traffic flow models: a unified approach. Transportation Research Part B 111, 1–18.

Jin, W.-L., Wada, K., 2018. A new cell transmission model with priority vehicles and special lanes. Transportation Research Procedia 34, 28–35.

Jin, W.-L., Yan, Q., 2019. A formulation of unifiable multi-commodity kinematic wave model with relative speed ratios. Transportation Research Part B 128, 236–253.
Jin, W.-L., Yu, Y., 2015. Performance analysis and signal design for a stationary signalized ring road. arXiv preprint. arXiv:1510.01216.
Jin, W.-L., Zhang, H.M., 2003a. The inhomogeneous kinematic wave traffic flow model as a resonant nonlinear system. Transportation Science 37 (3), 294–311.
Jin, W.-L., Zhang, H.M., 2003b. On the distribution schemes for determining flows through a merge. Transportation Research Part B 37 (6), 521–540.
Jin, W.-L., Zhang, H.M., 2004. A multicommodity kinematic wave simulation model of network traffic flow. Transportation Research Record: Journal of the Transportation Research Board 1883, 59–67.
Jin, W.-L., Chen, L., Puckett, E.G., 2009. Supply-demand diagrams and a new framework for analyzing the inhomogeneous Lighthill-Whitham-Richards model. In: Proceedings of the 18th International Symposium on Transportation and Traffic Theory, pp. 603–635.
Jin, W.-L., Wang, X., Lou, Y., 2020. Stable dynamic pricing scheme independent of lane-choice models for high-occupancy-toll lanes. Transportation Research Part B 140, 64–78.
Kerner, B.S., Konhäuser, P., 1994. Structure and parameters of clusters in traffic flow. Physical Review E 50 (1), 54–83.
Koshi, M., 1984. Traffic flow phenomena in expressway tunnels. IATSS Review 10 (1), 32–38. In Japanese.
Koshi, M., 1986. Capacity of motorway bottlenecks. Doboku Gakkai Ronbunshu 1986 (371), 1–7. In Japanese.
Koshi, M., Iwasaki, M., Ohkura, I., 1983. Some findings and an overview on vehicular flow characteristics. In: Proceedings of the Eighth International Symposium on Transportation and Traffic Theory, pp. 403–426.
Koshi, M., Kuwahara, M., Akahane, H., 1992. Capacity of sags and tunnels on Japanese motorways. ite Journal 62 (5), 17–22.
Krammes, R., Lopez, G., 1994. Updated capacity values for short-term freeway work zone lane closures. Transportation Research Record (1442).
Kulkarni, V., 1997. Fluid models for single buffer systems. Frontiers in Queueing: Models and Applications in Science and Engineering, 321–338.
Kuwahara, M., Akamatsu, T., 1997. Decomposition of the reactive dynamic assignments with queues for a many-to-many origin-destination pattern. Transportation Research Part B 31 (1), 1–10.
Kuwahara, M., Akamatsu, T., 2001. Dynamic user optimal assignment with physical queues for a many-to-many OD pattern. Transportation Research Part B 35 (5), 461–479.
Lanczos, C., 1986. The Variational Principles of Mechanics. Number 4. Dover Publications.
Laval, J., Daganzo, C.F., 2006. Lane-changing in traffic streams. Transportation Research Part B 40 (3), 251–264.
Laval, J.A., Leclercq, L., 2013. The Hamilton–Jacobi partial differential equation and the three representations of traffic flow. Transportation Research Part B 52, 17–30.
Laval, J.A., He, Z., Castrillon, F., 2012. Stochastic extension of Newell's three-detector method. Transportation Research Record: Journal of the Transportation Research Board 2315, 73–80.
Lax, P.D., 1972. Hyperbolic Systems of Conservation Laws and the Mathematical Theory of Shock Waves. SIAM, Philadelphia, Pennsylvania.
Le Boudec, J., Thiran, P., 2001. Network Calculus: A Theory of Deterministic Queuing Systems for the Internet. Springer-Verlag.
Lebacque, J., 2002. A two-phase extension of the LWR model based on the boundedness of traffic acceleration. In: Proceedings of ISTTT 2002.
Lebacque, J.-P., 1984. Semi-macroscopic simulation of urban traffic. In: Proceed. Int. AMSE Conf. "Modelling & Simulation", vol. 4, pp. 273–292.

Lebacque, J.P., 1996. The Godunov scheme and what it means for first order traffic flow models. In: Proceedings of the 13th International Symposium on Transportation and Traffic Theory, pp. 647–678.

Lebacque, J.P., Khoshyaran, M., 2005. First order macroscopic traffic flow models: intersection modeling, network modeling. In: Proceedings of the 16th International Symposium on Transportation and Traffic Theory, pp. 365–386.

Leo, C.J., Pretty, R.L., 1992. Numerical simulation of macroscopic continuum traffic models. Transportation Research Part B 26 (3), 207–220.

LeVeque, R.J., 1992. Numerical Methods for Conservation Laws. Springer Science & Business Media.

LeVeque, R.J., 2001. Some traffic flow models illustrating interesting hyperbolic behavior. In: SIAM 2001 Annual Meeting. San Diego, CA.

LeVeque, R.J., 2002. Finite Volume Methods for Hyperbolic Problems. Cambridge University Press, Cambridge; New York.

Li, J., Zhang, H., 2013. Modeling space–time inhomogeneities with the kinematic wave theory. Transportation Research Part B 54, 113–125.

Li, J., Fujiwara, O., Kawakami, S., 2000. A reactive dynamic user equilibrium model in network with queues. Transportation Research Part B 34 (8), 605–624.

Lighthill, M.J., Whitham, G.B., 1955. On kinematic waves: II. A theory of traffic flow on long crowded roads. Proceedings of the Royal Society of London A 229 (1178), 317–345.

Lopez, A., Jin, W.-L., Al Faruque, M.A., 2020. Security analysis for fixed-time traffic control systems. Transportation Research Part B 139, 473–495.

Mahmassani, H.S., Williams, J.C., Herman, R., 1984. Investigation of network-level traffic flow relationships: some simulation results. Transportation Research Record 971, 121–130.

Makigami, Y., Newell, G.F., Rothery, R., 1971. Three-dimensional representation of traffic flow. Transportation Science 5 (3), 302–313.

Mariotte, G., Leclercq, L., Laval, J.A., 2017. Macroscopic urban dynamics: analytical and numerical comparisons of existing models. Transportation Research Part B 101, 245–267.

McNally, M.G., 2007. The four-step model. In: Handbook of Transport Modelling, 2nd edition. Emerald Group Publishing Limited, pp. 35–53.

Moran, P., 1956. A probability theory of a dam with a continuous release. The Quarterly Journal of Mathematics 7 (1), 130–137.

Moran, P., 1959. The Theory of Storage. Methuen.

Moskowitz, K., 1965. Discussion of 'freeway level of service as influenced by volume and capacity characteristics' by D.R. Drew and C.J. Keese. Highway Research Record 99, 43–44.

Munjal, P.K., Hsu, Y.S., Lawrence, R.L., 1971. Analysis and validation of lane-drop effects of multilane freeways. Transportation Research 5 (4), 257–266.

Muralidharan, A., Pedarsani, R., Varaiya, P., 2015. Analysis of fixed-time control. Transportation Research Part B 73, 81–90.

Newell, G., 1982. Applications of Queueing Theory, vol. 733. Chapman and Hall, New York.

Newell, G., 2002. Memoirs on highway traffic flow theory in the 1950s. Operations Research 50 (1), 173–178.

Newell, G.F., 1961. Nonlinear effects in the dynamics of car following. Operations Research 9 (2), 209–229.

Newell, G.F., 1993. A simplified theory of kinematic waves in highway traffic I: general theory. II: queuing at freeway bottlenecks. III: multi-destination flows. Transportation Research Part B 27 (4), 281–313.

Newell, G.F., 2002. A simplified car-following theory: a lower order model. Transportation Research Part B 36 (3), 195–205.

Ngoduy, D., 2010. Multiclass first-order modelling of traffic networks using discontinuous flow-density relationships. Transportmetrica 6 (2), 121–141.

Ni, D., Leonard, J., 2005. A simplified kinematic wave model at a merge bottleneck. Applied Mathematical Modelling 29 (11), 1054–1072.

Osher, S., 1984. Riemann solvers, the entropy condition, and difference. SIAM Journal on Numerical Analysis 21 (2), 217–235.

Papageorgiou, M., 1990. Dynamic modelling, assignment and route guidance in traffic networks. Transportation Research Part B 24 (6), 471–495.

Papageorgiou, M., Diakaki, C., Dinopoulou, V., Kotsialos, A., Wang, Y., 2003. Review of road traffic control strategies. Proceedings of the IEEE 91 (12), 2043–2067.

Papageorgiou, M., Kosmatopoulos, E., Papamichail, I., 2008. Effects of variable speed limits on motorway traffic flow. Transportation Research Record: Journal of the Transportation Research Board 2047, 37–48.

Payne, H., 1984. Discontinuity in equilibrium freeway traffic flow. Transportation Research Record 971, 140–146.

Pipes, L.A., 1967. Car-following models and the fundamental diagram of road traffic. Transportation Research 1, 21–29.

Rakha, H., Ahn, K., Trani, A., 2003. Comparison of mobile5a, mobile6, vt-micro, and cmem models for estimating hot-stabilized light-duty gasoline vehicle emissions. Canadian Journal of Civil Engineering 30 (6), 1010–1021.

Rey, A., Jin, W.-L., Ritchie, S.G., 2019. An extension of Newell's simplified kinematic wave model to account for first-in-first-out violation: with an application to vehicle trajectory estimation. Transportation Research Part C 109, 79–94.

Richards, P.I., 1956. Shock waves on the highway. Operations Research 4 (1), 42–51.

Schaller, B., 2018. The new automobility: Lyft, uber and the future of American cities. Schaller Consulting.

Shalev-Shwartz, S., Shammah, S., Shashua, A., 2017. On a formal model of safe and scalable self-driving cars. arXiv preprint. arXiv:1708.06374.

Sheffi, Y., 1984. Urban Transportation Networks: Equilibrium Analysis with Mathematical Programming Methods. Prentice Hall, Englewood Cliffs, NJ.

Shladover, S.E., Su, D., Lu, X.-Y., 2012. Impacts of cooperative adaptive cruise control on freeway traffic flow. Transportation Research Record 2324 (1), 63–70.

Small, K., 2013. Urban Transportation Economics, vol. 4. Taylor & Francis.

Small, K.A., 1992. Trip scheduling in urban transportation analysis. The American Economic Review, Papers and Proceedings of the Hundred and Fourth Annual Meeting of the American Economic Association 82 (2), 482–486.

Small, K.A., Chu, X., 2003. Hypercongestion. Journal of Transport Economics and Policy (JTEP) 37 (3), 319–352.

Smith, B.L., Qin, L., Venkatanarayana, R., 2003. Characterization of freeway capacity reduction resulting from traffic accidents. Journal of Transportation Engineering 129 (4), 362–368.

Srivastava, A., Jin, W.-L., Lebacque, J.-P., 2015. A modified cell transmission model with realistic queue discharge features at signalized intersections. Transportation Research Part B: Methodological 81, 302–315.

Sun, D., Bayen, A.M., 2008. Multicommodity Eulerian-Lagrangian large-capacity cell transmission model for en route traffic. Journal of Guidance, Control, and Dynamics 31 (3), 616–628.

Tampère, C., Corthout, R., Cattrysse, D., Immers, L., 2011. A generic class of first order node models for dynamic macroscopic simulation of traffic flows. Transportation Research Part B 45 (1), 289–309.

Toledo, T., Zohar, D., 2007. Modeling duration of lane changes. Transportation Research Record: Journal of the Transportation Research Board 1999, 71–78.

Underwood, R.T., 1961. Speed, Volume and Density Relationships. Yale Bureau of Highway Traffic, New Haven, Connecticut, pp. 141–188.

van Leer, B., 1984. On the relation between the upwind-differencing schemes of Godunov, Engquist-Osher and Roe. SIAM Journal on Scientific and Statistical Computing 5 (1), 1–20.

van Lint, J.W.C., Hoogendoorn, S.P., Schreuder, M., 2008. Fastlane: new multiclass first-order traffic flow model. Transportation Research Record: Journal of the Transportation Research Board 2088, 177–187.
Vaughan, R., Hurdle, V.F., Hauer, E., 1984. A traffic flow model with time dependent o-d patterns. In: Proceedings of the Ninth International Symposium on Transportation and Traffic Theory, pp. 155–178.
Vickrey, W.S., 1969. Congestion theory and transport investment. The American Economic Review: Papers and Proceedings of the Eighty-first Annual Meeting of the American Economic Association 59 (2), 251–260.
Vickrey, W.S., 1991. Congestion in midtown Manhattan in relation to marginal cost pricing. Technical report. Columbia University.
Vickrey, W.S., 1994. Types of congestion pricing models. Technical report, mimeo. Columbia University.
Vickrey, W.S., 2019. Types of congestion pricing models. Economics of Transportation 20, 100140. Co-edited by Richard Arnott and W.L. Jin.
Vickrey, W.S., 2020. Congestion in midtown Manhattan in relation to marginal cost pricing. Economics of Transportation 21, 100152. Co-edited by Richard Arnott and W.L. Jin.
Wang, P., Wada, K., Akamatsu, T., Hara, Y., 2015. An empirical analysis of macroscopic fundamental diagrams for Sendai road networks. Interdisciplinary Information Sciences 21 (1), 49–61.
Wang, X., Jin, W.-L., Yin, Y., 2020. A control theoretic approach to simultaneously estimate average value of time and determine dynamic price for high-occupancy toll lanes. IEEE Transactions on Intelligent Transportation Systems.
Wong, G.C.K., Wong, S.C., 2002. A multi-class traffic flow model: an extension of LWR model with heterogeneous drivers. Transportation Research Part A 36 (9), 827–841.
Yan, Q., Jin, W.-L., 2017. Calibration and validation of non-FIFO unifiable lane-based fundamental diagrams in a multi-lane traffic flow system. In: Transportation Research Board 96th Annual Meeting. Number 17-06632. Presented.
Yan, Q., Sun, Z., Gan, Q., Jin, W.-L., 2018. Automatic identification of near-stationary traffic states based on the pelt changepoint detection. Transportation Research Part B 108, 39–54.
Yang, H., Huang, H.-J., 1997. Analysis of the time-varying pricing of a bottleneck with elastic demand using optimal control theory. Transportation Research Part B 31 (6), 425–440.
Yang, H., Huang, H.-J., 2005. Mathematical and Economic Theory of Road Pricing. Emerald Group Publishing Limited.
Yang, H., Gan, Q., Jin, W.-L., 2011. Calibration of a family of car-following models with retarded linear regression methods. In: Proceedings of Transportation Research Board Annual Meeting.
Yin, Y., Lou, Y., 2009. Dynamic tolling strategies for managed lanes. Journal of Transportation Engineering 135 (2), 45–52.
Yperman, I., 2007. The Link Transmission Model for dynamic network loading. PhD thesis.
Yperman, I., Logghe, S., Tampere, C., Immers, B., 2006. The multi-commodity link transmission model for dynamic network loading. In: Proceedings of the TRB Annual Meeting.
Zhang, H.M., Jin, W.-L., 2002. Kinematic wave traffic flow model for mixed traffic. Transportation Research Record: Journal of the Transportation Research Board 1802, 197–204.
Zhang, J., Chang, H., Ioannou, P.A., 2006. A simple roadway control system for freeway traffic. In: American Control Conference. IEEE.

Index

A

Acceleration
   process, 52, 86
   rate, 8, 19–21, 30, 33, 52, 61, 62, 72, 90, 170, 172
   rate increase, 62
   rate stationary, 61
Adaptive Cruise Control (ACC), 33
Anisotropic, 58
Anisotropic models, 168
Arterial roads, 7, 38, 64
Automatic vehicle re-identification (AVI), 24
Autonomous vehicles, 5, 7, 8, 39

B

Bathtub model, 7, 10, 55, 207, 208, 236–241
Beltway network, 129
Blue trips, 221
Bottlenecks, 6, 7, 10, 63, 75, 112, 178, 191
   network, 7
   road, 64, 191
   traffic, 67
Boundary
   downstream, 31, 34, 100, 113, 131, 158, 184
   flows, 150, 157, 165
   flux, 55, 76, 92, 94, 96–99, 106–109, 111, 112, 116, 121, 128, 157, 160, 183, 185, 192
   flux function, 10, 112
   upstream, 31, 34, 101, 113, 131, 158
Bureau of Public Roads (BPR), 204
   link performance, 204, 205

C

Capacity drop, 65
Capacity drop ratio, 66

Cell Transmission Model (CTM), 10, 109, 113, 117, 121–123, 133, 151, 157, 158, 161, 163, 177, 179, 192, 209
Characteristic
   curve, 135, 136, 166, 167, 208, 231
   distance, 230
   equations, 135, 148
   ordinary differential equations, 134, 166
   path, 136, 149
   travel distance, 208, 228, 229, 238, 239
   trip, 229
   trip distance, 208, 228, 230
   wave, 75, 85–88, 90, 91
   wave speed, 42, 43, 45, 49, 55, 82, 85, 86, 88, 91, 93–95, 119, 135, 166, 237
   wave speed upstream, 89
   wave upstream, 88
Commodity
   conservation law, 36
   density, 27, 50, 67, 80, 122
   density proportions, 27, 50, 122, 123, 125
   flows, 121
   speeds, 27, 69
   traffic streams, 69
Congested
   states, 66
   traffic, 7, 9, 39, 48, 56, 63, 66, 71, 84, 99, 111, 137, 174
   upstream initial conditions, 138
Congestion
   dynamics, 7, 8
   information, 107, 109
   level, 111, 116, 117, 130
   patterns, 4, 113, 209, 212
   pricing, 5, 7, 11
   situation, 113
   traffic, 4–7, 11, 15

Conservation
  equation, 35, 36, 60, 223, 226–228, 232, 234
  law, 7, 10, 33–35, 90, 105, 106, 124, 131, 134, 207, 208, 223, 225–227
  law commodity, 36
Constitutive law, 22, 23, 26, 40, 41, 76, 90
Critical (C) states, 148
Cumulative flows, 10, 16, 19, 22, 60, 67, 78, 106, 133, 134, 136, 137, 140, 151, 152, 156, 158, 180, 192, 195

D

Density
  commodity, 27, 50, 67, 80, 122
  downstream, 88, 101, 172, 173, 184
  traffic, 27, 37, 40, 86, 87, 90, 109, 133, 135, 143, 144, 156, 157, 192, 241
  trip, 232, 233
  upstream, 65, 71, 88, 90, 101, 172, 173, 184
  vehicle, 232, 233
Departure time, 4, 6, 7, 11, 14, 113, 191, 205, 207–209, 241
Departure time choice, 191, 200
Diverge models, 125
Downstream, 72, 147, 154
  boundary, 31, 34, 100, 113, 131, 152, 158, 162, 178, 184
  capacity, 61, 65, 131
  cell, 107, 109, 112, 117
  density, 88, 101, 117, 172, 173, 184
  destination, 113
  discharge flow-rate, 185
  dummy cell, 113
  end point, 138
  external supply, 159
  initial density, 159
  initial flow rates, 140
  initial states, 94, 95
  lanes, 61
  link, 15, 93, 95–98, 123, 125–127, 131, 151, 152, 157
  part, 72, 99

platoon, 58, 111, 130
region, 96
road, 65, 66, 110, 123
section, 138
states, 60, 72, 88
traffic density, 101
traffic state, 60
vehicles, 122
Dummy cell
  downstream, 113
  upstream, 113

E

Electronic toll collection (ETC), 24
Entropy condition, 10, 76, 87, 90, 95
Equilibrium, 41
  states, 70
  stationary states, 61, 70
  traffic state, 41

F

First-in-first-out (FIFO), 66, 67, 69, 71, 72, 80, 81, 102, 122, 125, 158
  diverge model, 129
  diverging rules, 129
  multilane traffic, 67
  principle, 67, 68, 71, 123, 149
  rule, 125
  traffic, 146, 157
  traffic flow, 151
  traffic stream, 67, 68
  trajectories, 30, 72
Flow
  exchange rate, 37
  rates, 140
  traffic, 5–13, 15, 17, 18, 29, 30, 33, 34, 53, 77, 80, 101, 102, 122, 168, 208
Freeway
  lanes, 29
  network, 4, 15, 66, 233, 241
  traffic dynamics, 66
Freight trips, 207
Fundamental diagram
  bivariate, 55
  concave, 46, 87, 88, 115, 130
  concave total, 128
  discontinuous, 54
  for night traffic, 54

Index

general, 40, 42, 60, 75, 76, 85, 105, 128
Greenshields, 43, 53, 55, 56, 76, 102, 118, 130, 149, 150, 182
LeVeque, 49
macroscopic, 149
network, 7, 51, 55, 164, 185, 187, 188, 232, 233, 236, 237, 241
normalized, 76
piecewise linear, 149
traffic flow, 7
trapezoidal, 51, 128, 233
unimodal, 112

G

Gipps acceleration model, 52
Godunov method, 108, 109, 127
Greenshields fundamental diagram, 43, 53, 55, 56, 76, 102, 118, 130, 149, 150, 182

H

Highway Capacity Manual (HCM), 38
Homogeneous
   LWR model, 95, 108, 130
   road, 70, 78, 122, 130, 133, 134, 147, 165, 179
   road section, 141
   signalized road networks, 159
Hyperbolic conservation laws, 76, 77, 84, 94, 97, 127, 149

I

Incremental Transfer (IT), 128
Inhomogeneous
   LWR model, 94, 95, 102, 103
   road, 49, 67, 70, 79, 109, 112, 120–122, 130, 134
   road fundamental diagrams, 49
Integral conservation equation, 231, 232
Intelligent Transportation System (ITS), 24

J

Jam
   density, 9, 37, 56, 64, 65, 72, 88, 98, 99, 107, 123, 135, 137, 174, 179, 186, 191
   spacing, 37, 53, 107, 167

Jammed
   road, 155
   upstream link, 152
Junction
   models, 7, 123, 127, 129, 157, 177
   network, 109, 112

K

Kinematic wave, 95
   models, 27, 91
   models network, 207, 209
   theory, 10, 99, 101, 128, 129, 138
   theory network, 7

L

Lane
   changes, 29, 36–38, 53
   closure, 65
   downstream, 61
   drops, 70, 98
   freeway, 29
   upstream, 61
Legendre transformation, 42, 43, 45, 135, 137, 166
LeVeque fundamental diagram, 49
Lighthill-Whitham-Richards (LWR) model
   for inhomogeneous roads, 76
   for network traffic, 208
   for network traffic flow, 129
   homogeneous, 95, 108, 130
   inhomogeneous, 94, 95, 102, 103
Link queue model (LQM), 10
Link Transmission Model (LTM), 10, 133, 151, 156, 191

M

Models
   queueing, 7, 10, 177
   traffic flow, 6–10, 33, 53, 58, 192
Multilane
   fundamental diagram, 49, 65
   road, 27, 28, 68, 80, 82

N

Network
   freeway, 4, 15, 66, 233, 241
   junction, 109, 112

kinematic wave models, 207, 209
kinematic wave theory, 7, 129
level, 211
queue, 208, 222, 223, 227
queue model, 208, 222
road, 4, 6, 7, 14, 15, 23, 29, 35, 51, 55, 66, 129, 163, 188, 191, 207–209, 212, 215, 217, 219, 223, 227, 228, 232
signalized, 55, 188
topology, 207–210
traffic, 133, 151
traffic flow, 123, 129, 157, 177, 191
trip flow bathtub model, 207
trip flow system, 222
Network fundamental diagram (NFD), 7, 51, 55, 164, 185, 187, 188, 232, 233, 236, 237, 241
Neumann boundary conditions, 113, 118, 119, 158
Night traffic, 40

P

Passenger
 travel demand, 4
 trips, 207, 232, 236
Peak period, 5, 11, 35, 66, 148, 202–204, 209, 239
Pedestrian traffic flow models, 10
Platoon, 31, 70
 downstream, 58, 111, 130
 upstream, 59, 87, 88, 110
 vehicles, 58, 170, 172, 173
Point queue model (PQM), 7, 10, 177, 191, 194–197, 204
Privately operated vehicle (POV), 4, 207, 232, 236

Q

Queue
 discharge problem, 71, 88, 171, 185, 187
 head, 101
 length, 6, 9, 103, 148, 199, 200, 205
 network, 208, 222, 223, 227
 size, 101, 155, 191, 193–196, 198, 205, 215, 231

spillback, 107
tail, 101
upstream, 62, 65, 66, 72
Queueing
 contents cumulative flows, 204
 cost, 201, 203
 dynamics, 147
 models, 7, 10, 177
 process, 7
 systems, 204
 time, 196, 197, 199–201, 203

R

Rarefaction wave, 76, 87, 89–91, 93, 95, 118, 119
Relative trip density, 215
Remaining trip distance, 14, 29, 208, 211, 216–221, 225, 227
Riemann
 problem, 9, 10, 58, 59, 76, 87–91, 93–97, 105, 108–111, 117, 118, 139, 150, 158, 159, 173
 solutions, 91–93, 102, 108, 129, 141, 149, 172
Ring road, 113, 159, 185, 210
Ring road signalized, 159, 160, 164, 185, 187
Road
 bottlenecks, 64, 191
 capacity, 162
 conditions, 52, 64, 126
 downstream, 65, 66, 110, 123
 expansion, 5, 11
 geometry, 38, 227
 homogeneous, 70, 78, 122, 130, 133, 134, 147, 165, 179
 inhomogeneous, 49, 67, 70, 79, 109, 112, 120–122, 130, 134
 link, 6, 15, 178
 network, 4, 6, 7, 14, 15, 23, 29, 35, 51, 55, 66, 129, 163, 188, 191, 207–209, 212, 215, 217, 219, 223, 227, 228, 232
 section, 118, 119, 130
 segment, 9, 15, 23–25, 31, 34, 35, 38, 64, 105, 113, 133, 137, 138, 145–147, 151, 161, 162, 165, 191–193

topology, 209
traffic flows, 109
transportation systems, 3, 4
upstream, 65, 66, 111, 130

S

Saturation headway, 38, 186
Schedule coordinates, 17, 21, 31
Secondary variables, 21, 22, 37, 46, 134
Served trips, 220
Shock wave, 59, 60, 70, 88–91, 93, 95, 99, 118, 138, 141, 163, 173
Signalized
  intersection, 6, 120, 171, 185, 189
  network, 55, 188
  ring road, 159, 160, 164, 185, 187
  road network, 66, 151, 159, 188, 205, 233, 241
Simple lead-vehicle problem (SLVP), 58–60, 71, 72
Space dimension, 10, 177, 191, 207–210, 216, 222, 223, 227, 239
Standing wave, 95
State
  downstream, 60, 72, 88
  equilibrium, 70
  stationary, 10, 40, 57, 60–63, 70, 76, 92–95, 102, 116, 117, 129, 151, 161, 162, 177, 182–184
  traffic, 18, 41, 51, 59, 62, 75, 78, 99, 109, 116, 169, 177, 188, 191, 209, 227
  unifiable, 71
  upstream, 60, 72, 88
  variables, 7, 157, 158
Stationary
  acceleration rate, 61
  cumulative flow, 161
  densities, 60, 93–99
  observer, 42
  states, 10, 40, 57, 60–63, 70, 76, 92–95, 102, 116, 117, 129, 151, 161, 162, 177, 182–184
Strictly over-critical (SOC), 147
  states, 42, 148
  traffic, 86

Strictly under-critical (SUC), 147
  states, 95, 148
  traffic, 86
Supersonic states, 53
Systematic lane changes, 29, 50

T

Time gap, 84
Traffic
  assignment problem, 6, 11, 209
  bottlenecks, 67
  characteristics, 90, 120, 121
  conditions, 16, 30, 37, 38, 77, 111, 138, 141, 143, 147, 151, 154, 158, 165, 177, 178, 211, 228
  congestion, 4–7, 11, 15
  control
    measures, 11
    policies, 227
    problems, 191
    strategies, 66, 71
  density, 27, 37, 40, 86, 87, 90, 109, 133, 135, 143, 144, 156, 157, 192, 241
  direction, 15
  dynamics, 75, 79, 81, 91, 99, 117, 129, 148, 151, 159, 178, 207, 209
  engineers, 7, 30
  FIFO, 146, 157
  flow, 7–10, 12, 13, 15, 17, 18, 30, 33, 53, 77, 80, 102, 122, 168, 208
    fundamental diagram, 7
    models, 6–10, 33, 53, 58, 192
    problems, 6
    theory, 5–9, 11, 12, 15, 29, 34, 53, 77, 101
  laws, 38
  light, 66, 88
  management, 208
  map, 15
  network, 133, 151
  rules, 33
  scenarios, 9, 13
  signal, 64, 171, 172
  state, 18, 41, 51, 59, 62, 75, 78, 99, 109, 116, 169, 177, 188, 191, 209, 227

state downstream, 60
stream, 22, 28, 35, 55, 57, 60, 72, 99, 100, 107, 120
surface, 21, 58, 82, 83, 85
systems, 11, 13, 15, 33, 35, 40, 41, 48, 70, 75, 79, 109, 120, 128, 133, 193, 208, 228
upstream, 99, 100
Traffic analysis zone (TAZ), 209
Transonic rarefaction wave, 94, 101, 102, 116, 119, 138, 143, 154, 159, 165, 172
Transonic rarefaction wave solutions, 130
Transportation network
  analysis methods, 11
  design, 208
Transportation Network Company (TNC), 4, 241
Transportation system, 3–5, 7, 12, 207
Transportation system analysis, 3, 209
Travel demand, 5, 6, 196, 207–209, 211, 212, 215, 241
  forecast, 12
  passengers, 4
Triangular
  fundamental diagram, 40, 43, 44, 46, 60, 61, 77, 82, 84, 105, 111, 112, 133, 137, 139, 151, 165, 166, 182, 184, 185
  shape, 40, 186, 187
Trips
  active, 221
  characteristic, 229
  characteristic distance, 229, 230
  demand, 211
  density, 232, 233
  distances, 14, 29, 207, 208, 210–214, 216–221, 225, 227, 230, 234, 237–239, 241
  distribution, 209
  generation, 209
  passengers, 207, 232, 236
  queue size, 208
  relative density, 216
  trajectories, 14, 208, 229

travel time, 211, 230
vehicles, 14
Tunnel bottlenecks, 65
TWOPAS acceleration model, 52, 55

U

Uncongested
  downstream initial conditions, 138
  traffic, 48, 49, 54, 66, 71, 108, 111
Undifferentiated
  roads, 227
  traffic conditions, 207
Unifiable, 69, 71, 80, 81, 102, 128, 151, 158
  equilibrium states, 69
  fundamental diagrams, 82
  states, 71
Upstream, 72, 147, 154
  blank region represents, 148
  boundary, 31, 34, 101, 113, 131, 152, 158, 162, 178
  capacity, 61
  cell, 107, 109, 112, 117
  characteristic wave, 88
  characteristic wave speed, 89
  demand, 65, 113, 117, 127, 131, 151, 161
  density, 65, 71, 88, 90, 101, 117, 172, 173, 184
  dummy cell, 113
  end point, 138
  external demand, 159
  initial density, 159
  initial flow rates, 140
  initial states, 94, 95
  lanes, 61
  link, 15, 93, 95–99, 123, 125–127, 131, 157
  platoon, 58, 59, 87, 88, 110
  queue, 62, 65, 66, 72
  road, 65, 66, 111, 130
  section, 138
  speeds, 65
  states, 60, 72, 88
  traffic, 99, 100
  traffic density, 101
  vehicles, 122

V

Variable Speed Limit (VSL), 38, 65, 70
Vehicles
   characteristics, 6, 33
   class, 31
   conservation laws, 35
   density, 232, 233
   downstream, 122
   emissions, 20
   platoon, 58, 170, 172, 173
   trajectories, 53, 58, 174
   trips, 14
   upstream, 122
Vehicular
   traffic, 11, 15, 58, 90, 233
   trips, 207, 232, 236

Printed in the United States
by Baker & Taylor Publisher Services